Kevin Hannafin, a native of Tralee, had a personal interest in this story due to family links with the Kerry IRA and Sir Arthur Vicars. He now lives in Dublin. John Cafferky, from Dublin, has been published in Canada, where he now lives.

SCANDAL & BETRAYAL

In 1907, coinciding with the visit of Edward VII to Ireland, an extraordinary discovery was made — the Irish Crown jewels had disappeared from Dublin Castle. Scotland Yard uncovered a complicated web of mystery, intrigue and scandal. The custodian of the jewels, Sir Arthur Vicars and his staff, including his co-tenant Frank Shackleton, brother of the explorer, came under intense scrutiny. The investigation revealed the existence of a homosexual circle within the Castle, including Vicars himself, Shackleton, Lord Haddo — the son of the King's Viceroy in Ireland — and the King's brother-in-law, the Duke of Argyll. A spectacular Irish burglary suddenly threatened to become an international scandal . . .

JOHN CAFFERKY & KEVIN HANNAFIN

SCANDAL

SHACKLETON AND THE IRISH
CROWN JEWELS

& BETRAYAL

Complete and Unabridged

CHARNWOOD
Leicester

First published in Great Britain in 2002 by
The Collins Press, Cork

First Charnwood Edition
published 2003
by arrangement with
The Collins Press, Cork

The authors would be happy to hear from readers
with their comments on the book at their website:
www.irishcrownjewels.com

British Library CIP Data

Cafferky, John
  Scandal & betrayal: Shackleton and the Irish
  crown jewels.—Large print ed.—
  Charnwood library series
  1. Edward, VII, King of Great Britain, *1841 –
  1910* —Friends and associates 2. Shackleton
  Frank 3. Vicars, Sir Arthur 4. Dublin Castle
  (Dublin, Ireland) 5. Jewel thieves—Ireland—
  Dublin 6. Scandals—Ireland—Dublin
  7. Large type books
  I. Title II. Hannafin Kevin
  364.1'323'0941835

ISBN 0–7089–4945–2

Published by
F. A. Thorpe (Publishing)
Anstey, Leicestershire

Set by Words & Graphics Ltd.
Anstey, Leicestershire
Printed and bound in Great Britain by
T. J. International Ltd., Padstow, Cornwall

This book is printed on acid-free paper

Dedicated to the Murphys of Kilmorna,
past and present

DUBLIN METROPOLITAN POLICE.

DETECTIVE DEPARTMENT,
EXCHANGE COURT,
DUBLIN, 8*th July*, 1907.

STOLEN

From a Safe in the Office of Arms, Dublin Castle, during the past month, supposed by means of a false key.

GRAND MASTER'S DIAMOND STAR.

A Diamond Star of the Grand Master of the Order of St. Patrick composed of brilliants (Brazilian stones) of the purest water, 4⅝ by 4¼ inches, consisting of eight points, four greater and four lesser, issuing from a centre enclosing a cross of rubies and a trefoil of emeralds surrounding a sky blue enamel circle with words, "Quis Separabit MDCCLXXXIII." in rose diamonds engraved on back.   Value about **£14,000**

CONTENTS

LIST OF ILLUSTRATIONS

Reward poster issued by the Dublin Metropolitan Police for the recovery of the jewels. (*courtesy Irish National Archives*) Ground Plan of the Office of Arms at Dublin Castle

1. Sir Arthur Vicars, Ulster King of Arms (*portrait by unknown artist, courtesy of the Genealogical Office*)
2. Kilmorna House, County Kerry
3. Mrs Mary Farrell, cleaning lady at the Office of Arms (*from a photograph lent by Seamus O'Farrell*)
4. Lord Ronald Gower, the Duke of Argyll's uncle and lifelong friend (*courtesy of National Portrait Gallery*)
5. Marquess of Lorne, (later ninth Duke of Argyll) in formal uniform (*courtesy of Glenbow Archives, Calgary*)
6. Francis Bennett-Goldney (Mayor of Canterbury) and Athlone Pursuivant
7. The Insignia of the Order of St Patrick, commonly known as the Irish Crown Jewels
8. Other valuables stored in the strong room at the Office of Arms
9. Michael Galvin, who was killed by British Forces, April 1921 (*courtesy of the Galvin Family*)
10. Left to right, Michael Murphy Jnr, (Sir

Arthur Vicars' valet), Michael Murphy Snr., and Billeen Murphy who also worked on the Kilmorna estate (*courtesy of Michael Murphy*)

11. The Crypt in Chichester, where Frank Shackleton operated an antique shop under the name Frank Mellor.

12. Frank Shackleton (right with umbrella) arriving in Liverpool, January 1913, with Detective Inspector Albert Cooper (in bowler) (*Hulton Archive*)

13. Chief Inspector John Kane of Scotland Yard (*courtesy of Alan Moss of Scotland Yard*)

14. Lord MacDonnell, Under-Secretary for Ireland (*by William Orpen, courtesy of the Hugh Lane Municipal Gallery of Modern Art*)

15. 'The' O'Mahony, half-brother of Sir Arthur Vicars at Grange Con (*courtesy of Colonel R. Page, Grange Con*)

16. The Royal party bids farewell to Lord Aberdeen at the end of their visit to Dublin in July 1907

17. The hoax stone found near the ruins of Kilmorna House in 1997

WHO'S WHO

This listing of characters is by no means exhaustive. Its only purpose is to assist the reader.

ABERDEEN & TEMAIR, (1847–1934). John Campbell Gordon. 1st Marquis 1915. 7th Earl of Aberdeen, Viceroy & Lord Lieutenant of Ireland for six months in 1886 and again in 1905–1915. Governor-General of Canada in 1893–1898; married 1877 Ishbel Maria Majoribanks youngest daughter of Lord Tweedmouth; Father of Lord Haddo.

ABERDEEN & TEMAIR, (1857–1939). Ishbel Majoribanks, Vicerine of Ireland; married 1877 Lord Aberdeen in 1877; President of International Council of Women 1893–1899 and 1904–1936; founded the Victorian Order of Nurses in Canada; mother of Lord Haddo.

ARGYLL, 9th Duke of. (1845–1914). Formerly the Marquis of Lorne, John Campbell; married Princess Louise, sister of King Edward V11 in 1871; Governor-General of Canada; Unionist MP South Manchester 1895; Nephew of Lord Gower and intimate friend of Frank Shackleton, the Dublin Herald.

BALFOUR, Arthur James (1848–1930). Chief Secretary for Ireland 1887–1891; British Prime Minister 1902–1905; due to his coercion legislation the Irish named him 'Bloody Balfour'.

BARRY, Redmond, K.C., M.P., Solicitor-General for Ireland.

BIRRELL, Augustine (1850–1933). Member of the Liberal Cabinet, President of the Board of Education 1905–1907; Chief Secretary for Ireland, Jan. 1907–1916; introduced the Irish Council Bill 1907; a London barrister and wit, he gave the name 'birrelling' to light essay-writing. He confined himself to day-to-day administration and took no part in major policy. His cabinet career was characterised by legislative failure. Found his assistant MacDonnell irksome. Mainly advised by John Redmond. Failed to realise the danger of the Sinn Féin movement and resigned after the Easter Rebellion of 1916.

BRYCE, James (1838–1922) Chief Secretary for Ireland 1905–1907; British Ambassador to Washington 1907–1913.

BURTCHAELL, Assistant to Sir Arthur Vicars.

BLACK AND TANS ('Tans'). 9,500 British ex-soldiers and sailors sent to Ireland to assist the Royal Irish Constabulary to pursue the IRA more vigorously. They were called the Black and Tans because of their Khaki military trousers and their dark green police tunics. They gained a fearsome reputation for brutality, which only helped alienate the population from the Royal Irish constabulary (RIC) as a whole.

CAMPBELL, J.H. ,K.C., M.P., Legal counsel for Sir Arthur Vicars, later became Lord Glenavy.

CAMPBELL BANNERMAN, Sir Henry. (1836–1908) Became Liberal Prime Minister in December 1905.

CARSON, Sir Edward. (1854–1935). Born Dublin. Solicitor General for Ireland 1892; Defended Queensbury in libel action against Oscar Wilde 1895; Solicitor General for England 1900–1905. Leader of the Irish Unionists in House of Commons 1910; Leader of movement for provisional government for Ulster 1911. His militant stand for the rights of the 'loyal minority' almost brought Ireland close to civil war by July 1914.

DILLON, John. (1851–1927). Supported John Redmond, the leader of the Irish Parliamentary Party; Chief member of the Irish Party cabinet in 1908.

DOUGHERTY, Sir James. (1844–1934). Assistant Under-Secretary for Ireland; replaced MacDonnell as the Under-Secretary for Ireland in 1908.

DUDLEY, William. (1867–1932). 2nd Earl. Lord Lieutenant for Ireland 1902–1906; Governor-General Australia 1908–1911.

EDWARD VII, King of England. (1901–1910). Known for his rakish lifestyle and overindulgence. His mother was Queen Victoria. Edward was succeeded by George V.

FARRELL, Mrs Mary. Cleaning lady of the Office of Arms. Her son was Seamus O'Farrell.

GLADSTONE, Herbert (1854–1930). 1st Viscount. Youngest son of Prime Minister Gladstone. Secretary of State for Home Affairs 1905–1910.

GLADSTONE, William E. (1809–1898). Tory MP; Prime Minister 1880–1885; proposed Home Rule Bill in 1886 but was defeated.

GOLDNEY, Francis Bennett. (1865–1918). MP (C) Mayor of Canterbury; Athlone Pursuivant in Dublin Castle in 1907.

GORGES, Captain Richard Howard. Saw Action in the Boer War.
Became musketry instructor at the Curragh Military Camp near Dublin. Intimate friend of Frank Shackleton.

GOWER, Lord Ronald Sutherland. (1845–1916). Sculptor. Brother of the 8th Duke of Sutherland and brother of the Duchess of Westminster. Uncle of the 9th Duke of Argyll. Friend of Oscar Wilde, Frank Shackleton and Sir Arthur Vicars.

HADDO, Lord. George Campbell Gordon (1879–1965). Eldest son of Lord and Lady Aberdeen. Marries Mary Florence Cockayne 1906; Becomes the 2nd Marquis of Aberdeen 1934; close friend of Sir Arthur Vicars.

HADDO, Lady, formerly Florence Cockayne, married Lord Haddo in 1906.

HARREL, William V. Royal Irish Constabulary 1886–1898. Inspector of Prisons 1898–1902; Assistant Commissioner Dublin Metropolitan Police 1902-?. Son of Sir David Harrel. Member of the Kildare Street Club.

HARREL, Sir David. Royal Irish Constabulary 1859–1879; Chief Commissioner Dublin Metropolitan Police 1883–1893; Under-Secretary for Ireland 1893–1902.

HEALY, T. Legal counsel to Sir Arthur Vicars. Became Governor-General of the Irish Free State in 1922.

IRISH REPUBLICAN ARMY (IRA), made up of Nationalist Volunteers, their purpose was to free Ireland from British rule. Linked to the political part called Sinn Féin (Ourselves alone). Their violent action led to the start of the Anglo-Irish War of Independence.

JONES, Chester. London police magistrate, Home Office appointee to the commissioner of inquiry.

KAISER, Wilhelm II, Emperor of Germany and nephew of King Edward VII; Intimate friend of Prince Philipp Eulenberg who was involved in the Berlin homosexual scandal.

KANE, John, (1852–1915). Chief Inspector from Scotland Yard who investigated the theft. Born in Prescott, Lancashire. Joined the London Metropolitan Police in 1874, Warrant number 58545, became Chief Inspector in 1906 and retired in 1911.

KERR, OWEN. Detective at Dublin Castle who made the nightly inspections of the Office of Arms.

KNOLLYS, Francis (1837–1924) 1st Viscount. Private Secretary to Prince of Wales and King Edward VII 1870–1910; Private Secretary King George V 1910–1913.

LONG, Sir Walter, (1854–1924). 1st Viscount cr. 1921. Chief Secretary for Ireland 1905–1906; MP(C) South Dublin 1906–1910.

LOWE, John. Police Superintendent Dublin Castle.

MACDONNELL, Sir Antony Patrick. (1844–1925). Born in County Mayo, Ireland. Educ: Queen's College, Galway; entered Indian Civil Service in 1865 where he had a distinguished career. Appointed by Conservative George Wyndham as Permanent Under-Secretary for Ireland, 1902–1908 with a special dispensation to initiate policy, although a civil servant, a Catholic, a Liberal and a home ruler 'in principle' whose brother was a Nationalist MP; devised devolution scheme in 1904 causing a strong reaction from Unionists, which in 1907 was expanded into the Irish Council Bill; became Lord MacDonnell of Swinford in 1908.

MAHONY, Peirce Gun. The Cork Herald 1905–1910, Sir Arthur Vicars' nephew; Shot July 26, 1914.

O'MAHONY, The. Peirce Charles de Lacy O'Mahony, Father of the Cork Herald, and half brother of Sir Arthur Vicars.

MAYO, Dermot. 7th Earl of Mayo; Knight of the Order of St. Patrick who organised petition to the King on behalf of Sir Arthur Vicars; Senator of the Irish Free State; Member of the Kildare Street Club.

MCENNERY, Peter. Worked in Dublin Castle. Close friend of Sir Arthur Vicars.

MEREDITH, Mr. G, solicitor to Sir Arthur Vicars.

PARNELL, Charles Stewart. (1846–91). A Protestant who led the Irish members of the British House of Commons in the fight for Irish self-determination. Always a thorn in the British establishment, who tried to snare him for involvement in the Phoenix Park murders. His downfall came after his adulterous affair with Kitty O'Shea was made public.

PITT, Frederick. Sir Arthur Vicars' coachman; Vicars paid his passage to America just before the inquiry in order to prevent him giving evidence.

REDMOND, John. (1856–1918) Born County Wexford. MP (N) Waterford since 1891; became leader of Parnell's group on Parnell's death in 1891; Chairman of the Irish Parliamentary Party; lost prestige for himself and his party when he did not support the Liberal Government's devolution scheme in 1906; secured the introduction of the third Home Rule Bill in 1912; helped recruit for the war effort in 1914.

ROSS of Bladenburg, Sir John (1848–1926). Chief Commissioner Dublin Metropolitan Police 1901–1914; Member of the Kildare Street Club.

SHACKLETON, Francis Richard. (1876–1941); Dublin Herald in 1905–1907; younger brother of Ernest Shackleton the famed Antarctic explorer; he was Sir Arthur's co-tenant at 7 St. James's Terrace, Clonskeagh, Dublin; after his release from jail, he assumed the name Mellor, and lived in Chichester where he operated an antique business.

SHAW, James Johnstone. Chairman of the commission of inquiry.

STARKIE, R.F. One of the three commissioners of the inquiry.

STIVEY, William. Messenger in the Office of Arms.

HORLOCK, Mr, Private Secretary to Sir Arthur Vicars.

VICARS, Sir Arthur Edward. (1864–1921). K.C.V.O. 1903; youngest son of Col William Henry Vicars and Jane Gun-Cunninghame; Knight Attendant on the Order of St. Patrick and Ulster King of Arms 1893–1908; married Gertrude Williford Wright 1917; shot by the IRA in 1921.

VICARS, Lady. Gertrude Williford Wright. Married Sir Arthur Vicars 1917; sister of the wife of Peirce Gun Mahony, the Cork Herald.

WILD GEESE, A term applied to those leaving Ireland to serve in foreign armies after the Siege of Limerick in the seventeenth century.

ACKNOWLEDGEMENTS

There are many who, with their recollections, provided us with insights into some of the main characters. Others provided historical research and photographs, while still others who thought they knew little of the facts still generously replied to our queries. We wish to thank them all; Audrey Bateman for her research on Francis Bennett-Goldney and for providing us with the transcript of the Vice-Regal Inquiry; Robert Barrett: Garda John Duffy, curator of the Garda Museum, who showed us around the Office of Arms; Desmond Gorges; Ken Green of Chichester Historical Society for tracking details of Frank Shackleton's life in Chichester; Ronald Guymer of the Ratner Safe Co.; Earl of Haddo; Lord Jenkins; Scott MacMillan, Herald of Arms, Ireland; Pamela Mahony; Mark Hughes-Morgan who met with some of the hoaxers; Alan Moss of Scotland Yard for information on Chief inspector Kane; Freddie O'Dwyer of Dúchas; Kevin O'Halloran, Enterprise Ireland for his analysis of the hoaxer's concrete slab; Colonel Page for the wonderful photo and history of The O'Mahony; Pamela Perry; Jonathan Shackleton for his hospitality, family history and photograph of Frank Shackleton; Garda Jim Sheridan who let us examine the original safe (which is now in Kevin Street police station); Seamus Shortall;

Noel Twomey of the *Kerryman* newspaper; Vivienne Waugh; Paddy Davies Webb, Kilmorna House, East Transvaal, for the photograph of Sir Arthur Vicars; Thomas Woodcock, Norroy and Ulster King of Arms for his help in heraldic matters; the Hugh Lane Gallery for their photograph of Sir Antony MacDonnell;

To Michael Murphy of Kilmorna and Sean Hannafin we owe a special debt for their researches into obscure details on our behalf and their continuous encouragement; a special thanks to John W. Maxwell who commented so generously on our manuscript, and Gaby Monaghan for also reading it in its early stages. We also wish to thank the staff and librarians at the Irish National Archives; the National Library of Ireland; the British Library for permission to quote from the Gladstone papers; the Bodleian Library for permission to quote from the MacDonnell Papers; Joanne Debes of the University of Delaware, for permission to read from the Brennan papers; University of Toronto Library; and Listowel Library, for details on Kilmorna House. Finally, a special thanks to our wives Bridgette and Meta for all their forebearance and patience over the course of this book.

PREFACE

The fact that many of our fellow Irishmen have never heard of the Irish Crown Jewels is not surprising; They are not the equivalent of the English Crown Jewels, but are in fact the regalia of the Knights of the Order of St Patrick, which for all practical purposes went into abeyance some 70 years ago after the formation of the Irish Free State.

Their disappearance from Dublin Castle in 1907 remains one of the great unsolved mysteries of this century. Fans of Sherlock Holmes will be glad to know that even Sir Arthur Conan Doyle, the great detective writer, tried his hand at solving the mystery. Conan Doyle was a relative of Sir Arthur Vicars, the custodian of the jewels, and it appears that Sir Arthur asked for his assistance. Conan Doyle went on to base his story the Bruce Partington Plan on the theft and some of the characters in his story can be identified with those in Dublin Castle. Even the use of a seance by Sir Arthur Vicars may have been inspired by Doyle's great belief in the medium.

Our efforts at trying to unravel the facts 90 years later were made extremely difficult by the fact that the authorities, primarily on the instructions of King Edward VII went to great lengths to cloak the affair. The Home Office still has not released certain files concerning the case

1

and we are shocked to learn that Chief Inspector Kane's report from Scotland Yard no longer exists. Even the Irish Free State Government's actions of holding up the release of the full text of Sir Arthur Vicar's will until twenty years ago indicates that they too were guilty in this regard.

Finally, we must make some mention of the elaborate hoax played on us while researching in Listowel, County Kerry, (see epilogue). Although the shenanigans of the hoaxers were most devious, we must congratulate them for the efforts they went to. The resultant media attention that followed from their prank played no small part in helping us to get this book published and we are most grateful to them on that score. Their efforts to deceive only further motivated us to try and solve the mystery. It is no wonder that the well-known author John B. Keane, who resides in Listowel, has such a rich colourful source on which to base his characters. We hope to meet the hoaxers some day and discuss with them some of the finer points of their deception, the logic of which still eludes us.

1

THE RISE AND FALL OF
ARTHUR VICARS

The principal participants in the Irish Crown Jewel affair range from virtually unknown men to major historical figures. Sir Arthur Vicars was the former custodian of the jewels, and Lord Haddo was the son of Lord Aberdeen, but few of us have ever heard their names. Frank Shackleton's claim to fame rests on his brother, Sir Ernest Shackleton, the great Antarctic explorer, rather than on the part he played in the affair. Meanwhile, King Edward VII, The O'Mahony of Kerry, Lord Aberdeen, Augustine Birrell and Herbert Gladstone have all played significant roles in history. Sir Antony Patrick MacDonnell was one of the most eminent Irishmen of his time, yet today he is all but forgotten. Each of these men played a major role in an affair that threatened to explode into a national scandal.

Caught in the centre of the storm was Sir Arthur Vicars. He was ruined by the affair and, in a morbid twist of fate, his changed circumstances led him to lose his life in the Irish War of Independence. While apparently separate calamities, the connecting link between these two events was the intractable political problem of the period.

Arthur Vicars was born the youngest of four children at Royal Leamington Spa in Warwickshire, England, in 1864. His father, William Henry Vicars, was a retired colonel in the 61st Regiment of Foot. In the sixteenth century, Arthur's ancestors represented Don Vicaro, a Spanish Cavalier who came to England in the suite of Katherine of Aragon. In his own times, Arthur Vicars could claim among his relatives the Nobel scientist, Lord Rayleigh, and the great detective writer, Sir Arthur Conan Doyle. Arthur's mother was Jane Gun-Cuninghame of County Wicklow, a family descended from members of both the Irish and French nobility. It was Jane's second marriage. Her first marriage had been to Peirce K. Mahony of Kilmorna House in County Kerry, where they had raised two sons, George and Peirce. When her first husband died, he bequeathed the Kilmorna estate to his eldest son, George.

When Arthur turned five years of age, his father died suddenly, leaving him emotionally scarred and insecure. His mother thought that the manly company of his two older Irish half-brothers, Peirce and George, would help Arthur come to terms with his loss and she sent him over to Ireland to spend his summer holidays at the Kilmorna estate. Peirce and George bonded immediately with Arthur, and they insisted on referring to him as their young brother, a most welcome development for his mother and one that the entire family accepted. George, in particular, became a father figure to the young boy, and he spent hours telling Arthur a highly-embellished romantic history of the Mahony family. George traced the family tree through a sequence of wonderfully chivalrous ancestors back to the High Kings of Munster in the time of Ireland's greatest King, Brian Boru. Vulnerable and easily impressed, young Arthur thrilled to these romantic tales, and unintentionally, George had inspired him with a passion for Irish genealogy.

After Arthur turned nine, the sudden death of his mother tore his world apart. Orphaned, he was sent off to boarding school to groom him in the ways of an English gentleman. At school he excelled in the classics, but suffered from loneliness and insecurity, leading him to crave the intimacy of his fellow students. Throughout these difficult years he always received a warm welcome in Kilmorna, and he became emotionally attached to Ireland.

Upon completing his studies, Arthur felt he lacked the manliness and physical build to follow the Vicar's tradition of pursuing an army career. Although he loved the pomp, ceremony and fine uniforms, a military life did not suit his artistic nature. He had developed into a sensitive and somewhat naïve young man. Listening to his heart, he followed his passion for genealogy and heraldry. He studied and honed his genealogical skills in London, before returning to Ireland, intent on researching the pedigrees of the great Anglo-Irish families.

Arthur pursued a career in the genealogical office in Dublin, known as the Office of Arms, with single-minded determination. He applied three times for a post in the Office of Arms, only to have an exasperated Irish administration refuse his request with increasing bluntness. Unable to obtain the coveted post on his own, Arthur persuaded Lord Rayleigh, a distant cousin, to act as his patron. Rayleigh talked to his personal friend, Arthur Balfour, and in 1893, the 29-year-old Arthur Vicars scaled the pinnacle of Irish genealogy by becoming Ulster King of Arms at Dublin Castle. As the Principal Herald of Ireland, he soon earned a knighthood for his services. In 1907, as a Knight Commander of the Victorian Order, Ulster King of Arms and Registrar to the Order of St Patrick, Sir Arthur, still only 44 years of age, had been that rare phenomenon — a perfectly happy man.

For centuries, Dublin Castle, with its fortified walls, army garrisons, police barracks and administration buildings, served as the nerve-centre of British rule in Ireland. Housed between its two main gates leading into Upper Castle Yard, stood the imposing Bedford Tower, home to the Office of Arms. Here, Sir Arthur and his staff confirmed the pedigrees of the landed gentry who sought the prestige of a coveted grant of arms. Vicars and his three junior heralds belonged to the English royal household, and functioned as an extension of the monarchy in Ireland.

Created by King George III in 1783, the Order of St Patrick consisted of at the most 22 Knights. King George founded the Order as a convenient means of rewarding his loyal Irish subjects, and to induce the loyalty of others who were less inclined. This Irish honour was equivalent to those associated with the Orders of the Garter, Bath and Thistle. The sky-blue robes and insignia of the Order derived from the Friendly Brothers of St Patrick, a quasi-Masonic brotherhood founded by James I. Officers of the Order consisted of the Monarch as its head, the Viceroy and Lord Lieutenant of Ireland as its Grand Master, and the Chief Secretary for Ireland as its ex-officio officer. Sir Arthur as Ulster King of Arms acted as the registrar and custodian of the seal, the archives and the Grand Master's regalia, more commonly referred to as the Irish Crown Jewels.

The so-called Irish Crown Jewels owed their existence to a delightful tale of squabbling ladies at the royal court. Comprised of diamonds and rubies, they were once the property of Queen Charlotte. However, George IV had given these jewels to his mistress, Lady Conyngham. When the King died, Lady Conyngham, displaying a touch of charming delicacy, returned the gems to Queen Charlotte through an intermediary. Vexed, the good Queen, considering the jewels irredeemably tainted, would have nothing to do with them, and handing them over to her son, William IV, insisted that he dispose of them appropriately. William initially had no idea what to do with the tainted baubles. In a moment of inspiration, he decided the Order of St Patrick in Ireland needed a fine Grand Master's Star and Badge that the Lord Lieutenant could wear on ceremonial occasions. He ordered the royal jewellers to fashion the star and badge and sent them to Ireland. Unfortunately, for the Order's great pride and dignity, the Crown Jewels of Ireland always retained the whiff of scandal, and less reverent Irish wits insisted on calling them the Queen's 'tainted baubles'.

On the afternoon of 11 June 1907, Sir Arthur Vicars, who had held the post of Ulster King of Arms for fifteen years, received a visit at the Office of Arms from his old friend John Crawford Hodgson, Librarian to the Duke of Northumberland. After exchanging news about mutual friends and acquaintances, the two men discussed the upcoming royal visit by King Edward VII to Dublin scheduled for 10 July. Sir Arthur revelled in giving his erudite friend a harrowing account of his increased workload brought on by the royal visit. He confided to Hodgson that the Lord Lieutenant of Ireland, Lord Aberdeen, had saddled him with preparing all the protocols.

Sir Arthur and Hodgson had a common interest in rare manuscripts and Sir Arthur took his visitor downstairs to the strong room to show off his extensive collection. While discussing the finer points of the documents, Vicars offered to show him the Crown Jewels, but the studious Hodgson declined. However, when Sir Arthur persisted, Hodgson, not wanting to offend his host, acquiesced. To Hodgson's great surprise, Sir Arthur did not keep the jewels in the strong room. Instead, they had to go into the adjoining library where he saw a large Ratner safe located between the two side windows which overlooked the sentries' post guarding the Main Gate to the

Castle. Hodgson kept to himself whatever misgivings he may have had concerning his host's eccentric security arrangements for the Irish Crown Jewels. Opening the safe, Sir Arthur removed the red morocco case containing the jewels. Despite Hodgson's habitual disdain for such things, he confessed that he had to admire the beauty of the Grand Master's Star and Badge (worth approximately £2 million in today's terms). The Star's rays were formed from Brazilian diamonds, its centre had a shamrock of emeralds superimposed on a ruby cross and encircled by the motto of the Order *Quis Seperabit* (Who will separate?). The Badge was of like splendour. Both pieces had intertwining harps and roses symbolically linking Ireland and England. After inspecting the jewels, the two men retired upstairs to Sir Arthur's office and resumed their learned discourse on the manuscripts. Two weeks later, on 27 June, another friend, Dr Finney, visited Sir Arthur, but he was not shown the jewels.

Mrs Farrell, who cleaned the Office of Arms, was a widow who appeared ten years older than her 40-odd years. Her husband, Jem, a mechanic, had died years earlier, leaving her destitute and fending for four young children. To survive, she sent the baby of the family to relatives in the country, and placed her three sons in a home before she herself went into service.

Sir Arthur learned of her plight while visiting the house where she worked, and assumed the role of the family's benefactor. He employed

Mrs Farrell to clean the Office of Arms, paying her the generous wage of 30 shillings a week. The income allowed Mrs Farrell to reunite her family under the same roof. For years her eldest son, Seamus, had helped her carry the coal buckets from the cellar to the offices upstairs, but recently, Sir Arthur had found him full-time work on the railway. Another son, Patrick, occasionally helped her with the office chores and Sir Arthur kindly put him on the office pay at twelve shillings and sixpence a month. He would, on occasion, also ask him to his house in Clonskeagh to clean the windows and do other odd jobs. Needless to say, the Farrell family thought very highly of Sir Arthur Vicars.

At 6:30am, 3 July, Mrs Mary Farrell, following a long established routine, set out for the Castle from her home in Mary's Abbey. As usual, she walked down Capel Street, and crossing the Liffey at Essex Bridge, passed up Parliament Street to enter Dublin Castle by the Main Gate. Neither the sentries nor the policemen guarding the gate detained her, for they saw her come and go six days a week. Just inside the gate, she walked the last twenty paces to the front door of the Office of Arms. Putting her key into the front door lock she found it already open with the latch bolt upright. This was unusual. Only William Stivey, the office messenger, ever put the bolt up, but that was after he normally arrived at 10:00am. Puzzled, she entered the building to find the offices empty.

Mrs Farrell, a working-class woman, had never before found the front door unlocked and she

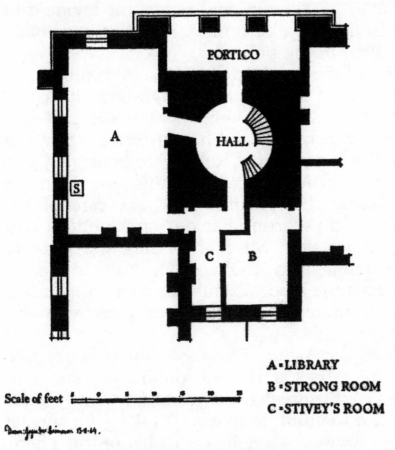

A · LIBRARY
B · STRONG ROOM
C · STIVEY'S ROOM

Scale of feet

S = THE POSITION OF THE SAFE

*Ground plan of the Office of Arms
at Dublin Castle.*

instinctively suspected a burglary. She knew that
Detective Kerr inspected the Office at 7:30pm
each evening, and always locked the door on his
way out. Someone, perhaps a prowler, had
entered the office late in the evening. Of course,
Mrs Farrell knew that she should report the
incident to the police, but she feared that if she
reported the open door, it might cause problems
for Sir Arthur. She decided that she should wait

11

for Stivey to come in, and report the incident to him. In that way, he could take the responsibility for calling in the police.

When Stivey arrived shortly after 10:00am, he found Mrs Farrell standing by his desk just in front of the strong room. At once she told him about her discovery and her suspicions. Stivey, a retired rating from the Royal Navy, normally had little time for Mrs Farrell, but this time she made good sense. He promised to take care of the matter, and escorting her out of the office, sent her on her way. Stivey now had the duty to report the incident to the police, but Mrs Farrell had sown the seed of doubt in his mind, and he decided to report the incident directly to his chief.

When Sir Arthur arrived at noon, Stivey told him that Mrs Farrell had found the front door unlocked. Surprisingly, he dismissed Stivey's tale with a disdainful 'is that so?' Taking no further action, he went straight up to his office. There, he continued working on the protocol for the upcoming royal visit, in particular the minute details concerning the investiture of Lord Castletown into the Order of St Patrick. Edward VII, who would personally preside over this ceremony, had a stickler's eye for ceremonial detail and tolerated no mistakes. Aware of this, Sir Arthur strove for perfection in every minutia. Downstairs, Stivey, in light of Sir Arthur's casual reaction, was relieved that he had not alerted the police.

Sir Arthur was the type of fussy individual who subscribed to a neat and orderly world where every routine had an exact purpose. He knew that even if he had inadvertently left the front door open the previous evening, Detective Kerr would have locked it after his nightly inspection. As a rule, Vicars would nitpick at even minor details, and ignoring the open front door went completely against his character. Even more strange, he had an exaggerated sense of duty, yet he failed to report the incident.

Later, when questioned by the police, Sir Arthur excused his omission by claiming that the plans for the upcoming royal visit had swamped him with work. Being the resident expert on formal protocol, Lord Aberdeen relied heavily on him to plan the ceremonies for the King. As Ulster King of Arms, he alone planned the details of Lord Castletown's investiture: to shine in the royal light was the very raison d'être of the Office of Arms. Only rarely did the King come on a state visit to Ireland, so Vicars had only the one chance of getting things right. Because of all these pressing concerns, he claimed that the incident of the unlocked door had just slipped his mind.

On 4 July, the Under-Secretary of State for Ireland, Sir Antony Patrick MacDonnell, returned from London to personally supervise the final preparations for the royal visit. The question of where their Majesties would stay while in Ireland had not yet been resolved. The King apparently preferred to stay at the Vice-Regal lodge in the Phoenix Park, even though the royal apartments in the Castle had been prepared. Although King Edward was popular among his Irish subjects, there always existed the possibility of an attempt on his life by an extreme Nationalist or an anarchist. For security reasons, Lord Aberdeen preferred the King to sleep on board the royal yacht, *Victoria and Albert*. MacDonnell, who ultimately had responsibility for policing Ireland, favoured Aberdeen's proposal. Later in the week, His Majesty reluctantly agreed to Aberdeen's proposals. MacDonnell felt confident that the royal visit on 10 July would go smoothly.

At 5.30pm on 5 July Stivey went upstairs to Sir Arthur's office, where he found him working with his private secretary, Mr Horlock. Stivey asked if he should lock the strong room for the night. Sir Arthur, handing him a manuscript to return to the strong room, replied 'Yes, you may close it'. After placing the manuscript inside, Stivey then closed and locked the outer door of the strong room, leaving, as usual, two keys hanging in the lock of the inner grille. After Stivey left for the day, Sir Arthur twice had to pass by the strong room to use the telephone, and out of habit, tested the strong room door and found it locked. Before closing the offices for the night, Sir Arthur made what he called his 'usual tour of inspection': 'I passed into the messenger's room, noticed the window was bolted and tried the handle of the strong room door and found the door was locked.'

After locking the front door on his way out, Vicars met a reporter in Upper Castle Yard, who jogged his memory about some detail of protocol. Sir Arthur excused himself because he wanted to call Lord Aberdeen immediately on the matter. Instead of re-entering his own offices, he decided to use the direct phone-line in the Chief Secretary's offices. He walked straight past the sentries on the Main Gate, entered the Chief Secretary's offices, bid hello to the night duty policeman, and made his call. Afterwards, he left by the Main Gate and stopped off at the Kildare Street Club before going home. Meanwhile, at 7:30pm Detective Kerr started his nightly inspection of the Office of Arms: he checked each room, including the cellar. All appeared to be in order.

The next morning, Saturday 6 July, Mrs Farrell made a second and more distressing discovery. Entering the Office at 7am, she checked for any instructions on Stivey's desk. As she entered his office, she found the strong room door ajar. Looking inside she saw the two keys in the lock of the inside grille. Unaware that Stivey always left these keys there, she removed them, and closing the outer door of the strong room, she placed the keys on Stivey's blotting paper, where she and Stivey sometimes left notes for each other. Though deeply troubled by her discovery, she again elected to pass the responsibility for alerting the police onto Stivey. Instinctively, she wanted to get away from the building in a hurry, and she rushed through her cleaning chores. Finishing just after 9am, she scribbled a note for Stivey outlining what she had found. She apologised for not staying to talk to him personally, explaining that she had to take care of an urgent domestic problem. Then she fled for the safety of home.

When Stivey arrived at about 10:20am, he found Mrs Farrell's note and the two keys tied with twine. He recognised them at once. The large key opened the lock of the inside grille, and the small key opened the presses in the Library. Stivey knew that he had shut the strong room the night before and had seen the keys in the grille lock. With the two keys now sitting on his blotting paper, the shocking truth of Mrs Farrell's note became obvious. She could only have reached the inner grille keys and removed them if the outer strong room door was open. Along with rare documents, the strong room contained other items of great value. These included three gold collars housed in a glass case, two state maces, the sword of state, a jewelled sceptre, a crown, and two massive silver spurs. Stivey immediately did an inspection and found everything in order. He knew that he should report the incident to the police, but a lifetime in the navy had impressed on him the importance of the chain of command and had atrophied his initiative. Incredibly, instead of going round the corner to the constables on duty at the Main Gate, or going over to the constable outside the Chief Secretary's offices, or going 50 yards to the headquarters of the Dublin Metropolitan Police, Stivey just sat at his desk wringing his hands anxiously as he waited for Sir Arthur to arrive. When Sir Arthur arrived at 11:30am, Stivey told him that Mrs Farrell had found the strong room open that morning. Sir Arthur casually replied 'Did she?' or 'Is that so?', and taking no more notice of the incident, went up to his office. Stivey, presuming that his chief had not grasped the seriousness of the situation, went to see him in his office, where he found him working with Horlock. Again Stivey related the message about the strong room, and again Sir Arthur took no notice.

Vicars' inaction baffled Stivey. As he understood the chain of command, his chief ought to have inspected the strong room personally. Under no circumstance should he have relied on Stivey's word that all was well and in its place. In the past, Sir Arthur had often complained that he bore an enormous burden of responsibility as custodian of the Crown Jewels, but on this occasion he seemed indifferent to the possibility that a prowler may have entered his offices. Stivey initially thought about alerting the Castle police himself, but years of taking orders in the navy had taught him to keep his own counsel. After all, he had no right to act alone or be presumptuous enough as to offer his superior unsolicited advice

If Stivey thought his chief had behaved most unusually that fateful Saturday, his biggest surprise still awaited him. On Saturdays, Stivey usually left the office early, so at 2:30pm he went to Sir Arthur' room to ask if he could leave for the day. He found Sir Arthur, Horlock and Miss Gibbon, the office secretary, working on the draft of a letter. Sir Arthur told Stivey he could leave and then picked up the gold collar worn by the late Lord de Ros, which had just been returned from the jewellers, and turning to

Stivey said, 'I wish you would take this collar and place it in the safe, we are getting overcrowded here'. Then Sir Arthur took his key chain, and singling out the key to the safe in the library, handed both the collar and the key to Stivey. If Sir Arthur had hit Stivey he could not have stunned him more. Sir Arthur never trusted anybody with his key to the great steel safe containing the Crown Jewels of Ireland. Yet here he was handing it over to the humblest member of staff.

Bewildered, Stivey descended the stairs. Entering the library, he walked over to the safe. He had never opened it before, but had watched Sir Arthur do so many times. The safe had two key slots, one for locked and the other for open. He placed the key in the locked slot, but try as he might, he could not get the key to work. Then he realised that the safe was not locked. Stivey's mind, hysterical with panic, refused to accept this fact. After a minute or so of frantic efforts to unlock an unlocked safe, he retreated towards the stairs. Overhead he heard footsteps, and as he arrived at the bottom of the stairs, Sir Arthur appeared at the top. Stivey called out to him: 'Sir Arthur, the last time you were at the safe you could not have locked the door.' Sir Arthur replied, 'I must have done.' 'Well,' said Stivey, 'I find that the safe door is unlocked.' Sir Arthur replied, 'Oh, I wonder if they are all right.'

Vicars hurried down, and snatching the key from Stivey, tried to insert the key into the 'locked' slot. At once he realised that the safe was already unlocked. He pressed on the handle

18

and the safe opened. Inside he saw the red morocco box containing the Crown Jewels. Lifting it out, he noticed the key in the lock. He never left the box with the key in the lock. When he opened it, the Grand Master's diamond star and badge were missing. 'My God, they're gone,' he cried. 'The jewels are gone!' If this were not sufficiently unsettling, he also found that the ribbon and clasp, normally attached to the Grand Master's diamond star, had been removed and carefully left in the box. He knew that this could not be done hurriedly, because it involved unscrewing the very small screws of the swivel and coaxing the ribbon off the hook.

Sir Arthur quickly examined the rest of the contents of the safe and found the gold collars of Lords Mayo, Enniskillen, Ormonde and Howth missing from their cases. The late Lord Cork's collar and enamelled badge had also disappeared, but the tissue paper in which they had been wrapped lay neatly folded in their box. Also taken was the small box containing his late mother's jewels, valued at £1,500. This box had been locked, and he had left the key with his brother George Mahony in Kilmorna. Stivey went to alert the police as Sir Arthur, shaken and dumbfounded, stayed by the safe. As if in mockery, the Letters Patent of the Order of St Patrick, under which Sir Arthur held office, stared back at him from the bottom of the safe.

Stivey had all of 50 yards to travel to reach the headquarters of the Dublin Metropolitan Police. He reported the theft, but in one of the many mysteries surrounding this case, the Dublin police experienced a period of complete inertia. Although no police officer rushed over to the Office of Arms to investigate the crime, word of the theft soon moved up the chain of command, and some time after three o'clock the news reached Assistant Police Commissioner William Harrel. At least 45 minutes after Stivey first reported the theft, Superintendent Lowe of the Dublin Metropolitan Police made his way over to the Office of Arms to investigate.

Lowe questioned Sir Arthur and his staff, taking down all the details. For some reason, Sir Arthur and Stivey neglected to tell Lowe about Mrs Farrell discovering the strong room door open that morning, or about finding the front door unlocked three days earlier. When questioned directly about the strong room, Sir Arthur replied, 'It is a modern safe, a Milner safe, and quite secure; it could not be opened but by its own key.'

Lowe left the office taking the morocco case with him, and made a swift verbal report to Harrel, who only then decided to walk over and investigate the crime. Harrel questioned Sir Arthur about the number of keys to the safe, and learnt that Vicars kept a spare key to the safe hidden at home in a locked drawer. He asked Sir Arthur to go home at once to check for the key, but Sir Arthur refused, promising to check later that evening and telephone the police. When he got home that evening, Sir Arthur rang the police to tell them the spare key was safe. Harrel briefed his superiors, Sir John Ross, the Chief Commissioner of police and Sir

James Dougherty, Assistant Under-Secretary of State for Ireland, and promised to vigorously pursue the investigation.

The next morning, 7 July, Detective Kerr, assisted by two officers, went round to Mary's Abbey to question Mrs Farrell. Without bothering to obtain a search warrant, they marched into Mrs Farrell's home and turned the place upside down as they searched for clues to the crime. In the process they discovered Republican literature belonging to her son Seamus, leading the police to keep the young man under surveillance for the next four months. Although the police did not suspect Mrs Farrell in the theft, Kerr interrogated her aggressively. Utterly intimidated and terrified, Mrs Farrell told Kerr everything she knew. She told him about finding the front door unlocked the previous Wednesday, and about finding the strong room ajar on Saturday morning. Under further questioning, Mrs Farrell revealed to Kerr that she saw a stranger in the office, early in the morning, just after the Christmas season. She identified the person as Lord Haddo, the son of Lord Aberdeen, the Lord Lieutenant of Ireland.

Mrs Farrell's statement to Detective Kerr threw the police into a state of confusion. They wondered why Sir Arthur and his staff had not informed them of the earlier intrusions into the office. This omission put Sir Arthur in a poor light and they wondered what else he may have neglected to tell them.

Harrel suggested posting a reward, the Castle authorities agreed, and the police circulated a notice offering £1,000 for the return of the jewels. Dougherty relayed all the news to his superiors, MacDonnell and Lord Aberdeen. By this time the royal train, with Their Majesties on board, had left Euston station en route to Wales, where the royal yacht lay waiting to ferry them to Dublin. Aberdeen worried that the theft might detract from His Majesty's visit, and that would annoy the King even more than the loss of his jewels. He discussed the matter in depth with MacDonnell, all the time insisting that the timing of the theft could not have been coincidental. Surely it had something to do with the King's visit? They decided to send a telegram to the Home Office, who would then relay the bad news to the King on board the royal yacht. It would be most improper if the King happened to read about the theft in the morning papers. They also asked Scotland Yard to assist in the investigation.

The 'vigorous' investigation promised by the Dublin police left much to be desired. Assistant Commissioner Harrel did not assign a lead investigator to the case. This resulted in haphazard questioning by different officers, and a lack of direction. During the first days of the investigation, the police and detectives neglected to take sworn statements from Sir Arthur and his staff. Because of a persistent lack of note taking, they had not cleared up who had what keys and when they had them.

The established security arrangements for the Castle were as follows. Every evening after 7pm, the police locked and placed sentries on all the side gates into the Castle. Only pedestrians could enter by these gates, and passing through a wicket, they had to identify themselves to the policeman on duty. The Main Gate beside the Office of Arms became the only entry and exit point for carriages. A detachment of police and soldiers manned this gate and had their guardhouse in the cellar of the Office of Arms. The main Castle guardhouse was next door to the Office of Arms. In the evening, the police had orders to identify every person entering or leaving the Castle. During the week before the royal visit, the Castle police received instructions to be more vigilant than usual, and an intruder ran a much greater risk of being questioned. After 7pm, all the offices were closed, leaving the Upper Castle Yard all but deserted, and the guards knew by sight the few remaining civilians. Furthermore, the police put a constable on duty in Upper Castle Yard at evening time, and he had specific orders to watch the vacant offices.

The greatest obstacle confronting a thief was the night constable patrolling the Upper Castle Yard. This man had the specific duty of guarding the offices at night. To enter the Office of Arms, a thief would have had to walk into the Bedford Tower's portico in plain view of the constable. Routine events can numb a guard's alertness to the point where he takes little notice but he would surely notice something unusual. At night, nobody had any business going into the offices, except Detective Kerr when he made his nightly rounds. When questioned, the night constable assured detectives that he had seen nothing unusual and that nobody had entered the offices while he patrolled the Upper Castle Yard. Despite the self-evident truth that an individual had entered the offices at least twice in the same week, the police did not press the matter any further.

For many years, Sir Arthur and his staff locked the office by slipping the bolt of the latch to shut the door, so that any person having a latchkey could still enter when the office was closed. The police had detected no signs of picking or forcing of the Yale lock, leading them to conclude that the intruder had a key. They ascertained that the following seven people possessed keys to the front door: Sir Arthur Vicars; Mr Burtchaell, Secretary; Mr P. G. Mahony, Cork Herald; William Stivey, the messenger; Mrs Farrell, the office cleaner; Detective Kerr, the nightly inspector; and John O'Keeffe, an employee of the Board of Works who lit the lantern above the Bedford Tower during the Dublin Season. The Season had ended on 24 March and he had not entered the Office of Arms since. Everyone possessing a key had perfectly valid reasons for having one.

Three departments shared responsibility for security in the Office of Arms. Sir Arthur had sole custody of the jewels. The Board of Works provided the safe and built the strong room, but had resisted replacing the large safe with a smaller one that would fit through the door of the strong room. In fact, the Board's furniture clerk emphatically refused to recommend a new safe because he thought the sentries on the Main

Gate provided 24-hour security for the offices. Therefore, the safe was placed in the library adjoining the strong room. The police had responsibility for the general security of the office, but surprisingly, as the professionals in these matters, they had no input on the safe-keeping of the jewels.

Four keys existed for the strong room's outer door. Stivey, Sir Arthur and Mahony had one each, and the fourth, which had been Burtchaell's, was hidden in an unlocked drawer inside the strong room. Inside the strong room door was a steel grille, and Vicars told Stivey to leave the key in the grille-lock when he was in the office, and to lock the grille and put the key in an unlocked drawer when he left the office on errands. Sir Arthur set up this routine to reduce the bother for himself, and his staff, in retrieving the manuscripts.

Following the discovery of the theft, two locksmiths examined the locks of the safe and the strong room. F. J. O'Hare, a Dublin agent of the Milner Safe Company, checked the strong room lock with great care. He took it apart and inspected the seven highly polished levers with a magnifying glass. He found no scratches on the levers, thereby concluding that no one had tampered with the lock. In a similar vein, Cornelius Gallagher, a locksmith from the Ratner Safe Company, examined the safe in the library. Removing the lock and chamber and taking the levers apart, he found no scratches from an alien key. Gallagher also concluded that no one had tampered with the safe lock.

The two expert locksmiths made similar reports. First, nobody had picked or tried to pick the locks. Second, the thief had used original keys, or perfect copies. Third, if the thief had used copies of the original keys, he did not fabricate them from wax impressions. The locksmiths claimed that although keys made from a wax impression could have opened the locks, small errors in the keys would have left pressure and friction scratches on the levers. Independently, the two locksmiths, basing their arguments on the absence of even minute scratches, categorically stated that the thief used the original key or a perfect copy. The police agreed with the men's findings.

The police concluded that the locksmiths' report about the keys, and the removal of the ribbon from the diamond star pointed to an inside job. They questioned the staff of the Office of Arms about their whereabouts from 2 July to 6 July. Frank Shackleton had been appointed the Dublin Herald two years earlier and Francis Bennett-Goldney had been appointed Athlone Pursuivant just four months previous to the theft. Neither man had keys to the office and had perfect alibis, as they lived almost full-time in England and had not yet crossed over to Dublin for the royal visit on 10 July. Mahony, the Cork Herald, had left Dublin in April for health reasons and had not returned until 4 July, so he could not have broken into the office on 2 July. Sir Arthur also had an alibi for 2 July as he dined at home at 8pm with a close friend, Mr McEnnery Jnr. The fact that the front door was found open the next morning meant that it had to be left open by the intruder after Detective Kerr had locked it when he completed his 7:30pm nightly inspection. This would not have left enough time for Sir Arthur to leave the door open and make it back to his house by 8:00pm. Thus each of the heralds had an alibi.

From the start, the police ruled out Mrs Farrell, Stivey and Ms Gibbon as possible suspects. They concluded that none of them had access to the safe key. This left the two assistants, Burtchaell and Horlock, both of whom satisfactorily accounted for their whereabouts. Also, the sentries would have noticed any of Sir Arthur's junior staff walking about the Castle after office hours. Therefore, the police concluded that the 'insider' on Vicars' staff must have had an accomplice who committed the theft.

While any member of staff could easily get hold of the keys to the front door and the strong room, accessing the key to the safe presented a problem. During the day, Vicars kept this key with him all the time, thus the thief could only get hold of this key, or the spare key, at his house, but only the heralds visited or stayed at Sir Arthur's home. Vicars often took long baths in the evening, during which time he left his keys in his bedroom. Thus, any man in the house on one of those evenings could swap a look-alike for the key. He could then make a copy and replace the key the next evening. Shackleton shared the house with Sir Arthur, so he had access to the key, as did Mahony who visited the house regularly. However, Goldney had only stayed with Sir Arthur for three days in May during the opening of the International Exhibition, and in that period Sir Arthur opened the safe at least twice. Thus, Goldney appears to have had no opportunity to take the key, get a copy made and replace it.

Given that the thief or his accomplice had to have been one of the heralds, and that he had to access the safe key in Sir Arthur's house, a more plausible theory presents itself. If the thief knew of the spare key hidden in the locked drawer then he could have taken Sir Arthur's key chain during one of his long baths, opened the locked drawer, and borrowed the spare safe key. After making a copy he could replace it in the same manner. This left the thief lots of time to make the copy away from Dublin. Both Shackleton and Mahony were close enough to Sir Arthur to have known the hiding place of the spare key.

Explaining the timing of the theft exercised the imaginations of the police. What normal thief, who already had all the keys he needed, would choose to steal the King of England's jewels just four days before he arrived in Ireland? Even the most daring thieves have strong survival instincts, and taking the jewels after the King's visit would have aroused less royal rage. The consensus among investigating detectives was that the thief deliberately timed the burglary to coincide with the royal visit and create a massive uproar.

The opening of the strong room also baffled the police. In a regular theft, greed is the prime motive and the thief takes as much booty as he can. A most striking fact of this case was that the thief ignored the valuables in the strong room. He had an accomplice on staff, so he must have known where to find the jewels. If the thief wanted to steal only the Crown Jewels, why had he bothered with the strong room at all? All the investigators agreed that the intruder left the front door open on 2 July, to precipitate the discovery of the missing jewels. If Mrs Farrell or Sir Arthur had acted normally and reported the open front door, the police would have begun their investigation without ever knowing that the thief had access to the strong room. This simple observation posed a profoundly puzzling problem for the police: Why go to the trouble of getting the strong room key if you don't intend to steal anything from it?

The best the police could offer was an alibi theory. They suggested that when the open front door did not cause an investigation, the thief returned three days later and left the strong room door open to force the discovery of the theft, thus leaving his insider accomplice with a solid alibi. However, this feeble theory had few supporters because the most obvious way of prompting the discovery of the missing jewels was to leave the safe door ajar. In reality, the thief had no need of the strong room key, nor had he any obvious purpose in opening the strong room door.

Adding more mystery to the crime, was the thief's removal of the blue ribbon and its swivel from the diamond star. Presumably the thief did this while in the Office of Arms, which meant he planned the removal beforehand, because he had to bring a very small screwdriver to undo the tiny screws of the swivel. Then he spent as much as ten laborious minutes teasing the ribbon off the hook. Why did the thief do this? Apparently he wanted to convince the police that the theft was an inside job, even though his accomplice would come under closer scrutiny as a consequence.

The greatest mystery of the theft concerns the thief's second entry into the Office of Arms. Smart thieves do not return to the scene of the crime but this brazen fellow readily did, even though it was continuously patrolled by soldiers and policemen. In all probability, his accomplice on staff was one of the heralds, but all three were away when Mrs. Farrell discovered the open front door on 3 July. We know that Vicars just ignored the incident, but how could the thief have learnt that? Obviously, by leaving the front door open, the thief expected Sir Arthur to react, so how could he be sure that he had said nothing to the authorities? If any possibility existed that the police had the Office of Arms under surveillance, only a daring thief would have gone back a second time. Yet if the thief's motive for leaving the strong door open was to create an alibi for his accomplice, he could easily have achieved the same result by telephoning the police and demanding a ransom for the jewels or by leaving the safe door ajar in the first place. Because the thief fearlessly re-entered the Office of Arms, one must conclude that he knew that Sir Arthur had not reported the open front door to the police.

The circumstances surrounding the theft of the Irish Crown Jewels from under the noses of the guards in Dublin Castle, arguably the most secure location in the United Kingdom, caught the imagination of the press. All the newspapers carried a detailed account of the burglary, while every man in Dublin appeared to have his own theory on who perpetrated the theft. His Majesty, King Edward VII, found himself twice victimised by the crime. First, the thief had stolen his jewels, and second, the uproar that followed the theft had all but eclipsed his visit to Ireland.

The King left Ireland thoroughly enraged by the affair. As the thief had clearly used one of Sir Arthur's safe keys, His majesty demanded the dismissal of the 'careless custodian of the Jewels'. However, Sir Arthur had no intention of going quietly, and for six months he resisted tenaciously. Trying to break his resolve, the Irish administration blackened Sir Arthur's name with rumours that he was a homosexual. They increased the pressure by offering him a generous pension in return for his resignation. Finally, the Irish administration set up a Commission of Inquiry with terms of reference so restricted that they could only investigate whether Sir Arthur had been negligent in his custody of the Crown Jewels. Expert witnesses testified that the thief used Sir Arthur's key, or a perfect copy, and the Commissioners found him guilty of negligence, whereupon he lost his treasured post.

The affair ruined Sir Arthur socially and financially, leaving him with neither position nor pension, and an appalling veil of suspicion hung over his head regarding his moral character. Coming to the rescue, his half-brother, George Mahony, invited him to live at Kilmorna House, in north Kerry. Sir Arthur, almost destitute and in need of escaping the pernicious Dublin gossip, accepted his generous offer. When George died in 1912, he left the estate to Sir Arthur's sister, Edith, who lived in London and had married the son of a rich Polish industrialist. She decided that Sir Arthur could live out his days in Kilmorna.

* * *

Kilmorna House stood proudly on a splendid estate four miles from Listowel in County Kerry. Mock battlements surrounded the Gothic-styled roof, twelve great chimneys defiantly pierced the sky, while terraced lawns with beds of exotic plants stretched down to the nearby salmon rich River Feale. At the beginning of the nineteenth century, a wealthy Anglo-Irish landlord had commissioned the ivy-clad manor comprising twenty elegant rooms, an armoury, and an elaborately decorated chapel. Toward the back of the mansion, the owner had constructed a stout strong room to store his valuables whenever he went away for any length of time. In 1839, the O'Mahonys of Kerry purchased the estate and made it their Kerry seat.

Living alone in Kilmorna, Sir Arthur found

companionship in his dogs. He began subscribing to an eccentric theology, asserting that dogs follow their masters to heaven. As a consequence, he walled off a small canine graveyard at the back of the house, where he laid to rest his cherished Yorkshire terriers, adorning each grave with a small headstone. To any visitor who cared to ask, he asserted that he would meet his little canine friends in the afterlife.

Gradually Sir Arthur recovered his self esteem and the new 'Squire of Kilmorna' began entertaining the local gentry. He was considered a caring landlord and paid his workers above the going rate. Generally he was well liked by the local community, however to the more Nationalist elements, he was a Unionist Anglo Irishman and dead set against Irish independence.

In 1917, Ethel Mahony, the wife of his late nephew, the Cork Herald died, leaving her sister Gertrude all alone. Feeling sorry for her and in need of human companionship, Sir Arthur, at 52, surprised everyone by marrying her and bringing her to live in Kilmorna.

After the Great War the Irish Republican movement grew in strength and eclipsed the more moderate Nationalists. In 1919 the Irish War of Independence began in earnest, gradually encircling Sir Arthur's rural oasis with bloodshed. By 1920 the struggle began to favour the Irish Republican Army (IRA), who, having mastered the art of guerrilla warfare, ambushed the British forces throughout the countryside. Britain retaliated by sending in the notorious 'Black and Tan' militia to suppress the

Republicans with force and terror. Raw force had always worked in the past, but now each brutal act by the 'Tans' only aroused greater sympathy and support for the IRA. The Irish refer to this period as the 'troubles', a time of ambush and retaliation. As the 'troubles' raged on, the IRA adopted a more persuasive tactic. They burnt down the great houses of the British and Anglo-Irish landlords, forcing them to flee Ireland permanently.

With the great houses burning, many local landlords, fearing for their own safety, adopted a low profile. But not Sir Arthur. He fervently believed in Unionism, the movement supporting the political union of Ireland and Britain. Like so many of his social circle, he abhorred the notion of the Catholic majority governing Ireland. Holding steadfast to his Unionist beliefs, he openly supported the local garrison of 'Tans' stationed in Listowel. In doing so, he knew that he ran the danger of incurring reprisals from the IRA, but he fervently believed that the great Nationalist reputation of his brother, The O'Mahony of Kerry, would protect him. On 30 April 1920, Sir Arthur's naïve delusions of immunity abruptly vanished when the 'troubles' came knocking at his door.

Under the cover of darkness, twelve armed IRA volunteers of the local Duagh Company descended on Kilmorna House searching for guns. As usual Sir Arthur had retired to his study when he heard a knock on the back door. After asking who was there, a muffled voice gave the name of a well-known District Inspector of the

Royal Irish Constabulary (RIC). Deeply suspicious that his friend, the District Inspector, would choose to use the rear entrance, Sir Arthur refused to open the door. Prepared for this eventuality, the men smashed down the door with large axes and forced their way in. Grabbing Sir Arthur, the intruders demanded the key to his strong room. To their astonishment, he calmly refused.

At first Sir Arthur's quiet resolve threw the raiders into complete confusion, but their leader, Jimmy Costello, quickly regained control. He pushed Sir Arthur against a wall, and ordered his men to form a firing squad. Obeying, ten men aimed their rifles. Costello began his count to ten slowly, one . . . two . . . three. The men became tense, trigger fingers became taut, but Sir Arthur, with his eyes fixed on Costello, remained calm. Just before the count of ten, Sir Arthur broke the tension by offering to show them the location of the strong room. However, after leading them to it, he threw them into total disarray by once again refusing to hand over the key.

Frustrated by Sir Arthur's unexpected nerve, the rebels attempted to enter the strong room from above by ripping up the floorboards of the bedroom overhead. Once they realised the strong room had a reinforced roof, they knew that any effort to break through with axes would be futile. Now angry and bewildered, the raiders turned again on Sir Arthur, but their previous indecision had convinced him to resist. After enduring their verbal rage, Sir Arthur with a steady voice, politely gave the raiders two choices — either shoot him or leave. Exasperated by this stubborn little man, the intruders made a half-hearted effort to break down the strong room door, but quickly gave up. Humiliated, Costello told his men to leave, and turning to Sir Arthur, he warned him that they would soon return. Delighted, Sir Arthur courteously insisted they exit by the front door.

Lady Vicars, shaken by the ordeal, begged her husband to heed their warning and leave Ireland, at least until the troubles had ended. Dismissing his wife's fears as groundless, Sir Arthur refused, though six days later, he prudently made his will and had it witnessed by his land steward, George Cuninghame, and his wife. With his affairs in order, he now proceeded to act in absolute defiance of the IRA. He wrote an embellished account of the incident to his friend, Lord Asketh, describing how he had stood up to 100 armed rebels. To great cheers from his fellow peers, Lord Asketh read aloud the letter in the House of Lords. Sir Arthur's closest friends, especially Canon Addersley, the Listowel Rector, were appalled by the recklessness of Sir Arthur's letter, an account of which appeared in *The Times*, and advised him to refrain from further antagonising the IRA. All advice to act prudently fell on deaf ears. Sir Arthur boldly continued to court the IRA's displeasure by inviting British army officers to tea and sending food hampers to the Listowel barracks.

No man can anticipate his reaction to danger until he confronts the real thing. When Sir

Arthur found himself put to the test, he discovered a deep sense of duty to his Unionist beliefs, and disregarding the IRA threats, he now started spying on their activities. He gathered information from within his own social circle and informers. Aided by his local knowledge, he applied his scholarly discipline to these snippets of fact, and supplied the army with reliable reports on the rebels' movements. Impressed with his efforts, the army command began sharing information with him. Sir Arthur knew the IRA would kill him if they caught him spying.

Although Sir Arthur repeatedly displayed great kindness to others, his single greatest failing was his inability to appreciate another person's point of view. Thus, as he embraced the Black and Tans, he not only enraged the IRA, but also offended the more neutral residents in the area. He utterly failed to comprehend how much the local population feared and loathed these undisciplined irregulars, and the more he befriended them the more he alienated his neighbours. At Christmas, he lost all remaining goodwill. While many in the area went without, he took it upon himself to deliver six fat turkeys to the 'Tans' in the Listowel barracks. The final straw came when a servant girl at Kilmorna House informed the IRA that Sir Arthur had received a written message from Dublin Castle praising him for his intelligence gathering.

In April 1921, the leaders of the local IRA, Kerry No. 1 Brigade, thought the moment had come to run Sir Arthur out of the county. Their sources in Listowel heard that he had invited a high-ranking British officer to tea, and that a Captain Watson and ten soldiers would provide a military escort. The Brigade thought they could frighten Sir Arthur by ambushing the soldiers and their distinguished officer as they left his estate.

On 7 April 1921, Sir Arthur entertained his distinguished guest. Nine IRA volunteers, including young Michael Galvin, secretly assembled for the ambush 100 yards west of the main gate. They took up strategic positions behind a ditch that provided a good line of fire and a quick escape. With each man in position, they waited patiently. The volunteers knew that they would have ample warning of the approaching soldiers because Sir Arthur always rode ahead to the entrance of the estate before giving the all-clear signal to his army guests. As evening fell, Sir Arthur came riding out to the main gate as expected. The rebels readied themselves for action.

On receiving Sir Arthur's signal, the escort of soldiers rode out ahead on bicycles. Constantly alert for an ambush, they cycled in duck-like formation. As they neared the bend, the IRA opened fire, but astonishingly, they only hit the two front riders. In their second volley of shots, they managed to hit Captain Watson in the forehead, and he fell to the ground. Then young Galvin, an inexperienced volunteer, made a fatal mistake. Wanting a better line of fire he stepped out from behind a pillar to shoot. With Galvin now fully exposed, Captain Watson, who had only received a graze to his head, shot him dead. As the British soldiers returned fire, the IRA quickly dispersed, leaving behind their dead comrade. After the skirmish, the escort divided into two groups, one going to Listowel to get support, the other moving their wounded to the nearby home of the Keane family.

Within the hour, a reinforcement of 'Tans' arrived. Anticipating a second attack, they had strapped a rebel prisoner, Florrie McCarthy, to the front of the armoured car to act as a human shield. They began scouring the fields for their attackers, but as night fell, they called off the search to return to the safety of their barracks. On their way back the 'Tans' strapped Galvin's body and chained it to the back of the armoured car for all the townspeople to see.

Back in Listowel, the 'Tans' displayed Galvin's bloodied body at the workhouse. They planned to avenge their wounded 'mates' by seizing any relatives who claimed the body. At a minimum, they intended to burn the family home and give the menfolk a savage beating. However, they waited in vain, for nobody came forward. The IRA had issued a standing order to Republican families never to claim the body of their relatives. Annoyed that nobody had come forward, the 'Tans' pressed the local police to identify the dead rebel. Fearing reprisals on their own people, the police reluctantly told the 'Tans' that the dead man might be one of the Galvins.

The 'Tans', not sure who to punish, rounded up all the Galvin family. Unknown to them, they had caught young Galvin's mother in their dragnet. No man can ever comprehend the secret thoughts of this unfortunate woman as the 'Tans' brought her to the workhouse. She knew she had to be strong to protect the rest of the family: she dare not evince the slightest emotion when she viewed the bloody body of her young son. However, nothing could have prepared her for what she saw when the soldiers brought her into that impersonal room. Her son lay on a cold marble table, his clothes bloodstained, his face bruised, and his hands still tied together. Her heart broke with grief, but outwardly she remained composed and told the soldiers that she did not recognise the young man. She acted the part well. Her calm demeanour convinced the 'Tans', and they let her walk away.

Finally, losing patience, the Tans defiled Galvin's body, and threw his bloodstained body into an unmarked grave. Within hours, his comrades discovered the burial site, and the following night, they secretly exhumed his body and buried him with military honours at Gale Cemetery.

The IRA were now more infuriated by Sir Arthur's stubborn determination to stay put. However, this paled in comparison to their feelings for Galvin's mother. Even for the 'Tans', this treatment had plumbed a new low. While the local IRA brooded, something snapped and they turned their anger on Sir Arthur with deadly intent. A week later at 9am on 14 April 1921, sections of the Duagh and the Knockanure units of the Kerry No. 1 Brigade assembled near the orchard wall of Kilmorna. Led by Paddy Deane and Jackie Brehany, some 30 men stole down through the fields towards Kilmorna House. The two leaders had been close friends of Galvin, and they had become enraged trying to comfort his mother.

Except for the servants going about their household duties, all was calm in the great house. Sir Arthur was still in bed as he rarely arose early. On this morning he felt poorly, as an attack of bronchitis had kept him awake, and he had his land steward, Francis Cuninghame, attend upon him in his bedroom.

Kitty Kelly, the cook, spotted the IRA men, guns drawn, converging on the house. She raced inside to alert Lady Vicars, who hurried upstairs to warn Sir Arthur. Throwing on his dressing gown, Sir Arthur shouted to Michael Murphy, his valet, to secure the front door. However, an advance party of masked raiders had already entered the house through the servants' quarters. Inside, the raiders caught Cuninghame trying to escape. Delighted with catching this particularly unpopular steward, they hit him with their rifles and locked him in a room. Terrified and fearing for his life, he managed to escape out a window and hid in the nearby woods. The staff now sensed the danger and panicked. One young servant girl began sobbing uncontrollably, while others tried to hide wherever they could. Lar Bruder, one of the raiders, caught hold of Sir Arthur's valet, and assured him that they had only come to burn the house and that no one would be harmed. While the IRA began dousing the house with petrol, Murphy reassured the staff and told them to leave the house.

Murphy remained calm. He had faced danger before, when, with Sir Arthur's encouragement, he had enlisted and fought in the Great War. Injured in battle, Sir Arthur had rewarded him with the position of valet. Murphy raced upstairs to assure his master that the IRA only intended to burn the house. Although relieved, Sir Arthur now started fretting about the family heirlooms. As smoke began to fill the house, he instructed his valet to save the family portraits by throwing them out a window onto the shrubs below. Murphy's calmness soon disappeared, and he shouted at Sir Arthur to forget the heirlooms and save himself. Finally, with their exit to safety almost cut off, Murphy began fearing for his own life. He caught hold of Sir Arthur and literally pulled him out the front door to safety.

Murphy brought his master down the front steps to the lawn below and into the hands of the waiting IRA. The commander gave a prearranged signal to three men. Immediately, they took hold of Sir Arthur and dragged him to a nearby tree. They told him to make his peace with God. Sir Arthur looked up into each man's eyes, but from the cold intensity he found staring back at him, he knew that this time there would be no hesitating. With just a hint of a smile, he played out his last act of defiance and told his executioners 'just get on with it'. They shot him five times.

Standing 50 feet from the tree, Lady Vicars witnessed the execution of her husband. She saw him thrown back against the tree as the first two bullets tore into his chest and head. For the longest moment, she stood transfixed and immobilised with horror, then, almost in slow motion, she collapsed to the ground in shock.

Meanwhile, a stable-hand, slipping away unnoticed to the nearby post office, alerted the army in Listowel. As the soldiers raced to Sir Arthur's defence, a single well-placed IRA sniper positioned at Shanacool Cross held them at bay for almost an hour. When the army finally got through, it was too late. They found the magnificent manor ablaze, and the rebels had made good their escape. Sir Arthur's body lay crumpled in a pool of blood just 30 yards from the house. Around his neck, the IRA had placed a placard bearing the inscription: Spy, informers beware. IRA never forgets.

Dozens of heavily-armed British soldiers watched helplessly as Kilmorna House turned into an inferno. The fire voraciously swallowed Sir Arthur's valuable documentation of family pedigrees and his collection of heraldic books. Steadily the blaze reached the top storey and tore through the roof to the accompaniment of crashing timbers. As the supporting walls buckled, one of the great chimneys surrendered, toppled and plunged almost gracefully into the waiting embrace of the engulfing flames below. Three months later, the signing of the cease-fire ended Britain's defence of the Union in Southern Ireland, and Sir Arthur's world vanished forever.

Sir Arthur's death raises the question of why such a decent man, albeit a highly eccentric one, had to die so savagely in the land he loved so dearly. In reality, the Irish War of Independence erupted after a long incubation of political bitterness. For decades, the conflict germinated in the fertile nursery of corrosive political bigotry. Home rule, the aspiration of Ireland's majority for self determination, dominated Irish politics for the 50 years preceding the War of Independence. Ireland became polarised into two tribes — the home rulers or Nationalists, and the Unionists who believed strongly in the union of Britain and Ireland. Irishmen had to take one side or the other, and this issue defined the individual and distinguished his friends from his enemies. Nobody could or would give an inch, and both sides adopted a policy of 'no surrender'.

The theft of the jewels, involving various political figures, took place in the midst of this corosive political atmosphere.

2

IRELAND: A LAND OF DISCONTENT

The agitation for Irish home rule began gathering strength 50 years before the War of Independence. Irish Catholics threw their support overwhelmingly behind home rule, and the Nationalists could expect to elect over 80 members to the English Parliament in every election. Opposing the Nationalists, the Protestant minority, driven by fear, rallied behind the Unionists. They believed home rule meant Rome rule, and they so dreaded the notion that they argued hell itself was a preferable option. As the home rule movement grew stronger, the Unionists resorted to every means, fair and foul, to thwart the aspirations of the nationalist majority.

For most of the nineteenth century, the Irish Nationalist members of parliament (the Irish Party) posed no threat, because the two English parties, the Tories and Liberals, firmly supported the Union of Ireland and Britain. As the century came to a close, English parliamentary cohesion on the Union cracked.

In 1884, 23 years before the Irish Crown Jewel affair, another Dublin Castle scandal came to light. William O'Brien, the fiery Irish editor of the *United Irishman*, published an unsigned article by T.M. Healy, an Irish propagandist for home rule. Hinting at unnatural vice, the article said that it was high time that 'the life and adventures, and what is known as the 'private character' of various Crown employees in Dublin Castle were fully laid before the universe'. The Liberal government retaliated against O'Brien. Hoping to silence him permanently by ruining his paper with huge court costs, the Liberals forced the officials named in the article to sue for libel, even though they knew the truth of the charges. They expected that O'Brien would be unable to persuade anyone to testify against the officials because the witnesses would have to implicate themselves in the scandal. O'Brien had an arduous job in defending himself against the libel writ. However, in a tense court case, he won. With only minutes to spare, his key witnesses agreed to testify against the plaintiffs. The court ruled for O'Brien, and the resulting 'widespread belief that homosexual 'vice' was rampant in official circles in Ireland did much to discredit Gladstone's Liberal administration at this time.'

Gladstone subscribed to the strangest (and perhaps contradictory) sexual morality of any British Prime Minister in history. The shocking revelations concerning British officials in Dublin Castle disillusioned him with the Irish administration. His scruples over the homosexual scandal brought to light by O'Brien led him to rethink his entire position on 'the Irish question'. Having investigated numerous problems as Tory Under-Secretary for the colonies in 1835, he came to believe the remedy for Ireland's unrest lay in local self-government. A member of the Conservative and Unionist Party, Gladstone later crossed the floor to join the Liberals, and during the 1860s he gradually developed his political ideal of liberty. Gladstone could not reconcile his ideals of political liberty and the reality of governing Ireland. While he and his Liberals advocated dignity and equality for the down-trodden in far-off fields, in Ireland he found himself policing the last feudal system in Western Europe. To coerce the Irish, the British stationed a huge complement of soldiers on the island which they augmented with the 10,000-strong Royal Irish Constabulary (R.I.C.). British law, with its fabled fairness, never saw the light of day in the Irish courts. To an urbane Englishman, the state of justice in Ireland gave cause for despair. In 1886, Gladstone shattered English solidarity over the 'Irish question' when he suddenly announced that he had converted to the cause of Irish home rule.

Gladstone's conversion split the Liberal Party, but with the support of Charles Stewart Parnell, the leader of the Irish Party he formed another administration. Prime Minister Gladstone put forward a Home Rule Bill that pleased nobody. Unionists felt outraged that the Liberals had betrayed the sanctity of the Union, while Parnell felt deceived that they had offered so little. Parnell pressed the Prime Minister to increase the provisions of the Bill, but Gladstone refused. Unwilling to compromise, Parnell withdrew his party's support from the Liberals. This precipitated a general election in which the Liberals went down to defeat at the hands of the Conservative and Unionist Party (Tories).

Unionists within the triumphant Tory elite decided that Parnell posed a real threat to the stability of the Union, so they devised a plan to ruin him. In 1887, they encouraged *The Times* to publish forged papers that linked him to the murder of two British officials in the Phoenix Park five years earlier. Parnell, suspecting that he would not receive justice in a British court, decided against suing the newspaper. With their prey refusing the bait, the Unionists arranged for a third party to sue *The Times*. In the sham trial that followed, the lawyers for *The Times* savagely attacked Parnell, even though he was not party to the suit.

Parnell, angered and offended at being convicted without a trial, relentlessly pursued the Government to set up a public inquiry to review the allegations against him. Over time, he convinced the British public that every accused man has the right to have his side of the story told, and the backlash compelled the Government to hold an inquiry. The Government, wanting to appear uninvolved, persuaded *The Times* to 'prosecute' the case. However, secretly they threw the resources of the state behind the newspaper, and they launched an extensive investigation into Parnell's public and private activities in Ireland. Parnell's friends in government circles warned him that the Government had instructed the police to compile a file on him for the inquiry. When Parnell questioned the

Prime Minister in the House of Commons about the Government's involvement, Lord Salisbury lied to Parliament and denied the Government's secret role.

During the Inquiry, *The Times* produced documents that almost swamped the proceedings. Counsel for Parnell constantly badgered the newspaper to produce its star witness and they finally brought forward Mr Pigott, the man who had provided them with the incriminating letters against Parnell. Parnell's counsel had bided his time for just this moment, and with Pigott under oath, he subjected the witness to an unrelenting, withering, cross examination. Pigott cracked under the merciless questioning and admitted that he had forged the letters. This admission from Pigott completely exonerated Parnell, and undermined the once-unblemished credibility of *The Times*. After testifying, Pigott fled to Spain, assisted by the newspaper owners. However, once the forger reached safety, he strangely took his own life — a most convenient and serendipitous outcome for his embarrassed patrons back in Britain.

The Unionist ploy to disgrace Parnell had backfired. As the icon of the British press, *The Times* suffered a severe blow to its prestige for knowingly publishing forged papers. The Irish leader sued the newspaper for libel and won an out-of-court settlement. In an unprecedented move, the Tory Government introduced a short Act of Parliament to protect the newspaper from further libel suits that might arise from the case. Meanwhile, Parnell's popularity soared in

Ireland whilst his victory only stiffened Unionist resolve to destroy him.

While delving into his private affairs they had discovered that Parnell was having an affair with a married woman, Katherine O'Shea. Lord Lansdowne persuaded her husband, Captain O'Shea, who was a member of the Irish Party, to name Parnell in a divorce suit. What happened afterwards exceeded everything the Unionists had ever anticipated. Gladstone took the moral high ground, rejected Parnell and gave the Irish Party a brutal choice — Parnell or home rule. The Liberal Leader got his wish when 60 of the Irish Party members deserted their leader, splitting the Irish Party into the Parnellite and anti-Parnellite factions. In Ireland the charge of adultery created an uproar, the Catholic Church's hierarchy denounced Parnell's private life and the Catholic people of Ireland abandoned their 'uncrowned king'. Parnell eventually married Katherine, but failed to hold the Irish Party together. He died some months later in Brighton, a broken man. For the next ten years, the Irish Party remained fractured and ineffective. Even when they reunited, they never rose to the same level of influence or power. The Unionists had discovered the ultimate political weapon — by destroying the man they also destroyed his cause.

When Arthur Balfour, under the Tory Government, ruled Ireland as the Chief Secretary, he earned the epitaph 'Bloody Balfour' from the Nationalists. He was largely responsible for the creation of a cadre of Irish Unionists, such as Sir Edward Carson, who lacked any scruples in defending the Union. After Chief Secretary Balfour left the Irish post, his philosophical mind took stock of the changing world about him. To the east he saw Europe marching into an enlightened age, while to the west he saw Ireland locked in a feudal quagmire. As Great Britain evolved into a modern society boasting of health and wealth, Ireland stagnated as a privy of superstition oozing with disease and want. As the British enjoyed the protection of their enlightened legal system, the Irish endured the tyranny of an anachronistic feudal system. With a new century dawning, Balfour and a small group of moderates within the party, including Lord Lansdowne, concluded that they could not shield Ireland indefinitely from the democratic forces of change sweeping through Europe and America. Abandoning coercion, Balfour tried to woo the Irish with a policy he called, 'killing home rule with kindness'.

In 1900, Balfour persuaded Lord Salisbury, the Tory Prime Minister, to send George Wyndham to Ireland as the new Chief Secretary. Wyndham, a long-time friend, enjoyed Balfour's total trust, and he agreed to implement the new policy. Balfour and Wyndham accepted that in modern Britain one could not continue indefinitely to rule the Irish majority without their support and against their will. Wyndham's mission was to forge a new political centre in Ireland by persuading moderate Unionists and Nationalists to work together. He had to strike a delicate balance. On the one hand, he had to bring in reforms to address the Nationalists' sense of injustice, while on the other, he had to govern firmly to allay Unionists' fears of desertion.

Wyndham understood Ireland and her politics. He had family ties to the country, and ten years previously, had served as Balfour's private secretary. His earlier work had prepared him for the inertia of the Irish administration. He foresaw that without a radical shake-up, he could only advance reform at a glacial pace. The Chief Secretary's office held only a feeble rein on the ad hoc mix of semi-independent boards that ran the country. As a politician, Wyndham had to spend more time in London than in Dublin, so he had to rely on his Permanent Under-Secretary, the chief civil servant, to run the country. In 1902, Sir David Harrel retired as Under-Secretary, giving Wyndham the chance to promote a civilian rather than a policeman to the top post in the civil service. He wanted Harrel's replacement to centralise the Irish administration and run the civil service like his counterpart in Britain. As before, the Under-Secretary had to keep law and order in Ireland, but Wyndham wanted a man capable of doing more than just police work; he wanted him to run the state as a civil enterprise.

3

SIR ANTONY PATRICK MACDONNELL AND DEVOLUTION

History has forgotten Sir Antony Patrick MacDonnell but in his day he was one of the most powerful men in Ireland. He played an important role in the Crown Jewels affair, but the background story of his proposed devolution scheme is crucial to interpreting the theft of the jewels. MacDonnell came to Ireland as a reformer yet his devolution proposals sparked a political crisis that almost cost him his career. Ultimately he failed to win support from either the Unionists or the Nationalists and his final devolution proposal was withdrawn just months before the theft of the jewels. As a political reformer, MacDonnell had become a spent force in Ireland and he seemed destined to retire quietly to London. Loathed by both political factions and detested by the Government ministers, even his greatest admirer at the time could never have anticipated that Mac-Donnell would spend his retirement in the House of Lords as Baron Swinford. Ironically, in taking care of the Crown Jewels affair, MacDonnell did more to please the Crown than in all his 40 years of loyal devotion to the Empire.

MacDonnell had returned to Ireland from India because George Wyndham, the Chief Secretary for Ireland, could not find a suitable man in England to be his assistant. Wyndham had combed the clubs of London looking for the right man to be his Under-Secretary, but found no takers. All the best men in London declined because the Irish post was one of the least envied jobs in the Empire. After exhausting *Who's Who* for likely candidates, he turned to his friend, Lord Lansdowne for help. Lansdowne advised Wyndham that no top man in London would touch the Irish post but suggested to him that he should approach Sir Antony Patrick MacDonnell, one of the ablest administrators in the Empire. Lansdowne gave Wyndham a glowing account of MacDonnell's 40-year career in India. However, his candidate had two serious drawbacks: he was an Irish Catholic, and more disturbing he was also some sort of 'home ruler'. Distasteful as these liabilities were, Lansdowne advised Wyndham to take the best man available, rather than appoint a second-rate individual.

MacDonnell's record impressed Wyndham. Born in 1844, in County Mayo, he was the eldest of a family of thirteen children. Though not rich, his father had accumulated enough land to become a petty landlord, enabling him to give his sons a good education. MacDonnell attended a Jesuit school, where he excelled at his studies, enabling him to graduate with honours from Queen's College, Galway. At 21 he entered the Indian Civil Service where he soared through the ranks. As a senior official in India, he had mediated ethnic feuds, initiated land reforms, quelled peasant unrest, and excelled in directing relief efforts during two great famines. Now, at the peak of his career, he awaited a seat on the Council of India and aspired to become the Governor of Bombay. Despite the prevailing prejudice against Irish Catholics, MacDonnell had enjoyed a stellar career. Wyndham, satisfied that MacDonnell possessed outstanding administrative skills, decided to offer him the post of Permanent Under-Secretary for Ireland.

However, before he could approach MacDonnell with the offer, Wyndham wrote a 'cypher message' seeking approval from Balfour, who had replaced Lord Salisbury as the Tory Prime Minister. Initially, Balfour demurred. He felt that the Irish Unionists within his party would resent a Catholic 'home ruler' occupying the top 'policing post' in Ireland. Worse still, MacDonnell professed himself a Liberal, had joined Liberal clubs in London, and his younger brother had sat as a Nationalist M.P. in opposition to the Tories. Balfour argued that while the Government might tolerate a man of MacDonnell's talent rising in the colonial services despite his religious or political persuasions, the same did not apply in Ireland because of the issue of trust. MacDonnell would never win the full confidence of the Irish Unionists.

Lord Lansdowne supported Wyndham's choice. Although he concurred with Balfour on MacDonnell's liabilities, he held that he had proved himself in India, where he repeatedly flashed a white hot temper but always used cool judgement. While discussing the 'Irish question', Lansdowne and Wyndham had both concluded that they needed a man who understood Ireland, and their man was 'Irish to the bone'. They readily conceded that MacDonnell had political drawbacks, but they concluded that his great abilities outweighed his political liabilities. Balfour's policy, of 'killing home rule with kindness' by winning Irish hearts, needed a strong and credible Catholic voice in the front line. Ideally, that credible Catholic voice should come from within the ranks of loyal Unionists, but no such man existed. To attract Catholics to their side, they had to appoint Catholics to office. Balfour, overruling his political instincts, decided that he could not break the mould in Irish politics without taking a risk, and therefore yielded to his lieutenants and sanctioned MacDonnell's appointment.

MacDonnell, however, had his own reservations about taking the post and initially refused the offer. He had sought the counsel of his friends at the Reform Club, and they all advised him to stay well clear of Ireland. They pointed out that an Irish Catholic appointed to office by the Tories would have no friends in Government circles. In contrast to the colonies, the chief civil servant in Ireland did little more than police the country, and he had no experience in this field. In every public disturbance, the Unionists would suspect him of pulling the reins on the police while the Catholics would accuse him of betrayal. He could never win. Moreover, they pointed out that he had great prospects by remaining on in India, where he could anticipate becoming a Governor.

MacDonnell knew that his friends had correctly assessed his prospects in the Irish post but he felt a sense of duty to his native land. He wrote to Wyndham; 'I am greatly attracted by the chance of doing some good for Ireland. My best friends tell me that I am deluding myself, and that I shall be abused by Orangemen as a Roman Catholic or home ruler, and denounced by the home rulers as a renegade, and that I shall do no good, and shall retire disgusted within a year.' In the same letter, he laid down several conditions that would make him accept the position. First, he wanted his seat on the Council of India left open for his return. Secondly, wanting to do more than just police Ireland, he asked for a freer hand than that which was normally granted to an Under-Secretary. He specifically asked that he 'should have adequate opportunities of influencing the policy and acts of the Irish administration.' Wyndham, eager to have the best man, agreed to MacDonnell's request for these wider powers.

Therefore, in late 1902, at almost 60 years of age, this stocky, rugged-faced Mayo Catholic became the Permanent Under-Secretary for Ireland and later played a leading secret role in covering up the Irish Crown Jewel affair. He quickly proved his worth by the manner and ease with which he carried out his duties. Just as his masters wished, he forged the core of a centrist axis in Ireland. With the support of moderate Unionists led by Lord Dunraven, a kinsman of

Wyndham, and a group of moderate Catholics, he helped put together the Land Reform Bill. Though limited in scope, this measure proved that moderate Irishmen could work together for the good of the country. After the success of his Land Bill, MacDonnell felt India call. His seat on the Council of India lay open, and even more enticing and financially rewarding, the newly-vacated Governor's post in Bombay was his for the taking. However, King Edward VII, acting on the advice of his ministers, blocked his return to India, promoted him to Knight Commander of the Victorian Order, and persuaded him to continue with his reforms in Ireland.

In 1904, Lord Dunraven asked MacDonnell to assist him in drafting a devolution plan for Ireland. In their plan, they sought to centralise the various boards that ran the country under one Irish Council comprised of both Catholics and Protestants. The plan embodied a logical blueprint for good government, leading Mac-Donnell to assume, naïvely, that all fair-minded men would support the initiative. What Mac-Donnell had not grasped was that the reformers in the Tory Government saw this whole exercise as the sending up of a 'trial balloon', with him as the pilot. Conveniently, Wyndham had left Ireland on 'sick leave' just before Dunraven released the devolution scheme.

When Dunraven released his plan, the reformers in Government felt for the pulse of the Unionist reaction. What they found dismayed them greatly, for the Irish Unionists responded with blind rage, viscerally voicing feelings of betrayal. Nobody cared about the common sense reforms in the proposal, while everybody resented the attack on the Union. A few days later, Wyndham wrote to *The Times* disowning the devolution scheme. He defended the Government and himself by claiming that Dunraven and MacDonnell had acted alone.

Privately, MacDonnell raged at being thrown to the wolves by his masters. For more than a year, he had discussed the gist of his devolution plans with Wyndham, so the scheme could not have surprised him, even if Dunraven really had kept him in the dark. The worst blow came from Lord Dudley, the Lord Lieutenant. MacDonnell had faithfully briefed his Lordship, the presumed head of the Irish administration, on every aspect of his dealings with Dunraven, but now Dudley claimed he had treated these briefings as private, and had not informed his colleagues. MacDonnell resented the cowardice demonstrated by his political masters and strongly resisted becoming their scapegoat.

The Unionists, feeling betrayed by their own party, wanted blood and above all they wanted to oust MacDonnell from office. Initially, Wyndham and Lord Lansdowne took the political heat, with Wyndham writing to Balfour arguing against dismissing MacDonnell. Instead, he suggested that the Government should let MacDonnell stay on for six months, after which he could quit his post with grace to take his seat on the Council of India. Balfour agreed, not least because he feared MacDonnell had damaging letters that would discredit his government's version of events. The reformers in cabinet, detached from the emotions of their Unionist allies, thought they could calm the political storm, but they had wildly underrated Unionist resolve, and how deeply their rank and file felt betrayed by the Government. Balfour, always a man to disdain emotion, never thought that his Unionist allies, in addition to hunting down MacDonnell, might also turn on their own Government.

Though the cabinet agreed that MacDonnell should leave office on his own terms, the hardline Unionists continued to fight for his immediate dismissal. At a meeting of the Ulster Unionist Council in March 1905, the members passed a motion: 'That the Ulster Unionist Members have the sanction of this Council in not supporting the Government until the Lord Lieutenant, Chief Secretary, and Under-Secretary be removed from Office'. The members further declared: 'That the Unionists of Ireland are hereby called upon to close up their ranks, subordinating all minor differences to the all-important question of the maintenance of the Union; and this Council emphatically declares the determination of Irish Unionists to oppose any scheme, no matter by what name designated, that would place the loyal minority at the mercy of the disloyal majority'.

MacDonnell was not a man easily bullied out of office. In India, his fierce resolve to face down one crisis after another led his colleagues to call him the 'The Bengal Tiger'. In Ireland, his admirers warmly referred to him as 'Antony Pat', his Unionist foes derisively nicknamed him 'The Fenian', and his enemies among the Nationalists referred to him as 'the Indian gentleman'. Ironically, leaving Ireland would have delighted MacDonnell, for he longed to go back to his work in India, but he wanted to go with full respect and honour.

As the Unionists intensified their efforts to oust him from office, MacDonnell wrote to Wyndham stating that the cause for the attacks did not stem from the devolution scheme. Instead he claimed that the attacks came from bigots and his enemies hated him because he was Catholic, and had promoted Catholic education. He argued that he was fighting the good fight, standing up to 'bigotry and intolerance' in Ireland, and that Wyndham had granted him exceptional powers to help champion that noble cause. By playing the religious card, MacDonnell had created a dilemma for Wyndham and Balfour. If they dismissed him they would turn him into a Catholic martyr, if they retained him they faced a Unionist revolt and the possible collapse of the Government.

The crisis for Balfour mounted, and, beset by other more pressing political problems, he decided not to risk dividing the Tories over Irish policy. His Unionist allies had played the 'orange card', and he caved in to their demands. He allowed the Unionists to force the resignation of Wyndham, whom the devolution crisis had reduced to the point of a nervous breakdown. Then he appeased them by appointing Walter Long as the new Chief Secretary of Ireland.

Balfour had chosen well, for Long was a true bigot. He hated the Irish Nationalists, and his loathing of Catholics matched the virulence of the hardest Unionist. Ten years earlier, in the House of Commons, he called the Nationalists 'whipped hounds' much to the delight of the Irish Unionists and the embarrassment of the Government.

After becoming the Chief Secretary in March 1905, Long charmed the Irish Unionists. Like so many of his kind, he strongly supported law and order, assured the police of his full backing, and urged them to firmly put down any unrest. To prove his true feelings, Long started a witch hunt in Dublin Castle for men with anti-union feelings, and began promoting Protestants exclusively to the higher positions. His loathing of Irish Catholics led him into conflict with Lord Dudley, the Lord Lieutenant. Appalled by the blatant bigotry, Dudley refused to co-operate with the Chief Secretary. Both men appealed to Balfour; however, the Prime Minister sided with Long, establishing the primacy of the Chief Secretary over the King's Viceroy.

Balfour's decision in favour of the Chief Secretary is critical to interpreting MacDonnell's later actions, when he set up a restricted Commission of Inquiry to investigate Sir Arthur's custody of the Irish Crown Jewels. One could not expect MacDonnell to treat the Lord Lieutenant as the head of the Irish administration, when Lord Dudley had let him down so badly, and when the Prime Minister had ruled that the Chief Secretary had primacy in the Irish administration. When the Liberals took power in 1906, they followed Balfour's precedent in this regard. MacDonnell had experienced personally the Lord Lieutenant's impotence in a confrontation with the Chief Secretary.

The Irish Unionists loved Long, but found his reluctance to dismiss his Catholic Under-Secretary infuriating. Long dearly wanted to comply with their wishes, but he had given his word to Balfour that he would leave MacDonnell in office. He solved his difficulty by emasculating the Under-Secretary's power and influence. While politely listening to MacDonnell's opinions, he ignored all his advice, and governed Ireland solely on the advice of his Unionist allies. Isolated from policy making and feeling the wrath of Irish Unionists, MacDonnell decided to take some sick leave, thereafter playing no further part in Long's administration.

MacDonnell returned to his home in London, where he spent the rest of the year resenting Walter Long, and brooding over his shabby treatment. This was the low point in his career, but he took some small satisfaction in watching the Tory Government stumble from one crisis to another. The next election would likely return the Liberals to power, and having no other choice, MacDonnell bided his time.

In the election of 1906, the Liberals trounced the Tories, and as the first returns came in, MacDonnell returned immediately to Dublin

Castle. The Liberals commanded a huge majority in parliament, and did not depend on the support of the Irish Party. Consequently they had no intention of tabling a divisive Home Rule Bill, but compromised by instructing MacDonnell to draw up a revised devolutionary scheme for the country.

Unfortunately, MacDonnell still seethed over the devolution crisis. He resented everybody involved: Balfour and Lansdowne for deserting him, Walter Long and the Unionists for savaging him, and John Redmond and the Irish Party for betraying a fellow Irishman. As he drew up the Irish Council Bill, he displayed none of the amazing powers of persuasion that he had shown previously. Instead, he seemed to antagonise everyone.

In his first mistake, MacDonnell dropped discreet hints in Dublin about letters he held, and that if these became public, they would demonstrate his absolute loyalty to the previous Government, and prove that senior members of the last cabinet had lied about their role in the affair. He suggested that only the threat of publishing these letters had protected him from outright dismissal by the previous Government. At the annual meeting of the Irish Unionist Association, Long replied to MacDonnell's charges. He gave his own reasons for keeping MacDonnell in office, then dared any man with sensitive papers to make them public. MacDonnell replied to the dare with this open letter to Long in *The Times*:

Sir, — The newspaper report of your speech yesterday at the annual convention of the Unionist alliance contains the following passages:

'But I say, if people have got these letters let them produce them instead of taking refuge in charges and threats. I say put the blame on the right shoulders, but do not be led away by this story that I was 'cribbed cabin'd and confin'd by any action of his.'

'The newspapers unanimously agree in naming me as the person to whom you alluded in the words I have underlined. Assuming that your remarks were directed to me, I desire to say that they raise two points — my possession of embarrassing letters, and my making charges and threats based upon them.

On the first point, I observe that the time has not come (if, in my discretion, it ever will come) for publishing the correspondence connected with the unsuccessful attempt to deprive me of office in 1904 – 1905. In challenging me to produce the correspondence, you have probably forgotten the refusal of the late Prime Minister to lay it on the table of the House of Commons . . . '

' . . . One word in conclusion as to my relations with yourself. At my first interview with you in 1905 you proposed that the agreement made with Mr Wyndham when I took office in 1902 should be cancelled. I told you that I regarded the agreement as made not with Mr. Wyndham alone, but with His Majesty's Government, and if it was cancelled

I should at once resign office. The agreement was left untouched.

Yours faithfully.

A.P. MacDonnell

MacDonnell may have had excellent personal reasons for writing this unprecedented letter, but politically he had made a grievous error of judgement and prejudiced his own cause. Everybody who knew MacDonnell felt confident that the letters existed and he would publish them if pushed. Reinforcing this conclusion, Wyndham, Lansdowne, and Balfour stayed stonily silent. Not one of them challenged him to publish the letters that he said he possessed. This only gave Long and his men ammunition, and they successfully bullied Balfour into moving the Tories to an even more uncompromising position on home rule and devolution. Sadly, MacDonnell had protected his own reputation at the expense of strengthening the men of hate who rent Ireland apart. After this incident, the voice of moderation within the Tories disappeared forever.

MacDonnell proved equally ineffective with his political initiatives. He urged the new Chief Secretary to push on one hand a Universities Bill, (for Catholic education) and on the other hand to push the Irish Council Bill, a measure to devolve government in Ireland. The Universities Bill antagonised the Protestant constituency supporting Trinity College, and the Chief Secretary elected to proceed with interminable consultations. The first draft of the Irish Council

Bill left John Redmond, the leader of the Irish Party, aghast. Redmond told the Prime Minister that it was sheer suicide for the Irish Party to support the Bill, because it gave no role to the Parliamentary caucus of the Irish Party. Exhausted by all the wrangling and fighting, the Chief Secretary abandoned his post and took the British ambassador's post in Washington.

To fill the empty position, the Prime Minister, unhappy with Augustine Birrell's performance as Minister for Education, demoted him to Chief Secretary for Ireland. Birrell, who prayed his stay in Ireland would be short, supported home rule. This stance and his smooth talking ways endeared him to the Irish Party. Early in 1907, Birrell told MacDonnell to draw up an amended Irish Council Bill that addressed Redmond's complaints.

Briefly what MacDonnell proposed in the revised Bill was that: the administration of Ireland would be centralised under one Irish Council. The composition of the 106 members of this Council would be proportional to the population. The Province of Ulster, where most of the Protestants in Ireland resided, would elect 23 members, while the rest of Ireland would elect 59 members. The Lord Lieutenant of Ireland would appoint 24 members. Over the years, the Lord Lieutenant had been superceded by the Chief Secretary, all but making his post redundant. MacDonnell's scheme would re-establish the Lord Lieutenant's influence in Ireland: he would chair the Irish Council, and had the power to nominate 24 members to the

Council. In effect MacDonnell's scheme proposed making the Lord Lieutenant the most powerful political figure in Ireland.

When Birrell released details of the Irish Council Bill, the Irish Unionists reacted violently. They saw the devolution scheme as the Trojan horse for home rule. Up and down the country, Irish Unionists organised meetings to protest the proposed Bill before the House of Commons. Unionists' hostility to the Bill can be seen in the following extracts from *The Times*.

The Times, 8 May 1907:
Sir Edward Carson for instance pointed out last night that the 106 members of the proposed Irish Council corresponded so nearly to the 103 members now sent by Ireland to the imperial Parliament that they (the Unionists) were perfectly entitled to assume that this council would be the nucleus of a future Irish Parliament. Ulster he said would be absolutely powerless in the new Council. Sir Edward pointed out that, Ulster being undenominational, and the rest of Ireland being Roman Catholic and denominational, it would mean that in this new Council, Ulster would have no chance and this would at once raise a conflict between Ulster and the rest of Ireland.

The Times, 11 May 1907:
A committee of the Irish Unionist Alliance met yesterday to make arrangements for a public demonstration to be held in Dublin at

as early a date as possible, with a view to offering the most strenuous opposition to the Irish Council Bill now before the House of Commons. The committee stressed that on the Chief Secretary's (Mr Birrell) own admission his proposals 'may pave the way to Home Rule'.

The Times, 16 May 1907:
A meeting of the executive committee of the Irish Unionist alliance was held at the offices in Dublin today where the Irish Council Bill was considered, and a resolution was unanimously adopted earnestly appealing to all Irish Unionists to offer the most uncompromising opposition to its proposals.

The Times, 25 May 1907:
Sir Edward Carson said the Bill produced by Mr Birrell was a cowardly Bill and it was a dishonest Bill. It was a cowardly Bill because it was produced by men who told them that the only remedy for Ireland's troubles was Home Rule and who did not have the courage to proclaim their convictions in the English constituencies. It was a dishonest Bill, because it meant to convey to one party that it was a Home Rule Bill, whereas it was meant to convey to another party that it had nothing on earth to say to home rule.

The Times, 27 May 1907:
A demonstration of the Unionists of South Armagh was held in Portadown on Saturday

afternoon at which the principal speakers were Mr Walter Long, MP Chairman of the Irish Unionist Party. Alluding to the Irish Council Bill, he said 'its unfortunate remains were about to be interred, and he wondered who would be the mourner'. 'He did not think anyone would be found sympathetic enough to drop a single tear on the poor bantling's grave.' Dealing with education coming under the influence of an Irish Council, Long commented that the educational system would come under party influence and votes, a prospect which they could not contemplate without grievous doubts and misgivings. The motto of the Unionist party was written on many a wall and many a placard but more deeply in their hearts, and it was 'No surrender'.

The Times, 5 June 1907:
At a meeting of the executive committee of the Irish Unionist Alliance held in Dublin yesterday, the following resolutions were passed:
1. That in view of the Prime Minister's announcement in the House of Commons today that the Irish Council Bill has been abandoned, the monster demonstration of Irish Unionists to be held on Friday next in Dublin be postponed until further notice. But we avail ourselves of this opportunity to reiterate our continued hostility to any proposal calculated or intended to weaken the Imperial tie or directly or indirectly to lead the way to Home Rule.

The Irish Nationalists were unhappy with MacDonnell's proposals as well. At a meeting in the Mansion House in Dublin, they voted to reject the Irish Council Bill. When Birrell brought the Bill to the floor of the House, he lacked support from either side of the Irish divide and thus the Government withdrew the Bill on 3 June 1907.

All along, Walter Long, Sir Edward Carson and their Unionist colleagues interpreted the proposed devolution scheme as being home rule in disguise. Over eighteen months they had noticed that each of the three proposed devolutionary schemes had progressively shifted towards home rule. They strongly believed that the next Liberal proposal would be an outright Home Rule Bill, and they resolved to resist it fiercely.

In case anyone might mistake Unionist determination as simple posturing, one need only refer to their reactions to Prime Minister Asquith's Home Rule Bill from 1912 to 1914. The Leader of His Majesty's loyal opposition, Bonar Law, became so incensed by the Bill that he incited sedition. Fifty-seven officers in elite British regiments stationed at the Curragh Military Camp in County Kildare mutinied by refusing to coerce the Province of Ulster. The police and army turned a blind eye to the Larne gun running by Northern Unionists; and high officials in the British police and military committed treason by helping Sir Edward Carson escape to Northern Ireland. The passion that drove these 'loyalists' to rebel against home rule simmered in the Summer of 1907.

4

THE ABERDEENS RETURN
TO IRELAND

No British Lord wanted to be Irish Viceroy as much as Lord Aberdeen, yet when the Crown Jewels débâcle erupted, no Viceroy was so tormented in office. One suspects that the whole business haunted Aberdeen for the rest of his life. Just like Sir Arthur Vicars, Aberdeen found himself dragged onto centre stage as a most unwilling principal actor in the drama. His reactions and behaviour are so thoroughly incomprehensible that one can only surmise that the dread of scandal had paralysed his ability to act.

The Liberals swept into power in an enormous landslide victory in 1906. For the next two years, the Aberdeens reached the peak of their political influence. Some of their closest political allies sat in cabinet. As well, Lady Aberdeen's brother, Lord Tweedmouth, had received the Admiralty post, while their son-in-law, Jack Sinclair, had received the Scottish post. Through Jack Sinclair they had direct access to the Prime Minister because Campbell-Bannerman publicly attributed his political success to Sinclair's loyalty and support.

When Sinclair proposed Lord Aberdeen for

Irish Viceroy, the Prime Minister readily agreed. Campbell-Bannerman's political judgement failed him on this occasion. He and his Liberal colleagues had received no electoral mandate for Irish home rule, yet the Aberdeens were the most ardent supporters of home rule in the Liberal party. Their appointment could only antagonise the Unionists and frustrate the Nationalists.

For Ishbel, Lady Aberdeen, returning to Ireland represented a chance to relive the glory days of 1886. During Gladstone's short-lived administration of that year, he had appointed Lord Aberdeen as the Lord Lieutenant of Ireland. Initially Ishbel resented going to Ireland but within days of arriving she embraced the Irish and became their champion. The Aberdeens spent six months in Ireland but in that short time, and unlike any Viceroy before them, they won the hearts and minds of the Irish people. Bewitched by Ishbel's warmth and charm, the Irish began referring to her as the 'real queen of Ireland', much to Ishbel's public embarrassment, and Queen Victoria's annoyance.

When the Liberal Government fell, they had to leave Ireland, and all Dublin thronged the streets to bid them God's speed. Dubliners packed the farewell route from Winetavern Street to College Green, all giving the popular couple a grand send-off amid cries of 'home rule'. In honour of the Aberdeens, half of Dublin donned the ivy of the Gordon clan in their lapels. The city became stricken with 'ivy fever', with even the jarveys adorning their horses' heads with wreaths of ivy. Ishbel, just a young woman, felt profoundly moved. As the ship bearing the Aberdeens pulled away from Kingstown, she wept while she listened to the band playing the 'Aberdeen March' to the tune of the 'Shamrock and Thistle'.

After her triumphant six months, Ishbel longed to return to Ireland. Her great friend and mentor, Gladstone, formed his last administration in 1892, but he could not persuade John Morley the Chief Secretary to accept Lord Aberdeen as his Lord Lieutenant, though there is no official reason for Morley's rejection of Aberdeen. Morley wrote a two-volume memoir, but never mentioned the incident. Ishbel confronted him about his attitude, but he gave her no satisfaction — at least she never recorded any specific reason other than Morley's argument that he wanted a free hand to promote home rule. Thus Ishbel had to wait twenty years before she could fulfil her dream of returning to Ireland. She supported home rule, education, land reform, employment initiatives and public health, as well as a host of other smaller issues. If ever the Irish people had an English champion, then Ishbel Marjoribanks Gordon, Lady Aberdeen, was that champion.

Although she lived in a period when women faced insurmountable social and political barriers, Ishbel made her voice heard in politics through her innate leadership skills and raw determination. Her thinking was ahead of her time, as she championed the downtrodden, promoted public health, peace, social justice, women's rights and education, and brought a feisty energy to all her endeavours. Politically, she committed herself to the Liberal Party, and counted three British, and two Canadian Prime Ministers among her personal friends. Among the many recognitions of her public service, Ishbel received the Grand Cross of the British Empire in 1931, which made her a Grand Dame of the Empire.

Ishbel might have exerted even greater influence had she married a more effective husband but at best Lord Aberdeen was inadequate. In their latter years, this highly incompatible couple became deeply attached to each other, and to their credit their relationship reached a level of true devotion. However, in the early years, their marriage had quickly degenerated into a convenient arrangement. Social taboos prevented divorce, so to preserve their social status they kept up public appearances despite their domestic difficulties.

While Ishbel had endured difficulties in childhood, her husband, John Gordon, Lord Aberdeen, grew up psychologically maimed by his upbringing. The Gordons of Aberdeen can trace their ancestry back seven centuries. The 4th Earl of Aberdeen, who served as Britain's Prime Minister between 1852 and 1855, was one of the more distinguished members of the family. All too often the sons of great men turn out dismal failures, and John Gordon's father was one such man. The 5th Earl of Aberdeen, failing to live up to expectations, lived his entire life in the glare of his illustrious father's disapproval.

Lacking even minimal civility, his exasperated father rebuked him: 'Endeavour to feel that it is always indispensable to be civil and attentive to a woman, be she old or young, ugly or pretty. A savage and morose manner to anyone is a real misfortune, to a woman it is barbarous.'

The more he failed in life, the more dysfunctional he became. Constantly complaining of psychosomatic illnesses, he retreated into a morbid puritanism, and ruled his unfortunate family with all the determination that he lacked in his worldly endeavours. He ruthlessly policed the moral upbringing of his six children, ensuring they gained all the burdens of religion and none of the benefits. Though wealthy, he provided few comforts for his family, and ran the home on a frugal budget. This lugubrious man banned jokes from the house, refused to give his children toys, and appears to have viewed joy in any form as an insidious vice that required instant eradication. On his hierarchy of human vice, sexual immorality reigned supreme. In his only notable contribution to parliament, he proposed a motion to remove a £100 grant to art colleges on the grounds that their use of nude models was morally offensive. His enthusiasm for stamping out sexual vice led him to improve the hovels inhabited by his tenants, although he raised the rent to cover his costs. He screened his tenants to admit 'none but those whose character was free from that blot which he so anxiously wished to see removed from the face of society in the district.' While devoting his joyless life to stamping out vice, he gradually became obsessed with death. Very fittingly, just before he died at the ripe old age of 47, he indulged his morbidity with the printing of a dismally macabre leaflet entitled: 'Death May Be Near'.

Predictably, the children of this fine home grew up troubled and disturbed. Lacking self-esteem and confidence, they exhibited unnatural levels of anxiety, found the world a truly menacing place, and felt so overwhelmed by life that they could not face up to responsibility. The oldest son, George, succeeded his father, and became the 6th Earl of Aberdeen. For two years he struggled to lead the life of an aristocrat and run the estate, after which he abandoned his privileged position and ran away to America. In Boston he signed on as a seaman under the name of George Osborne. Occasionally he wrote to his mother, but he gave no forwarding address.

The second Gordon boy, James, seemed to have his feet firmly anchored on the ground. Unlike his older brother, he had a winning personality and got on well with people. He made many friends through his sporting activities for which he displayed considerable talent. Leaving home, he went to Cambridge to carve out a career for himself. While there, some friends persuaded him to run for parliament. The details are obscure, but this political venture unhinged young James. Two weeks after he announced his bid for parliament, he became depressed, and shot himself in his rooms.

Following James' suicide, Mrs Gordon tried to strengthen the family by bringing home the runaway Earl. Not having an address, she sent his former tutor to America in search of him. After five months of searching, the tutor discovered that the Earl of Aberdeen used the name George Osborne. Armed with a name, he took only a short while to discover that George had lost his life at sea during a storm — at least that was the story he brought back to the family.

John Gordon described the untimely death of his two older brothers, as the 'dark portal' through which he came to inherit the ancestral estate and become the 7th Earl of Aberdeen. His character developed in total opposition to that of his father. This extremely nervous man possessed impeccable manners, and always treated women with the utmost courtesy and respect. He cultivated a sense of humour and loved to tell entertaining yarns. Even in old age, he relished a good story, and published *Jokes Cracked* by Lord Aberdeen in 1929. In another drastic departure, John enjoyed socialising with gentlemen friends in his London clubs, and showed none of his father's horror of tobacco and alcohol.

Mrs Gordon, having lost two sons, took great care of her last surviving boy. When John attended the House of Lords, she went down with him to London, and invariably at least one of his sisters accompanied her. Instead of buying a house in the town, they chose to rent for the duration of the parliamentary season. This ritual, whereby the young Earl found himself protected by a phalanx of female Gordons, continued until he reached the age of 30. During this time John became strongly attached to his mother, generating a powerful bond that lasted until she died.

Mrs Gordon made one supreme request of her son — to produce an heir for the family. Lord Aberdeen always acknowledged his dynastic obligations to the family, but he attended to this 'duty' with a singular lack of zeal. Though he was an eminently suitable, rich bachelor with a title, he successfully evaded London's army of high-society matrons seeking a suitable match for their debutante daughters. Without fail, he would treat every young woman with consummate courtesy but he never displayed a lasting interest in any of them. He attended some of the social parties and dances, but he much preferred the social life in his London clubs.

Not far away in London, Ishbel, ten years John's junior, grew up in fashionable Mayfair, the daughter of Dudley and Isabella Marjoribanks. Her father had succeeded in business, amassing a fortune in the brewing industry. Reputedly, Marjoribanks had a savage temper, and his wife regularly bore the brunt of his rage. As so often happens, Ishbel became the victim of her parents feuding. At a young age she idolised her father, but her mother successfully undermined this relationship and turned her permanently against him. From then on, seeing herself in the role of a protector, she always sided with her mother. Ishbel's biographer, Doris French, says of this corrosive relationship: 'She professed to hate her father (even at his death in 1897 she was unforgiving).'

Religion made up the other great influence in Ishbel's formative years. Her mother came from a particularly devoted Christian family, and she gave Ishbel a firm religious and ethical upbringing. Ishbel's uncles enthusiastically contributed to Ishbel's moral formation, and she referred to them as 'a source of Christian inspiration'. From a modern perspective, Isabella Marjoribanks' religiosity suffered from a strong puritan influence. For example, in her teens, Ishbel fell seriously ill. While she convalesced away from home, Isabella wrote to her daughter about receiving her first communion in the Church of England:

> . . . Satan is ever at hand to snatch what he can of blessed privilege from us. Therefore fail not to fill up every smallest interval of time with prayer and holy meditation . . . You know you must take off the glove from your right hand as you approach the altar . . .

The passage cited lacks the tenderness and compassion one would expect a mother to write to her recuperating daughter who was far from home.

Paradoxically, though Ishbel thoroughly disliked her father, she followed him in his political allegiance. Dudley Marjoribanks sat as a 'silent' Liberal backbencher in the House of Commons. As a wealthy Liberal, Marjoribanks often entertained the leading Liberals at his home. Ishbel met these men, and admired William Gladstone, leading her to believe fervently in his particular brand of politics which she saw as Christianity in action. By her early teens, Ishbel committed herself to the Liberal Party — a commitment that she honoured with 60 years of devoted service.

According to Ishbel's journals, she fell in love with John Gordon at the age of fourteen after they met while riding in Hyde Park. Three years after this meeting, Ishbel told her mother that she would like to marry Lord Aberdeen. Isabella Marjoribanks approved of her daughter's choice and set about arranging the marriage. They changed churches so that they could meet Lord Aberdeen more frequently. Over the next two and a half years, mother and daughter contrived to meet and entertain Lord Aberdeen at every possible opportunity. In her journals, Ishbel speaks of intense love such as 'to have as a friend (at least) one whom I could love so intensely.' Having met John Gordon on so many occasions, one must assume that Ishbel became fully acquainted with quirks of his personality, particularly his shy nervous disposition.

A major obstacle confronted Ishbel's marriage plans — John Gordon never indicated that he reciprocated her feelings. After two and a half years she confronted him and they all but agreed to go their separate ways. However, her mother made one last desperate effort and sent a stern letter to Lord Aberdeen in Scotland which she concluded:

In conclusion I venture to tell you that I am sure you are deceiving yourself. What is the evidence of love but the seeking of companionship? Continual introspection is a fatal error. For your own sake I would not have you throw away a priceless blessing.

No record exists of the role played by the aging Mrs Gordon at this critical juncture, but we suspect that she too intervened. By this time her son had reached the age of 30, and she must have despaired at his lack of matrimonial progress. If she permitted him to let Ishbel slip through the net, she faced the prospect of dying without seeing the Gordon heir. In any event, with a suitable amount of prodding, John Gordon changed his mind and proposed to Ishbel. She recorded her reaction to Aberdeen's love as: 'deep, holy, deferential, tender, heavenly . . . the waiting had not been a scrap too long as a preparation for such paradisaical happenings.' They married in November 1877.

Through remarkable resolve and tenacity, Ishbel succeeded in marrying the man of her dreams, but she tired of him within five years. At the age of 25 she began a fourteen-year-long extra-marital liaison with the love of her life, Henry Drummond, giving birth to his son Archie in 1884. Ishbel tried to camouflage Archie's paternity in her journal, by putting the date of her first meeting with Drummond as 1884. However, Drummond's papers reveal that their first meeting occurred in 1883. As Archie was the last of her children, we infer that from this point on, Ishbel and Lord Aberdeen no longer made love.

Ishbel never attempted to conceal her intense feelings for Drummond. Apparently, by the fifth year of her marriage, Ishbel had secured from her husband a free hand in the company of men, a most extraordinary arrangement for any period in history, let alone Victorian England. Ishbel's biographer, Doris French, summed it up as follows:

> In the pattern made familiar by the philandering of the Prince of Wales, the existence of the extramarital lover was both concealed and acknowledged. It is difficult not to conclude that the Aberdeens and Drummond gained all three.

After considering the record, we have concluded that Aberdeen's activities in his London clubs lay at the heart of Ishbel's marriage breakdown. It appears that Lord Aberdeen indulged in some sort of behaviour that Ishbel found repugnant. Divorce offered no escape, because with it came social ruin. After realising that she was trapped in an unorthodox marriage, she had no scruples about having an affair, and Aberdeen, for his part, had no objections to her cultivating male friends. We also believe that Ishbel committed a great deal of her marriage problems to her journals, and her daughter Marjorie, if she had not already known, learned all about her father's failings. She also learned the depth of Ishbel's bitterness about the situation, for in reality, Aberdeen had used her solely to fulfil his dynastic obligations of producing an heir.

Ishbel gave birth to four children, George — Lord Haddo, Marjorie, Dudley, and Archie. Her youngest son Archie was her favourite and he could do no wrong in her eyes. In contrast, this most empathetic of women struggled to love her eldest boy. Haddo came into the world a sickly baby, and as a delicate boy he began having epileptic seizures. Apparently, Haddo failed to excel in any activity. By the time Haddo had reached the age of seventeen Ishbel had given up on him. Her biographer, French, comments: 'Ishbel admitted Haddo's incapacity obliquely. It looked she wrote, 'pretty different to what might have been expected if one looks back to Jan. 20 1879' when the bells rang out at Haddo House as at the birth of a prince.'

Haddo craved Ishbel's affection, and he exploited his illness to evoke her sympathy. French comments on this relationship when Haddo was twenty years old:

Poor Haddo was having a difficult time of it. In a weak and ill-formed hand he wrote frequently to 'My Dearest Mother', signing himself 'Mother's own St George' in what seems to be a pathetic attempt to live up to the name she used to inspire valour. He apologised to her for the epileptic recurrences which he called 'warnings': ' . . . Mother will understand that these attacks do the contrary to helping me with my work. I can't rouse my head to work when it is so full of nerves going on like they do . . . '

Noticeably, George attributes his lack of academic success to his ailment. Haddo attended Oxford for a while, but the intellectual demands of university study proved far beyond his ability. He dropped out of college and became infatuated with faith healers in a vain attempt to find a cure for his epilepsy. He made one major effort to stand on his own two feet when he ran for parliament. However, the effort exhausted him and he abandoned national politics.

Ishbel apparently displayed an appalling harshness to Haddo that virtually contradicts everything else she did during her life. The 'official story' from the Gordon archives as told by Doris French is that by 1905, Ishbel decided to resolve the 'Haddo' problem. She believed that his epilepsy was hereditary, and forbade him from marrying and producing degenerate offspring. French writes:

Ishbel and her husband were greatly concerned that Haddo's condition might be hereditary, and were firmly opposed to Haddo producing an heir. They had given him heavy advice on the subject to which he replied in confused and rebellious letters. He seemed to hint that the joys of marriage could be his, while avoiding parenthood, but Ishbel apparently thought this much too risky. He was in love with a girl called Evelyn, and believed he had 'many evidences of her affection'. He recognised his 'responsibility to the family'; he believed there was danger of 'bringing disease into the world', but he could not accept that he must never marry. Evelyn became engaged to another man — Haddo could not promise not to 'direct my thoughts to somebody else.'

Ishbel's solution to the problem proved peculiar. While at Oxford, Haddo had met Florence Cockayne, the mother of a classmate. Florence was a widow with an extremely kind disposition, who liked Haddo in a motherly way. In his letters home, Haddo wrote highly of Florence which led Ishbel to invite her to Haddo House for Christmas. When Haddo dropped out of Oxford he took a flat in London. Ishbel persuaded Florence to take an adjoining flat with a communicating door. While Haddo stayed in London, Florence kept Ishbel informed of her son's uncertain liaisons with young women. To put an end to Haddo's flirtations Ishbel suggested to Florence that she marry Haddo. Florence would not hear of the suggestion, and refused to even mention the subject to Haddo. Having failed with Florence, Ishbel recruited her own mother to coerce Haddo into proposing to Florence. Haddo apparently resisted, but Lady Tweedmouth had her way, and the young man agreed to marry Florence, a woman the same age as his mother. Ishbel arranged for a private wedding in 1906.

This version of the story puts all involved in a poor light. By agreeing to an unwanted marriage, Haddo appears wimpish. Yet as the years went by, Lord Haddo played a constructive role in local politics, suggesting that he was not as weak as this account makes him out to be. And if the issue concerned Haddo's care, the Aberdeens could easily have afforded to hire a permanent housekeeper for the young man.

Ishbel emerges from this account with little honour. From an early age she committed herself to Liberal principles, yet her treatment of Haddo portrays her in the light of a fascist committed to eugenics. Lady Tweedmouth's role in the affair compounds the problem. Is one to believe that she too subscribed to strong eugenic principles? One has to wonder why she concerned herself so forcefully in maintaining the purity of the Aberdeen line when the Gordon family did not appear too concerned by the issue.

After weighing the evidence, we have rejected the eugenic story as told by Ishbel's biographer, Doris French. We believe Ishbel concocted this version of the story to camouflage another problem with her son. Haddo had many homosexual friends, and we believe that he too was of the same sexual persuasion. Ishbel became aware of this some time around 1905 and it presented her with a staggering social problem. If Haddo were ever exposed, he faced total ostracisation by his own class. The revelation would also smear the whole family and would cause serious political problems for herself and her husband.

We believe that as the effective head of the family, Ishbel had to protect the Aberdeen's social standing by suppressing all traces of Haddo's sexual preferences. Initially she wanted Florence Cockayne to act as a chaperone or housekeeper for Haddo. The presence of this respectable woman would chase away Haddo's undesirable friends. One problem persisted throughout. Haddo retained some dynastic ambitions of his own, and he wanted to find a young woman who would bear him a child. This proved too much for Ishbel. She refused to countenance Haddo's marrying a young woman and thought that this amounted to abuse of any woman involved.

To pre-empt Haddo's dynastic ambitions, Ishbel insisted that he marry Florence and he refused. Exploiting the danger of a major social scandal engulfing the family, Ishbel prevailed upon her own mother, to influence him and he agreed to marry Florence in an effort to protect the family name. Ishbel needed to explain why her son had married a woman twice his age and she invented the eugenic explanation.

In an ironic twist, the theft of the Crown Jewels seems to have succeeded where Ishbel failed. The affair appears to have given Haddo such a shock that afterwards he severed all links to his homosexual friends and, embracing religion in a major way, he became a church elder.

When the Aberdeens returned to Ireland in 1906, few people knew about their domestic difficulties. MacDonnell had not previously worked with them, but he had high hopes for their tenure in Ireland. He felt that they would make great allies, because like him, they too were loathed by the Tories. Before his posting to Ireland, Lord Aberdeen had been the Governor

General of Canada. While in Canada the Aberdeens had helped the Liberal, Wilfred Laurier, win power by conspiring against the ruling Canadian Tories. Most rumours gave Ishbel all the credit for the shrewd schemes that led to the defeat of Sir Charles Tupper, whom the English Tories backed. However, when the Tories won the next British election, they avenged Tupper by ousting Aberdeen. This Tory malice followed the Aberdeens to Ireland as they began their second tour of duty. To add to this, the Aberdeens' home rule stance provoked the Irish Unionists to open hostility.

When MacDonnell first met Lord Aberdeen, he warned him that the country had changed greatly since their 'miraculous' six-month tour of duty under Gladstone. He advised Aberdeen to prepare for a chilly reception from the Unionists and to expect nothing but cynical mistrust from the Nationalists. Irish politics had polarised into two camps that fed on bigotry, racism and fear. His Excellency would quickly discover that in this rigid land, 'no surrender' had become the battle cry of Unionist and Nationalist alike. The Aberdeens soon discovered the truth of MacDonnell's predictions when they found themselves virtually ostracised by the Irish Unionist establishment.

Despite the Unionist hostility, the Aberdeens settled down well in Ireland, but they found it necessary to discourage Lord Haddo from spending too much time in Dublin. When in Ireland, Haddo immediately began socialising with Sir Arthur Vicars, with whom he became great friends. However, over the Christmas of 1906, he brought a bit too much attention to this close relationship. During a party in Sir Arthur's offices, Haddo removed the keys from his highly inebriated host, took the Crown Jewels from the safe, wrapped them in brown paper, and placed them on Sir Arthur's desk for him to discover the next morning. While Lord Aberdeen, along with the entire Castle, thought the prank was outrageously funny, Ishbel thought otherwise. She guessed correctly that Sir Arthur was another of Haddo's 'confirmed bachelor' friends, and mindful of the 1884 homosexual débâcle in Dublin Castle, she told her son to return to Scotland.

Whatever Ishbel said when sending Haddo away, it had a profound effect on him. One would have expected him to come to Dublin for the opening of the International Exhibition in May 1907, and even more so to come for the Royal visit in July. However, Haddo came for neither event, and had the good fortune not to return to Ireland between the Christmas season and the royal visit in July. This unanticipated absence provided Haddo with his strongest alibi during the Crown Jewels affair.

5

HOMOSEXUALITY WITHIN THE ROYAL HOUSEHOLD

Being a homosexual in Victorian or Edwardian times forced an individual to lead a double life. Fear of being discovered by a friend, let alone an enemy, could have disastrous consequences. Oscar Wilde was jailed for his homosexual acts and at least one prominent general committed suicide rather than face exposure. Ishbel, Lady Aberdeen had guessed correctly that Sir Arthur Vicars was a homosexual, yet aided by a powerful patron, Vicars, at just 29 years old, had assumed the highest heraldic post in Ireland when he became Ulster King of Arms in 1893. He quickly proved himself a competent genealogist, and innately grasped the subtleties of protocol. As Registrar and Knight Attendant of the Order of St Patrick, he instilled in their ceremonies a new gravitas and dignity. The Knights of the Order appreciated the added polish, pomp, and professionalism which he introduced, and within four years Queen Victoria rewarded him with a knighthood. A decade later, King Edward VII bestowed on him the honour of Knight Commander of the Victorian Order.

In 1903, Sir Arthur 'preoccupied with tidiness and precision of detail', began revising the archaic and obsolete Statutes or Regulations of the Order. In 1905, the Knights ratified the new Statutes and King Edward VII signed the Warrant. In his revision, Sir Arthur gave himself tenure for life as Ulster, and to complement his new importance he revived some lapsed heraldic posts. He tried to assign the custody of the Crown Jewels to the Lord Lieutenant, but his Lordship firmly rejected the proposal. Thus, Statute 27 specifically states that Ulster King of Arms was to be the official custodian of the jewels, thereby leaving Sir Arthur with the sole responsibility for their safekeeping. Statute 20 ordered that they be kept in a steel safe inside the strong room of the Office of Arms.

1903 proved to be a busy year for Vicars, as along with revising the Statutes, he had the pleasure of moving his office from the dowdy Fisheries Building into the imposing Bedford Tower, just inside Dublin Castle's main gate. Undoubtedly Vicars, with his appreciation for the finer points of architecture, exploited King Edward's 1903 visit to coax or shame the Irish administration into providing him with more dignified offices befitting a member of the King's household. Unfortunately, some of the pleasure of the move faded when Sir Arthur discovered that the Board of Works had blundered in the reconstruction of his new offices. When building the strong room, they made the doorway so narrow that his safe would not fit through. They offered to correct their error, but aghast at the thought of more disruption, Vicars declined. In addition, upon reviewing the situation, Sir

Arthur concluded that the large steel safe would take up too much space in the strong room. He discussed the situation with the Board, and agreed to leave the safe in the adjoining library until such time as they would provide him with a smaller safe that would fit into the strong room. As is wont to happen, this 'temporary' arrangement, whereby the safe containing the Crown Jewels of Ireland sat in the library instead of the strong room, became permanent.

Four full-time staff carried on the day-to-day work of the Office of Arms. Vicars' assistant, Mr Burtchaell, started his working life as a lawyer in Dublin. He had established a good practice, but the onset of epilepsy forced him to abandon the law and seek a career that would better accommodate his frequent attacks. Vicars, upon hearing of Burtchaell's plight, offered him the less stressful assistant's post. Plagued by ill-health, and in dire need of an income, Burtchaell gladly accepted the offer. Stivey, a retired Royal Navy rating, held the position of office messenger, though no one knows what lured him to Dublin. Miss Gibbon, a spinster in her forties, performed the secretarial duties. A prim and proper lady of Anglo-Irish descent, Gibbon adored Sir Arthur. However, no question of impropriety ever arose, as she had the reputation of being a devout devotee of the Church of Ireland, with impeccable morals. In 1907, Sir Arthur placed an advertisement for a personal secretary in a London newspaper. A Mr Horlock applied for the job, and apparently provided such a glowing testimonial from his clergy that Sir Arthur felt fortunate to engage him.

In 1905, after receiving the royal warrant for the revised statutes, Vicars began to create a small heraldic court appointed exclusively from within the ranks of his homosexual friends. He appointed his nephew Peirce Gun Mahony as the Cork Herald, Francis Richard Shackleton as the Dublin Herald and Francis Bennet-Goldney as the Athlone Pursuivant. These honorary posts demanded nothing more of their holders than to attend the occasional major ceremony in Dublin. Thus, living full-time in England, Goldney attended to his duties as Mayor of Canterbury, and Shackleton, spending only two months of the year in Dublin, was able to attended to his 'investment' business in the City of London.

Frank Shackleton, younger brother of the famed Antarctic explorer, loved the world of heraldry and genealogy. He spent two years working for Sir Arthur as an unpaid assistant before getting a commission in the Royal Irish Fusiliers and fighting in the Boer War. The two men had developed an intimate friendship and wrote regularly to each other while Frank fought overseas. Shackleton appears to have been in serious trouble in South Africa and had to resign his commission. Fortunately the incident was hushed, and he returned to Britain claiming that he had been invalided out of the army. Back in London, Frank set out to become a wealthy businessman.

Despite being occupied with his many business ventures, Shackleton maintained a keen interest in Sir Arthur's heraldic world. He loved the pomp, pageantry, ceremonial dress, and above all the tabard, the official heralds' coat that was emblazoned with the Arms of the King. In 1903, during the visit of Edward VII to Ireland, Vicars took the opportunity to make his friend Shackleton a Gold Staff Officer. Two years later, Sir Arthur, vouching for his friend, had the pleasure of appointing him the Dublin Herald. In appreciation, Shackleton suggested that Vicars deserved to live in better surroundings, and they both agreed to share a fine Georgian house at 7 St James' Terrace in Clonskeagh, a half-hour carriage journey from Dublin Castle. Shackleton quickly discovered that his new status as Dublin Herald opened doors into influential circles.

While fighting in South Africa, Shackleton befriended Captain Richard Gorges, a fellow Anglo-Irishman and homosexual. However, Gorges was not only homosexual, but also a paedophile who preyed on young boys. An orderly once caught Gorges having sex with a young drummer boy. The incident was reported to General Thornycroft who gave the order to literally boot Gorges out of the regiment. The regimental officers formed two lines and as Gorges walked between them, each officer applied his boot to Gorges' backside. The Gorges family had a distinguished Norman pedigree and had kinship with some of the most established families in Great Britain. Using their influence, they had the Captain's disgrace in South Africa hushed up, allowing him to return to Ireland to take up a full-time musketry instructor's post at the Curragh Military Camp near Dublin. Shackleton tried to introduce his friend Gorges into Sir Arthur's circle, but found his way resolutely blocked. Sir Arthur had heard about Gorges' indiscretion, probably from his relative, Sir Arthur Conan Doyle, who was also served in the Boer war, and banished him from visiting his house in St James' Terrace. Afterwards, he advised Shackleton to have nothing to do with 'that bad lot'.

Vicars filled the last of his heraldic posts when he appointed Francis Bennett-Goldney as Athlone Pursuivant. Goldney's father, Sebastian Evans, had married the wealthy Elizabeth Bennet-Goldney, daughter of the founder of the London Joint Stock Bank. When Goldney reached his twenty-seventh year, an aunt, on his mother's side, willed him a fortune if he adopted her surname, so he obliged, taking the name Bennett-Goldney. Financially secure, he developed a keen interest in history, and became an collector of rare artifacts. Though wealthy, Goldney had few friends due to his lugubrious and tedious personality. Through his Masonic connections, Goldney gained entry to a web of London gentlemen, nominally headed by Lord Ronald Gower. This was no ordinary circle of homosexuals, for it included men who came from some of the most illustrious families in England.

Goldney first met Sir Arthur in Gower's circle, and to his delight, discovered that as members of the society of Antiquaries they shared a common passion for collecting old artifacts. He craved Sir

Arthur's friendship, and upon hearing of the Athlone Pursuivant post, he plagued Vicars for the appointment, even though he had no connection with Ireland. Vicars did not relish the prospect of Goldney's company, and tried to put him off by demanding that he supply a reference from an eminent individual. Goldney rose to this challenge by producing some fine references, among them, a sterling testimonial from the Duke of Bedford.

With the completion of his heraldic court, Sir Arthur anticipated a blissful life. His salary of £500 allowed him many comforts and most evenings on his way home from the Castle, he stopped off at the Kildare Street Club, the home of Irish Unionism. This exclusive establishment had the reputation of keeping the best table in Dublin. When oysters were in season, the club had them shipped up daily from its own bed in Galway, and they also made every effort to have the finest wine cellar in Dublin. All the members came from the same religious, social and political background. Only two home rule MPs had joined the club, and both were Protestants, as none of their Catholic colleagues could or would join. The club served as a focal point for the most powerful landlords and Unionist politicians in Ireland.

Naturally, Sir Arthur did everything he could to further his intimate friend's career in business. He brought Shackleton into his circle of 'confirmed bachelor' friends in London, many of whom could help further his business ambitions. He introduced him to the most influential contacts, including Lord Ronald Gower, the 'club's' nominal patron. A contemporary described Gower as 'a promiscuous homosexual, who shocked his more discreet friends by openly whoring after guardsmen in the underpaid Services'. Gower had been a close friend of Oscar Wilde and served as the real-life subject for the character of Lord Henry Wooton in *The Picture of Dorian Grey*. Shackleton possessed unusually good looks, complemented by a winning personality, and following Gower's lead, members of the 'club' took a great liking to him. One of them said of him that he was 'extremely good looking . . . and extremely depraved'. Before long, Shackleton took full advantage of his good fortune and somehow acquired a luxuriously appointed flat in Mayfair at 44 Park Lane. After his appointment as the Dublin Herald, Shackleton soon took on the role as the go-between for Sir Arthur and Lord Gower.

Lord Gower's nephew, John (Ian) Campbell, the ninth Duke of Argyll and brother-in-law of the King, took a particular liking to Shackleton, and the two men met regularly at Gower's country estate. Ian Campbell's father, the eighth Duke of Argyll, had married Elizabeth Leveson-Gower, daughter of the Duke of Sunderland and together, the two families ranked among the most influential and wealthy families in Britain. As his father's heir and nephew to the Duke of Sunderland, Ian Campbell's birthright gave him access to the highest tiers of society at home and abroad.

When his father became the eighth Duke of

Argyll, Ian Campbell assumed the courtesy title 'Marquess of Lorne', after which his contemporaries referred to him simply as Lorne. He had a sheltered upbringing, socialising primarily with his own family, the Leveson-Gowers, and occasionally the royal family. His greatest formative influence came from his mother Elizabeth, with whom he maintained almost unnaturally strong emotional bonds well into his adult life. His uncle, Ronald Gower, became the second formative influence in his life. Fate or destiny threw these two individuals together for the greater part of their lives. Though uncle and nephew, the two men were born in the same house just four days apart. As Gower became an uninhibited homosexual, he brought Lorne into his exciting underworld of like-minded friends.

Eton College left two indelible marks on Lorne. While playing cricket, a ball broke the bridge of his nose, leaving him to speak with a nasal twang for the rest of his life. At Eton he also encountered the world of homosexuality. Though he never mentions any schoolmaster in particular in his 1907 autobiography, he included a full page photograph of Eton's most infamous homosexual master, William Johnson. From this we may deduce that Lorne had been one of Johnson's intimates. An old Etonian described Johnson: 'Johnson was averse to the company of women, while among men he was attracted to the bold, gay, confident alert and beautiful.' This particular master joined the Eton staff in 1845, but had to leave in disgrace in 1872.

Lorne spent his life in the shadow of his father. The eighth Duke of Argyll served in cabinet, played an important role in politics, thought deeply about his views and commanded society's respect at large. In contrast, his son sat silent in parliament, failing to give even one significant speech in his entire career.

Lorne might have overcome his inability to walk in his father's shoes had fate not contrived to exacerbate the problem. Queen Victoria's middle daughter, Princess Louise, had a mind of her own. Rather than marrying into a European royal family, she wished to remain in her own country and wanted to marry a member of the English aristocracy, something a royal princess had not done for three and a half centuries. The overbearing Queen had tired of the feuding in her family and agreed. Mother and daughter drew up a list of five possible suitors: Lord Rosebery, Lord Stafford, Lord Fitzroy, Albert Grey and the Marquess of Lorne. All five men received invitations to visit Balmoral in September 1870. Few aristocrats would have wanted to marry a royal princess and live at a lower social rank than his wife, or take on Queen Victoria as his mother-in-law. The first four suitors duly obeyed the summons to Balmoral but made every effort to deflate the amorous intentions of the Princess and escape the embrace of her formidable mother. Suitably unimpressed, Victoria peremptorily dispatched each of these suitors.

Lorne proved different. His father appears to have considered the prospect of his son marrying royalty with great enthusiasm. Thus, never having shown any interest in women before, and probably already a confirmed homosexual, the Marquess of Lorne presented himself at Balmoral Castle, fully intending to win the hand of Queen Victoria's daughter, Princess Louise. Lorne married Louise on 21 March 1871, a decision that ultimately sealed his fate.

No one person's influence extended over nineteenth-century Britain as much as Victoria's, and she suffocated the newlyweds. Making matters worse, the other members of the royal family never accepted Lorne as an equal. Bertie, the Prince of Wales, disliked Lorne personally and they argued over everything. The principal cause of their disagreements came from their different sexual orientations. Bertie prided himself on his virility, and he detested Lorne's effeminate ways. For Lorne the worst feature of the marriage was simply that his wife outshone him on every level. She held a higher social rank. Lorne now lived his life not only in the shadows of his father but also in the shadows of Queen Victoria, the royal family and his wife.

Only once did Lorne break free of the shadows, during his tenure as Governor-General of Canada. Despite the rigours of the emerging nation, Lorne thoroughly enjoyed his time there, as he could live up to the limited demands of the post. In this new country, away from the English court, he discovered the joy of being his own man, whereas in Britain, he became utterly frustrated. His marriage to Louise broke down, but owing to the Queen's influence they kept the appearance of living together while living separate lives. Robert Stamp, who wrote a biography on the royal couple, commented; 'Princess Louise had a high sexual drive. Certainly she got on well with her male relatives and in-laws and artistic acquaintances. She liked Louis Battenberg ... she got on well with the Kaiser — indeed with any man — she ran after anything in trousers.' The Marquess of Lorne escaped into the homosexual world of his uncle, Lord Ronald Gower. Lorne's homosexual proclivities became so notorious that Louise had a window in Kensington Palace boarded up to prevent him slipping out at night to meet guardsmen. By the 1890s, Gower played a major role in the lives of both Lorne and his Princess.

Princess Louise's golden years occurred during the reign of her brother, Edward VII. Stamp comments: 'The Duchess of Argyll (Louise) may have been the King's favourite sister, but her husband was certainly not his favourite brother-in-law ... Bertie led a decidedly heterosexual life ... He could neither understand nor sympathise with Lorne's homosexual drives.' While the Crown Jewels imbroglio began to threaten his reputation, Lorne, now the ninth Duke of Argyll, continued his forays into Gower's social world. Stamp remarks: 'While the country buzzed with rumours, the gay weekends continued at Hammerfield (Gower's home). Lorne's homosexual life was another royal secret and he was now connected intimately to Frank Shackleton, the Dublin Herald and co-tenant of Sir Arthur Vicars.

King Edward VII dreaded public scandals. A man of double standards himself, he had discovered, as Prince of Wales, that the tolerance shown to his heterosexual infidelity was sorely absent when homosexual problems arose. When the Cleveland Street scandal broke in London, Edward had to use all the influence of the royal family to suppress the allegations that his son, Prince Albert Victor, was involved.

In 1889, the British public first learned that aristocrats procured young boys for sex in a male brothel at 19 Cleveland Street. The case revolved around Lord Arthur Somerset, third son of the Duke of Beaufort. Somerset belonged to the Prince of Wales' private club, the Marlborough Club. In 1885, the Prince appointed Somerset as his equerry which brought him into constant contact with Prince Edward's personal household.

The police first became aware of the brothel when a young telegraph boy admitted receiving money for having sex with a gentleman at the Cleveland Street house. They interviewed four boys, one of whom alerted the proprietor of the brothel before the police could arrest him. Subsequently, the police learned that the proprietor had fled to France. During the next two weeks, Scotland Yard put the house under surveillance, and officers observed many gentlemen attempting to gain admission to the brothel.

Scotland Yard built a strong case against Lord Somerset, who frequented the establishment, and the Director of Public Prosecutions wanted to have him arrested but the politicians had other ideas. Prime Minister Salisbury, acting as Foreign Secretary, made only feeble efforts to have the proprietor of the brothel extradited from France. The evidence suggests that he shared a common cause with Somerset in his wish to see the proprietor flee to America. Meanwhile the senior law officers in the Government, the Attorney General, the Solicitor General and the Home Secretary prohibited the police from arresting Somerset.

On 15 September, the Director of Public Prosecutions felt so exercised by the political interference in the case that he wrote a vigorous letter of protest to the Attorney General, which concluded:

> . . . in my judgement the circumstances of this case demand the intervention of those whose duty it is to enforce the law and to prevent the children of respectable parents taken in the service of the public, as these unfortunate boys have been, from being made victims of the unnatural lust of full grown men — and no consideration of public scandal owing to the position in society or sympathy with the family of the offender should in my judgement militate against this paramount duty.

H. Montgomery Hyde, an authority on the case comments: 'This must be one of the strongest letters ever addressed by a Director of Public Prosecutions to a Government Law Officer on the subject of a case involving unusual political and social features.'

Somerset and his father, the Duke of Beaufort, did not command the political clout to persuade the Prime Minister and his ministers to go against the strongest representations of their law enforcement officials. One suspects that only the royal family wielded that level of influence. The name of Prince Albert Victor (Prince Eddy), the elder son of the Prince of Wales, surfaced repeatedly in the case. He appears to have visited the brothel on at least two occasions. If Somerset ended up in open court, Prince Eddy's name might be mentioned, and seeking to avoid this calamity, the Prime Minister and his colleagues tried to suppress the affair.

Somerset's solicitor and counsel advised him to leave the country, but he decided to stand his ground and fight the case in open court. He thought that he would win because the prosecutor had nothing against him except the tainted evidence of other suspects in the case. Somerset had great support among his homosexual friends, particularly from Reginald Brett, later to become second Viscount Esher and the eminence grise in King Edward's court. Somerset's extensive correspondence with Brett gives us a running commentary on the developments in the case.

Once Prince Eddy's name surfaced in connection with the Cleveland Street affair, two members of the Prince of Wales' household became involved. Sir Dighton Probyn, Comptroller and Treasurer, and Sir Francis Knollys, private secretary to the Prince of Wales, began assessing the potential danger of the case to the royal household. They questioned Somerset, who assured them of his innocence.

On 18 September Somerset changed his mind and fled the country before the prosecutor could obtain a warrant for his arrest. The only man he spoke to on this fateful day was Montagu. We surmise that Montagu persuaded Somerset that he must leave England to protect the reputation of Prince Eddy. Somerset knew that running away amounted to his admitting guilt in the affair, but nonetheless, with the assistance of Montagu, he left England.

Despite Somerset's admission of guilt by fleeing the country, the Prince of Wales and his advisors attempted to persuade the Government to drop the charges against him. Sir Dighton Probyn wrote to Prime Minister Salisbury:

> I write now to ask you, to implore of you if it can be managed to have the prosecution stopped. It can do no good to prosecute him. He has gone and will never show his face in England again. He dare never come back to this country.
>
> I think it is the most hateful, loathsome story I ever heard, and the most astounding. It is too fearful, but further publicity will only make matters worse. I have of course telegraphed to the Prince, and am writing full particulars of this calamity to HRH.
>
> The Prince will be terribly cut up about it ... I felt that in writing to you I am only doing what the Prince would wish.
>
> I do not write with a view of trying to save

the man. He has gone — he is beyond punishment, or rather out of reach of the law. I only want if possible not to increase the fearful disgrace which has fallen on his family.

For the man, in his defence, I can only trust that he is mad.

The Prince of Wales, believing Salisbury favoured dropping the charge, wrote to ask the Prime Minister the following:

I don't know whether I am asking what I have no right to ask, but, if I may ask the question, I shall feel greatly obliged by your kindly letting me know whether the man might return to England now, or at any future date, without fear of being apprehended on this awful charge. I have no idea where he has gone, or if he would ever dare to show his face in England again even if he were free to do so, but I would like if I may, to let the Family know if their relative will at any time be at liberty to visit his native country.

Until I receive your reply giving me permission to speak, neither the Father, nor any of the Family shall ever know from me that I have been in correspondence with you on this painful subject.

Somerset expected the Prince of Wales to treat him kindly. Although he had absconded the country to avoid facing the charges against him, he wrote to the Prince of Wales asking for a recommendation for employment. However, the

Prince refused. Edward and his advisors had become thoroughly disenchanted with Somerset's explanations for leaving England. In a letter to Somerset's mother, Sir Dighton Probyn expressed the Prince of Wales' displeasure:

> Nobody accused your son of having mentioned Prince Albert Victor's name, but his excuse to everybody for having to leave England is that he has been forced to do so to screen another and that his lips are closed! The only conclusion therefore people can draw from this is that he is sacrificing himself to save the young Prince. Who else is there for whom he could make such a sacrifice? Hence the false reports dragging Prince Albert Victor's name into the sad story.

Probyn and others in the Prince of Wales' household pressurised Somerset to alter his explanation for leaving England. Montagu, his former commanding officer, wrote a savage letter to Somerset in which he berated him for causing harm to Prince Eddy.

Somerset, deeply upset by Montagu's tone, explained his position to Reginald Brett:

> I cannot see what good I could do Prince Eddy if I went into Court. I might do him harm because if I was asked if I had ever heard anything against him — whom from? — has any person mentioned with whom he went there etc? — the questions would be very awkward. I have never mentioned the boy's

name except to Probyn, Montagu and Knollys when they were acting for me and I thought they ought to know. Had they been wise, hearing what I knew and therefore what others knew, they ought to have hushed the matter up, instead of stirring it up with all the authorities . . .

What Oliver does not seem to see is that, if I could tell him my reasons for not going into Court, I could not go in. Nothing will ever make me divulge anything I know even if I were arrested. But of course if certain people laid themselves out to have me arrested and succeeded, I might possibly lose my temper and annoy them.

Of course, it has very often, or may I say constantly occurred to me, that it rests with me to clear up this business, but what can I do? A great many people would never speak to me again as it is, but if I went into Court and told all I knew no one who called himself a man would ever speak to me again. Hence my infernal position . . .

I did what I then, and still, believe was the best for all concerned. If they don't mind, they will make a hash of the whole thing yet, and then I suppose they will say I did it. At all events you and Newton can bear me witness that I have sat absolutely tight in the matter and have not told my own father anything.

With Somerset safely living in France, and the proprietor of the brothel living in America, Prince Edward managed to convince the entire

British public that he had always desired the most frank and open disclosure of all aspects of this case. Even Labouchere, a radical liberal and perpetual irritant to the royal family, fell for this posturing. Labouchere called for a debate on the scandal in Parliament and had the following to say about Edward and his son, Prince Eddy:

> I have seen the name of a gentleman of very high position mentioned in foreign newspapers in connection with the case, but having, as I have just said, looked very narrowly into the whole matter, I am absolutely certain that there is no justification for the calumny. In connection with this I may add that a still more eminent gentleman, closely connected with the gentleman to whom I have alluded, has used all his efforts to have the highest publicity given. I think that it is due to that eminent gentleman that the government have at last been forced into the qualified action which has been taken against Lord Arthur Somerset. I think this ought to be known . . . I honour and respect the eminent gentleman to whom I have alluded for his action in this matter. I consider it wise and noble and worthy of the great position he holds.

This exoneration from one of the most outspoken radicals in the British Parliament must have pleased the Prince of Wales. Thus Edward suppressed a scandal that threatened the future of the monarchy, and simultaneously won public credit for trying to 'clear the air' and have maximum publicity brought to bear on the affair. Nonetheless, this public relations triumph had come at great cost, and it is said that a few years later, officials in the royal household heaved deep sighs of relief when Prince Albert Victor died prematurely. The affair left its mark on the future King. Though a legendary philanderer in his own right, he had learnt to distance himself quickly from homosexual scandals.

6

THE KING'S ARRIVAL

The theft of the Irish Crown Jewels threw the arrangements for the royal visit into confusion. His Majesty had agreed to initiate Lord Castletown into the Order of St Patrick on 11 July but with the Grand Master's Regalia now stolen, Lord Aberdeen, in his capacity as Grand Master, cancelled the ceremony. While the Castle authorities hastily rearranged the King's schedule, the royal yacht, *Victoria and Albert*, dropped anchor in Kingstown harbour at 3:30am, on 10 July 1907. On board, King Edward VII, Queen Alexandra and Princess Victoria, oblivious to their arrival in the Emerald Isle, still slept soundly.

Although the Home Office had telegraphed the King about the theft of the Crown Jewels, His Majesty never suspected that the crime would eclipse his visit. The headline in *The Times* that day read:

'The Jewel Robbery at Dublin Castle.'

. . . The Office of Arms where the jewels were kept is exactly opposite to the state entrance to the Vice-Regal Apartments in the Upper Castle Yard. Just round the corner of the building, a soldier and a policeman are on duty by night and day, and a few yards away at the entrance to the Chief Secretary's Office another policeman is stationed during office hours. The headquarters of the Dublin Metropolitan Police, the headquarters of the Dublin detective force, the headquarters of the Royal Irish Constabulary, and the head office of the Dublin military garrison are all within a radius of 50 yards of the Office of Arms. In a word, there is no spot in Dublin, or possibly in the United Kingdom, which is at all hours of the 24 more constantly and systematically occupied by soldiers and policemen ... Some person got access to the safe ... and escaped without leaving any trace behind him ...

This was Edward's third visit to Ireland since becoming King. During his 1903 visit, a supposed account of a conversation between the King and MacDonnell, the Under-Secretary for Ireland was widely circulated before his arrival:

The King: Are the Irish disloyal?
MacDonnell: No, Sir, but they are discontented.
The King: What do they want?
MacDonnell: They want education and they want security in their land.
The King: I shall come to Ireland with an Education Bill in one hand and a Land Bill in the other.

That previous visit had been a great success with his Irish subjects and had been memorable despite the official snub from Dublin Corporation who had voted against an official address of welcome. Afterwards, he relished relating the yarn regarding his visit to Maynooth Seminary in County Kildare. The nationalist rector Dr Mannix, averse to flying the Union flag, chose instead to hoist the King's racing colours. Edward was tickled pink that the Catholic Church should endorse his zest for the turf so openly. The only displeasure on that visit had been a domestic tragedy during the night, which the King noted in his diary: 'The King's faithful Irish terrier Jack dies suddenly at 11pm.'

Edward also remembered fondly his sojourn in Ireland in 1861, when he had spent some months training at the Curragh Military Camp near Dublin, attached to a battalion of the Grenadier Guards. Here, the nineteen-year old Prince of Wales lost his virginity to the young actress Nellie Clifden, when officers had smuggled her into his bed. Nellie later bragged about the episode. Unfortunately, the resulting publicity of his first foray into carnal pleasure caused great distress to his parents as his father, Albert, died shortly after hearing of the sordid details and his mother, Queen Victoria, always blamed her son's loose conduct for her husband's untimely death.

However, this visit was more of a challenge to the King's popularity because the nationalist elements in Ireland were restless for home rule. King Edward abhorred the idea, and disapproved strongly of the 'Gladstone Liberals' who kept promising to push through the initiative. His official biographer commented that 'he was convinced that the grant of home rule to Ireland was incompatible with the maintenance of the integrity of the Empire, and that coercion of the disaffected Irish was an essential safeguard of the Union.'

Although angered over the theft of the Crown Jewels, King Edward determined to make this visit an enjoyable one. The Racing Commission, no doubt swayed by the increased turnout that his attendance would bring, had delayed the Leopardstown Races to coincide with his visit. This gesture pleased him greatly, as horse racing was his ultimate sporting passion.

All of Kingstown had prepared for the royal visit by decorating their homes. Festoons of laurels decked the Town Hall from top to bottom. Mottoes of 'God bless our King', 'God bless our Queen', in crimson and gold, draped over the balconies of the large terraced houses and small hotels along the route.

By 10am, crowds of Dubliners began to congregate, and lined the route into the city. Shortly after, the Lord Lieutenant dressed in military uniform, decked with a badge of the Order of St Patrick, and Lady Aberdeen arrived, and received a great welcome from the crowd. They were followed by the Chief Secretary, Birrell, and the Under-Secretary, MacDonnell.

A troubled Lord Lieutenant then prepared to

officially welcome the royal party. As soon as the King had shaken his hand, Aberdeen became conscious that His Majesty was scrutinising a badge of the Order of St Patrick (which had escaped the thief's haul). Aberdeen, knowing that King Edward was a stickler for detail, was afraid the badge might have been incorrectly placed and trembling, he remarked, 'Is it not right, sir?' 'Oh yes,' said the King, 'but I was thinking of those Jewels.' Apart from that slight remark, the King, true to form, did not want this catastrophe to mar his visit.

When their Majesties came ashore they received a warm official welcome. In attendance were the Irish nobility, many of whom were Knights of the Order of St Patrick. The King, a leader in fashion, wore morning dress and top-hat, and to honour the Irish linen industry, he had donned a green poplin tie. Her Majesty the Queen was in high spirits and wore a black and white dress, with a light grey wrap, a toque trimmed with red roses and a feather boa. A few paces back the Naval Band played the National Anthem, and the guard of honour gave the Royal salute.

Lord Aberdeen escorted their Majesties to the royal carriage to begin the five-mile trip to Ballsbridge, where King Edward was scheduled to tour the International Exhibition. After arriving at the Exhibition grounds, the King briefly inspected the pavilions, before sitting down to a musical reception in his honour. The choir and orchestra, comprising 500 choristers and 120 instrumentalists performed an ode of welcome set to the music of 'Come Back to Erin'. The King and Queen, with programme in hand closely followed the song:

'Come back to Erin' and 'Cead Mile Fáilte'.
Welcome our King to Hibernia's green shore.
True hearts will greet thee and brave hands will meet thee.
'Come back to Erin' and 'welcome galore'.

The royal party then entered the Royal Palace Restaurant for luncheon. In the afternoon, Their Majesties attended a garden party at the Vice-Regal Lodge in the Phoenix Park. During the festivities, however, another tragedy struck, when his darling Irish terrier 'Pat' died unexpectedly. On the second day of his visit, despite the death of his dog, the King attended Leopardstown races.

To the outsider, the royal visit seemed to have gone well and pleased the Castle's senior officials, all of whom seemed to bask in its success. However in reality, the theft of the Crown Jewels had enraged the King, and embarrassed the Irish administration. For the theft to have occurred at all proved humiliating, but when it stole attention from the royal tour, it only further fuelled the King's fury. While His Majesty made his public rounds, the press paid scant heed and at times went so far as to ignore him. Instead of reporting on the royal ribbon cutting they chose to write stories concerning the theft. Edward, like all royals, loved the limelight, and resented being upstaged. By the third day of his visit, Edward felt that he had endured enough injury, and before leaving Ireland commanded Lord Aberdeen to bring the thieves to justice. In turn, Aberdeen relayed the royal rage to Birrell and MacDonnell.

7

THE KANE REPORT

The detectives might well say that it is an affair for a Sherlock Holmes to investigate.

Sir Arthur Vicars, in an interview published in the *Daily Express*,

15 July 1907

From the outset, the Irish administration had requested Scotland Yard to assist the Dublin police in their investigation. In response, the Yard assigned Chief Inspector John Kane to handle the case.

Born in Lancashire, Kane started his career walking the beat in the east end of London. Poisonings, stabbings, bodies in boxes, 'money or your life', blackmails, all had come his way over the last 30 years. Ironically for a man who had spent his career proving the guilt of criminals, Kane's most celebrated case involved proving the innocence of a convicted man. In the most astonishing case of mistaken identity, Adolph Beck was twice convicted of crimes committed by a man who could almost pass as his twin. When Kane saw the real culprit, he recognised the uncanny resemblance he bore to Beck. Despite the lukewarm support of his superiors, Kane insisted on investigating the matter in

1904, oftentimes getting into trouble with his superiors and Home Office officials who had no desire to reopen the case. With the help of Thomas Gurrin, a handwriting expert, Kane forced the Home Office to recommend a pardon for Beck in July 1904. Despite stepping on toes in the Home Office, and the upbraiding of his superiors, Kane was promoted to Chief Inspector two years later.

In 1907, the Yard had created a specialist squad known as the Central Office Criminal Investigation Branch, later nicknamed the 'Murder Squad', because of the number of murders they investigated. Superintendent Frank Froest commanded the new squad, and initially his force comprised four Chief Inspectors, including Chief Inspector Kane. Froest chose his team based on their wide experience of criminal activity, their knowledge of forensic aids and their specialised training. The new squad received a special mandate from the Home Office to assist provincial police forces that often lacked trained or experienced detectives.

In assisting the Dublin police investigate the greatest jewel theft in Irish history, the new squad received a baptism of fire, but Kane's superiors felt that he could handle this sensitive political case. Kane's colleagues found this choice surprising. They readily acknowledged Kane's superior skills as a detective but even his admirers admitted that he always had some grievance or other to air. He had a particularly severe temperament, and he was especially caustic with what he called 'amateur detectives'.

Surprisingly, the Yard sent Kane to Dublin on his own, not even bothering to provide him with a couple of CID men, even though the missing jewels were valued at £30 000 – £50 000 (over £2 million in today's terms).

Kane took his time crossing over to Dublin, arriving on 11 July, five days after the Yard had been called in. Before leaving London, he first studied the files of well-known jewel thieves to see if he could detect the signs of their handiwork. These professionals often trailed royal visits with the intent of swooping on the big houses while their owners attended gala balls. The Dublin theft did not fit this pattern. These 'smart boys' from London always struck on a night when a major function distracted everybody, including the police. They would never have struck five days in advance of the royal visit, a time when Dubliners and their police went about their routine business.

After reading the initial reports made by the Dublin police, Kane agreed with their theory that the thief must have had an accomplice in the Office of Arms. A background check of the staff turned up nothing unusual, until Kane's superior allowed him to review a highly classified report on a group of upper-class homosexuals.

This report mentioned that Vicars associated closely with Lord Gower and his coterie of London gentlemen. For over a year the Yard had enlisted the help of the Dublin police to keep Sir Arthur's house at 7 St James' Terrace under surveillance, and they reported that several known members of the London clique had

121

stayed there. Frank Shackleton, the Dublin Herald, appeared to act as an intermediary between Lord Gower and Sir Arthur. Though not mentioned by name, Kane presumed that both Mahony and Goldney also belonged to this homosexual club. Two other names in the file immediately caught Kane's attention, namely Lord Haddo, Lord Aberdeen's eldest son, and the Duke of Argyll, the King's brother-in-law. The Yard's investigators believed that Lord Aberdeen's son, Lord Haddo, appeared to be a good friend of Sir Arthur Vicars, while Frank Shackleton associated intimately with the Duke of Argyll.

When Chief Inspector Kane arrived in Dublin, he had already decided how he would conduct his investigation. He considered that the thief's willingness to spend time removing the blue silk ribbon from the diamond star and leaving it neatly wrapped in the Jewel box gave a crucial clue to the puzzle. Superintendent Lowe took Kane to interview Vicars at the Office of Arms. At this first meeting, Sir Arthur emphasised the thief's removal of the ribbon, to which Kane remarked:

The thief was in no hurry to leave the premises. If my opinion is worth anything, this gentleman, (pointing to Superintendent Lowe) must remain to look for the thief in this building, because what he has described to me would be utterly impossible, to my mind, on the part of an ordinary or outside thief.

However, Kane disputed Vicars' estimate of the time required to remove the ribbon. While Sir Arthur calculated the intruder needed ten minutes, Kane thought that half that time would be adequate.

Kane, just like the Dublin police and the entire Irish population, wondered how the thief entered the Office of Arms unobserved. Virtually every commentator on the crime remarked that the theft took place in the most policed and heavily guarded location in Ireland. Yet the dozens of soldiers and policemen who passed through the Upper Castle Yard on the nights of 2 July and 5 July had seen nothing unusual. Unlike the Dublin police, Kane professionally interrogated the officers and sentries who guarded the Main Gate and Upper Castle Yard during the week of the theft, and he also interviewed the policemen who had handled the initial inquiry. All the evidence pointed to an inside job, and therefore Kane tried to compile a list of Castle employees who had been seen by the sentries after 8pm. However, more than a week had passed since the theft, the King had come and gone, and the sentries could not remember the movements of the Castle staff.

At this juncture, the Chief Inspector, for some unknown reason, abandoned his attempt to identify the thief. Of all the theories and rumours concerning the theft — and they are many — none has ever advanced a credible theory to explain this detail.

Kane now turned all his efforts to identifying the thief's accomplice within the Office of Arms.

After two or three days, he had eliminated all the junior members of staff as suspects, and focused on those men who had possible access to Sir Arthur's safe key.

Detective Kerr told the Chief Inspector about his questioning of Mrs Farrell on 7 July. Specifically he related her story about seeing Lord Haddo in the Office of Arms early one morning. She had told Kerr that about six months earlier while cleaning the upstairs offices, she heard a man walking about downstairs. Unaccustomed to having someone in the offices, while she worked, she became nervous, and looking over the landing, saw the man entering the library. He looked up and said to her 'It's all right'. She positively identified the man as Lord Haddo, the eldest son of Lord Aberdeen.

When in Ireland, Lord Haddo had the use of the state apartments in the Castle, but this did not explain how he had been able to enter the Office of Arms before office hours. Mrs Farrell always left the door locked while she worked inside, implying that Haddo had to use a key to let himself in. The police listed seven people who held keys to the front door but Haddo was not among them. Kane had heard about Haddo's Christmas prank at the Office of Arms, when Haddo removed Sir Arthur's keys from around Sir Arthur's neck as he was in a comatose state from too much drink, then removing the jewels from the safe, Haddo had left them on Sir Arthur's desk in a brown bag for him to discover the next morning. In fact Haddo's prank was widely known by Castle officials. Now Mrs Farrell's revelation that she had seen Haddo in the office early one morning prompted Kane to investigate Haddo thoroughly, even though he knew that in doing so, he would antagonise his father, Lord Aberdeen.

Kane discreetly inquired into Lord Haddo's movements from 11 June when the jewels were last seen to 6 July, when the theft was officially discovered. He learnt that Haddo had stayed at Haddo House in Scotland during that time and confirmed that Haddo had not used his apartment in the Castle, nor had he stayed with his parents in the Vice-Regal Lodge in the Phoenix Park. If the Chief Inspector uncovered any incriminating evidence on Haddo, it never became public. Despite Haddo's alibi, Kane retained him as a suspect in the crime. He appears not to have been particularly discreet about his suspicions because within days, half of Dublin knew. Considering the potential for political interference, one would have expected Kane to have been more cautious about whom he suspected.

Chief Inspector Kane submitted his first report to the Dublin police on 16 July, just five days after he had arrived. This and any subsequent reports have 'disappeared' from the files of Scotland Yard, the Home Office, and the Dublin Metropolitan Police. Only one reference to Kane's activities in Dublin occurs, and this is a brief note in the Chief Secretary's files acknowledging receipt of the report on 16 July. Kane continued his work in Dublin until 2

125

August, and presumably kept the Dublin authorities abreast of his activities. At this stage the authorities summarily sent him home to London.

The substance of the Kane report became the focus of multiple rumours, and in many respects, it lies at the heart of the Irish Crown Jewel affair. The exact details of Kane's theory are not known but we do know that it so provoked the Irish administration that they removed him from the case and sent him back to London. Obviously the Liberal authorities had something to hide but they had no reason to defend the Unionist heralds within the Office of Arms. Augustine Birrell, the Chief Secretary, took no part in these early decisions by the Irish administration, leading us to infer that the Lord Aberdeen personally authorised Kane's dismissal. Following this line of reasoning we conclude that Kane suspected Lord Haddo, and in the process threatened Lord Aberdeen's position as Lord Lieutenant.

Since Kane's report is so critical, we have tried to reconstruct it, by drawing on his later testimony, leaks from the police and rumours in the press. The following is some of the detail we believe Kane included in his report to the Dublin authorities.

Kane exposed Sir Arthur's homosexual court and its ties to Lord Gower's circle in London. Far worse, from the Dublin authorities' point of view, he associated Lord Haddo with Sir Arthur and Lord Gower. The problems for Vicars began with Haddo's Christmas prank. Everybody in the Castle thought the prank was hilarious, but in private Sir Arthur had a ferocious row with Haddo as a result. In the heat of this bitter exchange, Sir Arthur, knowing Haddo's vulnerability, sneered at Haddo's intelligence, epilepsy and his mother's prohibition on his having children. Haddo turned absolutely vengeful towards Sir Arthur, and set out to destroy him.

From the rumours afloat in Dublin we suggest that Kane may have made the following accusations. Haddo's first move was to fake a reconciliation with his enemy. Inviting Sir Arthur to his apartments, he made conciliatory overtures and Vicars, never a man to bear a grudge, accepted the apology. Naturally Haddo plied his unsuspecting guest with whiskey until he became so inebriated that he passed out. Haddo, aided by a loyal servant from his father's household, removed Sir Arthur's keys, and made plaster of Paris copies. The servant arranged the cutting of the keys. Before he left for Scotland, Haddo made a foray into the Office of Arms to check that the keys worked. Unfortunately he had not known how early Mrs Farrell came to work and she saw him in the offices. By the time Mrs Farrell looked over the balcony, he had already verified that the copies of the front door key and the safe key worked.

Haddo knew his father wanted the King to open the International Exhibition in early May. Staying in touch, he would have learnt that His Majesty had declined and then later agreed to come over on 10 July. He wanted to exploit the publicity of the royal visit to make as much trouble as possible for Sir Arthur. The loyal servant entered the Office of Arms on or before 28 June, (the king's birthday) and, removing the blue ribbon, left with the jewels. When Sir Arthur failed to discover the theft, the servant returned on the night of 2 July and left the front door open to precipitate the discovery. When this too failed, Haddo instructed the servant to unlock the safe and to leave the strong room open. Maintaining his alibi, Haddo remained in Scotland, and did not travel over to Dublin even for the King's visit.

We do not state that Kane's theory of the crime was exactly as above but we do believe that this is the gist of what he said. Obviously Lord Aberdeen would not appreciate any theory along these lines, and so had Kane removed from the case.

Some obvious problems arise concerning the theory that Haddo orchestrated the theft. No evidence exists that Sir Arthur and Haddo had a falling out. The idea that Haddo took plaster of Paris impressions of the keys suggests a level of sophistication that Haddo never previously or subsequently displayed. Also, one suspects that amateurs would be incapable of making perfect copies of the safe and strong room keys using impressions. The theory does not explain why Haddo took impressions of the strong room key — a key he had no need of to carry out his plan. Finally, we have no idea how Haddo and the servant communicated with each other. Kane would surely have checked for telegrams and phone calls, and the post would have been too slow.

While Kane suspected Haddo of the theft, another set of rumours pointed the finger at Frank Shackleton. Kane dismissed these rumours outright, and from the beginning of the case, firmly asserted that Shackleton played no part in the theft. Somewhat inconsistently, Kane argued that Shackleton had a perfect alibi for the time, and he therefore could not have taken the jewels. Apparently, to Kane's way of thinking, Shackleton's perfect alibi proved his innocence while Haddo's equally perfect alibi proved his guilt.

Many good reasons existed for suspecting Shackleton:

• Francis Richard Shackleton, Dublin Herald, appeared to have prophetic gifts. At a luncheon, given by Lady Ormonde in London two days prior to the discovery of the theft, Shackleton remarked to one of the guests concerning the jewels: 'I shall not be surprised to hear if they are stolen some day.' He was the only herald who had mentioned even the possibility that the jewels might be stolen.

• When Sir Arthur discovered the theft, he telegraphed Shackleton to come over to Dublin immediately. Upon arriving, Shackleton proceeded to burn an undisclosed number of letters and documents. Goldney informed Kane about the burning, but the Chief Inspector took no notice.

• As co-tenant with Sir Arthur at 7 St James' Terrace he had the greatest opportunity of borrowing the spare key to the safe.

• Decorated for bravery in the Boer war, he had proved himself a man of action and courage, definitely desirable qualities in a thief.

• Shackleton had serious financial problems in his business dealings, and living beyond his means, had borrowed heavily from the London money lenders, Wilton & Co. At the time of the theft, he was on the brink of bankruptcy.

• He lacked discretion as a homosexual, thus leaving himself easy prey to a blackmailer.

• By 1907, Shackleton had developed a dubious reputation in London. His partner in one of his ventures had repudiated him over some shady share transactions. Kane took the unusual course of ignoring Shackleton's known dishonesty and lack of scruples. At the time of the theft, Shackleton was the only herald known to have developed criminal tendencies.

• He promised his brother Ernest financial support for the Antarctic Expedition scheduled to depart in August 1907.

• The Office of Arms insider needed an accomplice to carry out the theft, and unlike the other heralds, Shackleton had the ideal man. His intimate friend in Ireland, the infamous Captain Richard Gorges, was stationed just twenty miles from Dublin. Dressed as an army officer, he ran far less risk of being questioned by the Castle sentries. Based on Gorges' past military record he had both the nerve and the daring to pull off the burglary. Gorges also bore a personal grudge against Sir Arthur for banishing him from St James' Terrace.

• Unlike Haddo who provided his wife and domestic staff as alibis, Shackleton produced a glittering sample of London's high-society, including Lady Ormonde, Lady Butler, Lord Gower and the Duke of Argyll. Equally suspicious, Shackleton documented precisely his movements from the time of the International Exhibition in May to the time of the discovery of the theft in July. Remarkably, while in London, he signed the register in at least one of his London clubs every day, while out of London he made a point of writing thank-you notes to people he visited.

★ ★ ★

Surprisingly, nothing on this list influenced Kane in the least. On the contrary he forcefully insisted that Shackleton was absolutely innocent of the theft, saying that Shackleton was no more implicated in the theft than he himself was.

8

INFERNAL TELEGRAMS

A week after the King left Ireland in a rage, Sir Arthur Vicars became involved in a bizarre incident. He received a note from a medium working in the Italian section of the International Exhibition who told him that her daughter had a vision concerning the Crown Jewels. Like his famous kinsman, Sir Arthur Conan Doyle, Sir Arthur appears to have had considerable faith in the occult and asked his friend Shackleton to go to the Exhibition and verify the young lady's visionary abilities. Shackleton obliged, went to see the young lady, returned to Sir Arthur with a favourable report and advised him to accept the clairvoyant's assistance. Vicars, proud holder of the title Ulster King of Arms, invited the young clairvoyant to hold a seance at his home in St James' Terrace. Even more astonishing, the police cooperated in this extraordinary affair by providing, from the criminal evidence file, the original key to the safe, which Sir Arthur assured them had more potency in these matters.

The young psychic duly arrived at Sir Arthur's home accompanied by a small entourage of spiritualists. In the darkened drawing-room, the clairvoyant slipped into a trance and gave the following message: 'the missing jewels are hidden near a tombstone which stood not far from the entrance to an old and disused churchyard in the direction of Clonsilla.' The following day, Sir Arthur, along with Mahony, and Sergeant Murphy of the Dublin police, drove to the Clonsilla and Mulhuddart graveyards. They spent the day wandering about the two graveyards but at last, a dejected threesome admitted defeat and returned gloomily to Dublin. Six months later, when news of the incident became public, Sir Arthur had to endure savage criticism from Marie Corelli in the *London Opinion*:

As for Sir Arthur Vicars, he must have been what is called 'a figure of fun'. Indeed groping about for the jewels in two cemeteries at the behest of a 'clairvoyant!' If there is anything to be specially quoted against him beyond his evident carelessness, it is this outrageous display of utter stupidity, which has certainly exposed him completely to popular contempt. For the bulk of the British people are still sane and healthy, and can see through a thing or two. They are wide awake to the fact that while God is blasphemed in the press and Christ 'preached down' in many pulpits, the 'upper' classes are giving themselves over to such superstitious observances as degraded even the paganism of a barbarous age. They view with unutterable scorn men who, placed in positions of trust under government, are found dabbling with conjuring tricks of 'clairvoyant'; humbug . . .

During Chief Inspector Kane's short stay in Dublin, Sir Arthur assured him repeatedly that he had complete confidence in his staff at the Office of Arms. However, just days before Kane's curt dismissal, Vicars abruptly lost faith in his friend and co-tenant, Frank Shackleton. This change of heart stunned his friends, and they pressed him to explain his new-found suspicions. He revealed that a close friend of his had alerted him that there was a shady side to Shackleton. Specifically, he mentioned the young man's growing disrepute in the City of London over dubious share dealings coupled with rumours that he lived well beyond his means. These questions of character convinced Sir Arthur that Shackleton may have had a hand in the theft.

Both Kane and the Dublin police inquired into Vicars' new accusations against his friend. They questioned Sir Arthur and his confidant, Peter McEnnery, the man who had given the damning report on Shackleton. McEnnery, who worked in the Castle, and also frequented Sir Arthur's parties, moved in the same circle of 'gentlemen' and knew Shackleton well. He bluntly told the police that he suspected Shackleton but could not support his charge. He told the police about the Dublin Herald's shady share dealings in London, about his extravagant lifestyle, and harped on the incident at Lady Ormonde's luncheon where Shackleton had predicted the theft of the jewels. The police already knew everything McEnnery had to tell them, and wanted more substantial evidence. After questioning McEnnery for hours, the unconvinced detectives dismissed his charges as groundless.

While the junior police may have had reason to dismiss McEnnery and Sir Arthur's accusations against Shackleton for want of hard evidence, the more senior officers, such as Kane and Harrel, ought to have viewed them in a different light. They had the advantage of knowing about the homosexual links between the heralds. Just as Shackleton had mentioned the possibility that the jewels might be stolen some day, he had no doubt said the same to his 'friends' in London. Presumably, one of these friends tipped off McEnnery about what Shackleton had said. If this information was obtained under compromising conditions, then McEnnery could not tell the police the full story. Harrel and Kane could have figured that much out themselves. As policemen they could never hope to penetrate the secret world of the homosexual community, and ought to have considered it an important breakthrough when two of the 'circle' tried to turn in one of their own. Instead they ignored Sir Arthur's accusations against his erstwhile friend and lover.

It is surprising that Kane, a CID officer who had been selected to join the 'Murder Squad' because of his great experience with criminal investigations, simply dismissed the accusations against Shackleton as a personal vendetta. In doing so, Kane suggested Shackleton's airtight alibis proved his innocence. However, as far as the historical record shows, all of the heralds and Lord Haddo had airtight alibis for at least part of the time. To account for this the police had theorised that two men committed the crime — the thief and his insider partner. If Kane worked along those lines then the alibis did not count for anything, unless he had evidence to discount one of them, yet evidence is not apparent that Lord Haddo's alibi had been cracked. A few years later, Kane confided in a close friend that he might have solved the case if there had not been so many amateur detectives in Dublin.

Again, the numerous commentators have all raised questions about Shackleton's possible role in the theft. Only four weeks after Kane's dismissal, the Dublin police promoted Shackleton to prime suspect in the case yet right up to the end of the investigation, Kane vouched for Shackleton's total innocence. Five months later at the Commission of Inquiry, the Chief Inspector assured the Commissioners that Shackleton was no more guilty than himself. Ironically, just over two years later, revelations again surfaced that Shackleton had defrauded his closest friends, but this time he was charged and subsequently went to prison. Kane was the principal source for all the rumours against Haddo, while in contrast, virtually every independent commentator came to suspect Shackleton of having been involved.

Although we do not know the details of McEnnery's story, we can measure its persuasive force from Sir Arthur's reaction. He instantly turned on his long-time friend and lover, thereafter resolutely accusing him of the crime, and, thirteen years later, inserting the accusation in his last will and testament.

In mid-August, Goldney, who had guaranteed two loans for Shackleton, wanted to be released from these obligations. When he met Shackleton in London, Shackleton mentioned that Sir Patrick Coll, former Chief Solicitor of Ireland, had told him that the police had found the jewels. This stunning statement inflamed Goldney's suspicions, and he immediately reported Shackleton's story to Kane. The Chief Inspector ignored Goldney, stating that Shackleton's alibis between 11 June and 6 July proved that he had not been in Dublin during these dates, so he could not have personally stolen the jewels. Kane told Goldney he thought Shackleton was innocent and that he did not plan to pursue him.

Goldney travelled to Dublin for Horseshow Week in late August, and was shocked to find Sir Arthur's spirits had sagged so badly. Sir Arthur related McEnnery's accusations to him, and their persuasive force easily convinced Goldney of Shackleton's guilt. Goldney thought Vicars was teetering on the brink of a nervous breakdown so he invited Sir Arthur to Canterbury to recoup his spirits. The two men travelled there together, and dissected their former friend's character and corrupt dealings. Rumours soon surfaced in Dublin that Goldney had started stalking Shackleton.

A dramatic turn of events occurred on 28 August, when Lord Aberdeen received an unsigned telegram at Dublin Castle, stating: 'jewels are in box, 9 Hadley Street, Dublin.'

Aberdeen ordered the police to investigate but no Hadley Street existed in Dublin. Displaying uncharacteristic tenacity, Aberdeen would not let the matter drop and ordered Sir James Dougherty, the Assistant Under-Secretary of State, to ask the Home Office to find the handwritten telegram form and forward it to Dublin for examination. Dougherty sent the request to the Home Office who only sent a routine query to the Postmaster General. In replying, the post office stated that the telegram came from either Malvern or Great Malvern — information the Dublin authorities already knew from the telegram. Aberdeen refused to accept this answer, and on 30 August, Dougherty sent another request to the Home Office. Home Secretary Gladstone, aware by now of Aberdeen's interest, issued a warrant to the post office to search for the form. After finding it, the post office forwarded the document to the Home Office along with the miffed note: 'since it was the addressee who wished to see the original, no warrant had been necessary.'

At this juncture, the Home Office took an unusual course of action. Aberdeen had asked to see the original form; nonetheless, ignoring the Lord Lieutenant's request, they decided to investigate the matter in London and the Home Office chose Chief Inspector Kane to investigate the matter. In returning Kane to the case, the Home Office, for reasons unknown, decided to ignore the existing conflict between the Chief Inspector and the Dublin authorities.

Kane took possession of the telegram form and returned to Scotland Yard. He had all the forensic expertise of the Yard at his disposal, including the new breed of handwriting experts. In his greatest triumph, the Adolph Beck case in 1904, Kane had worked closely with Thomas Gurrin, a handwriting expert. However, Kane, for all his acquaintance with the new forensics, decided to work alone.

Kane appears to have had no doubt about who wrote the telegram and immediately went in search of Shackleton at his London clubs. Finding him, he asked the young man to accompany him to Scotland Yard, where he 'wanted to show him something'. He than produced the telegram and showing him just the one word 'Dublin', he asked Shackleton if he could identify the writing. Shackleton replied 'That is mine'. The Chief Inspector then opened the telegram, whereupon Shackleton denied having written the message. Kane asked him to explain its contents. Agitated, Shackleton denied all knowledge of the message. Kane, convinced that it was Shackleton's handwriting, cautioned him that this was a serious matter, and ordered him not to leave London.

Kane next sent for Sir Arthur, who was still staying with Goldney at Canterbury. The following day, Sir Arthur along with his brother, Major Vicars, arrived at Kane's office, only to find Shackleton there as well. The Chief Inspector showed Sir Arthur the word 'Dublin' on the telegram and asked him if he could identify the handwriting. Sir Arthur looked at the script for a moment and then, turning to Shackleton said, 'You, I suppose'. The Chief Inspector opened the telegram for Sir Arthur to read. Without hesitation, Vicars identified the writing as Shackleton's, who retorted, 'You might believe it was mine'. Then Shackleton asked Vicars, 'You do not believe it is mine do you?' To which Sir Arthur replied, 'Yes I do'. Shackleton then said, 'You may think the writing is like mine, but you do not think I wrote it do you?' Vicars replied, 'Well, I do think you wrote it, you have not assisted the police.'

Kane intervened. 'Now Mr Shackleton, you will not be astonished at whatever position the police assume, or what notice they take of this statement.' Kane went on to warn Shackleton that he was now under suspicion and may be arrested at any time. He then ordered Shackleton to keep him posted of his movements in London.

In the most remarkable twist of the saga, the spectre of clairvoyance descended upon the investigation for the second time in five weeks. The next day, 4 September, Aberdeen received a second telegram with the same message; however, this time it bore the name of the sender, Mr A. Bullock Webster from Great Malvern. Aberdeen notified the Home Office, and they again asked Kane to investigate. After making inquiries, Kane reported that he had questioned Mr Bullock Webster, and that this gentleman, a man of the highest repute in Great Malvern, confirmed sending both telegrams. Apparently his wife, who believed she possessed clairvoyant powers, had a dream about the jewels and she told her husband to disclose her revelations to the Dublin authorities. When they had found no reports in the newspapers concerning the first telegram, Bullock Webster elected to send the second one, this time bearing his name and address.

Although Kane had cleared Shackleton, he neglected to convey the good news to the young herald. Instead, he allowed Shackleton to go about his daily business believing that he faced imminent arrest. Later, when Sir Arthur and Major Vicars pressured the Chief Inspector, Kane insisted on Shackleton's innocence. Testifying at the Inquiry, Kane described Sir Arthur's persistence as badgering. However, Shackleton told the Commissioners: 'I was never informed or relieved of the suspense and unpleasantness I felt with regard to that telegram; but I have been informed since, but not till quite a long time afterwards that Scotland Yard had completely investigated the matter . . . '

Miss Corelli, who had already commented on Sir Arthur's use of a clairvoyant's assistance, went on to castigate the upper class in general for their belief in spiritualism, when she reported the Bullock-Webster story:

Perhaps if the visionary had been the wife of a gentleman of less repute, no attention would have been paid to her statement. Friends of the humbler class will take note by this how good a thing it is, my brethren, to be of 'high repute'. You can do everything then. You can

141

dream dreams, and they will actually be accepted as important facts by Government officials. Think of It! What a grand vista opens out before the dazzled eye!

Almost certainly referring to the Bullock-Webster telegram, Sir Arthur later wrote to his friend Fuller on 29 June, 1909:

Shackleton, when he was suspected, worked the alleged scandal for all he was worth and even blackened his own character! threatening to produce a social scandal and involve high persons.

Who were these 'high persons?' One would expect Shackleton to have aimed his threat at Lord Gower and the Duke of Argyll. Presumably when somebody is threatened they are aware of the fact. For all his contacts, including the King, Gower never heard of the threat, and remained on close terms with Shackleton throughout the affair. Likewise for the Duke of Argyll, he continued to visit Gower at his country estate, and met Shackleton there regularly. These men had no knowledge that Shackleton had threatened to expose them. The one man who gave every indication of having received a threat was Lord Aberdeen. He reacted to the Hadley Street telegram with such uncharacteristic determination and vigour that he must have been threatened.

9

'I'LL HAVE NO SCANDAL'

No record exists of how King Edward reacted to Chief Inspector Kane's dismissal from the case, but we can infer that he received a scathing report on the actions of the Dublin authorities. His Majesty gave the Dublin police just three weeks before he instructed Lord Knollys, his private secretary, to convey his displeasure. Knollys wrote to Lord Aberdeen on 26 August, commenting that the police had a 'certain lukewarmness' for catching the culprits which displeased the King. He also commanded the Lord Lieutenant to punish the careless custodian of the jewels.

One can hardly fault the King for insisting on punishing Sir Arthur. Having authored the revised statutes of the Order, Sir Arthur had assigned to himself, albeit involuntarily, full responsibility for the jewels. The thief had extracted the jewels with Sir Arthur's safe key or a perfect copy. Somehow Sir Arthur had given the thief access to the key, and for this he should have accepted responsibility. Furthermore, he had to account for his failure to report the open front door on 3 July.

In a surprising development, Lord Aberdeen did not act upon the King's command to dismiss

Vicars. Petrified that punishing Sir Arthur might open a Pandora's box of scandals, Aberdeen did nothing. He left the police to work at their own pace, and ignored the royal command to punish Sir Arthur. Aberdeen must have calculated that more pressing matters of state or even pleasure would soon distract his Sovereign.

An intriguing aspect of Aberdeen's actions is that he never alerted his wife to the situation. From late August until December, Lady Aberdeen played no role in the affair. Considering that contemporaries usually referred to 'the Aberdeens' in recognition of Ishbel's contribution, one has to conclude that Aberdeen deliberately kept Lady Aberdeen in the dark, possibly because he could not discuss homosexual issues with his wife.

Three weeks later, Aberdeen discovered how he had misjudged his King. Though Edward thoroughly enjoyed indulging his pleasures, he, or his advisers, kept an eye on Dublin's foundering investigation. On 17 September, Aberdeen received a follow-up letter from Knollys, again advising him of the King's displeasure and demanding Sir Arthur's dismissal. Concluding his letter, Knollys commanded Aberdeen to attend His Majesty at Balmoral on 24 September, so that he could personally present his report on 'the unwelcome topic'.

The King's intrusion into the affair worried the Lord Lieutenant. Aberdeen liked Vicars and had no desire to dismiss him. On a more pragmatic level, Sir Arthur might cause

144

Aberdeen problems for his son Lord Haddo. Aberdeen also had to think of the police. Vicars' dismissal might inspire them to investigate his character and lifestyle more closely, possibly bringing to light aspects of his secret life and close association with Lord Haddo. However, Aberdeen had to take some action, because he could not evade a royal command to punish Sir Arthur or to press the police for results.

Instead of dismissing Sir Arthur, Aberdeen elected to try subtly blackmailing the King into backing off. Though the press had stayed quiet on the matter, London's high-society gossipped continuously about the Duke and Duchess of Argyll. Considering the 'delicate' nature of Argyll's relationship with Shackleton, Aberdeen found it surprising that His Majesty had intervened so forcefully in the case. Naturally, King Edward wanted to retrieve his jewels, but he also shared the Lord Lieutenant's aversion to public humiliation and disgrace. As Prince of Wales, he had suffered a multitude of embarrassments over his own philandering. The antics of his son, the Duke of Clarence, in the Cleveland Street affair had brought chagrin to the royal family. In general, the public tolerated their aristocrats having mistresses, but homosexual liaisons remained utterly taboo and were liable to criminal prosecution. It was clear to Aberdeen that His Majesty's desire to catch the thief and to punish Sir Arthur might prove disastrous for both their households.

Aberdeen turned to MacDonnell for advice. Obviously he assured MacDonnell that his son had neither homosexual inclinations nor anything to do with the crime. Together, the two men reviewed the facts of the case. They agreed that in assessing Shackleton with his burgeoning financial difficulties, his apparent access to the safe key, his growing disrepute as a man of few scruples, and his ruptured relations with his intimate friend, Sir Arthur, combined to make him the prime suspect. Despite having a perfect alibi, the Dublin herald could easily have supplied an accomplice with the keys, and his unwholesome friend, Captain Richard Gorges, surfaced in the discussion as a possible partner. MacDonnell and Aberdeen felt confident that the handwriting on the mysterious telegrams belonged to Shackleton, although Chief Inspector Kane seemed determined to shield the young herald. They concluded that Scotland Yard had received instructions to protect the royal household from scandal. Shackleton apparently had found the perfect sanctuary through his intimate association with the Duke of Argyll.

What remained unclear was whether the King had been informed of the more sensitive details of the case. Believing he shared a common cause with the King, Aberdeen determined to convince His Majesty of the inadvisability of pressing the police too hard. He believed that once the King realised that his brother-in-law's liaison with Shackleton would become public in any criminal proceedings, he would clamp down on the entire investigation. To this end, he persuaded MacDonnell to write a report on the homosexual activities in the Office of Arms, which he would present to the King during their meeting at Balmoral. In his report, MacDonnell would outline the reasons for suspecting Shackleton, and then he would examine the dangers involved in exposing any of the heralds for fear that their innocent acquaintances would become tarred with the same brush.

MacDonnell agreed to write the report. However, independently of Aberdeen, it appears that he decided to take a calculated gamble. In all probability, His Majesty would recoil in horror from the report, but he would become even more determined to dismiss Vicars from his household. MacDonnell thought it prudent to blacken Sir Arthur's name among the general public and the Unionists in the Kildare Street Club. Thus, when the time came to oust Vicars, few friends would stand up in his defence.

The Under-Secretary for Ireland wasted no time. Well versed in the workings of Dublin's gossip mills, he sought known vultures to unknowingly assist him in spreading the rumours. While piling praise on Sir Arthur's achievements, he would mention his reprehensible sexual preferences. Thus, MacDonnell played the strangest role in his career. For two weeks the Bengal Tiger turned into an Irish Machiavelli; renowned for his fearless honesty and blunt directness, he now spent his time slyly smearing Sir Arthur's character. He hoped that these rumours would cause Sir Arthur's supporters to abandon him, and, more importantly, they might even shame him into resigning voluntarily.

MacDonnell planted his slanderous seeds in fertile ground and little time passed before the confidential whispers began sprouting all sorts of calumnies against the hapless Vicars. In a small city like Dublin, rumours grow of their own accord and spread swiftly. Soon Dublin's high-society, those who called themselves 'the quality', believed that Sir Arthur lived a truly depraved life, indulging in late night orgies in the Castle.

Within days, MacDonnell began reaping a rich harvest of rumours that flowed back to the Castle from all over Dublin. Having published two books of his own, he had no trouble selecting the best stories to include in his report. Thus he embellished dry police reports with sordid slurs and slander, and wrote it all in the cold drone of a mandarin. As planned, he made a point of highlighting Shackleton's leading role, and named him as the prime suspect in the theft. He also mentioned the well-placed homosexual circle in London, to which both Shackleton and Sir Arthur belonged. Among other notables, he listed Lord Gower and the Duke of Argyll as their associates. Finally, he ended by urging the Lord Lieutenant to tread with the utmost care in arresting either Sir Arthur or Shackleton on the grounds that they could not control what might come out in a public trial. Aberdeen and MacDonnell hoped that the report would convince the King of the inadvisability of pushing the Dublin investigation too far.

Meeting the King at Balmoral, Aberdeen, despite his nervous character, handled his testy

Monarch with surprising skill. With imperious ire, His Majesty ordered Aberdeen to explain the desultory pace of the police probe and why he had not obeyed the royal command to dismiss Vicars. Handing over MacDonnell's report, Aberdeen gave a verbal account of its sordid contents, and argued that he had acted in the best interests of the Crown. He finished by noting that this report came from one of the most respected administrators in the empire, a man whom His Majesty greatly trusted and had honoured with a knighthood. While the King had scant regard for Aberdeen, he held MacDonnell in the highest esteem, and therefore thought it prudent to read the report.

His Majesty's reaction dispelled any doubts that the King was aware of the 'more sensitive aspects' of the case. Banging on the table, the King thundered 'I will have no scandals! I will never come to Dublin again! I will give nothing (honours)'. He impressed upon Aberdeen the absolute necessity to avert a scandal at all costs, insisting that the name of the Duke of Argyll must never surface in connection with that of Mr Shackleton. Needing time to digest the full import of MacDonnell's report, His Majesty agreed to extend the deadline for Sir Arthur's dismissal by two weeks. However, he saw the presence of the homosexuals in his household as a threat, and commanded that when the deadline came, Aberdeen must remove not only Sir Arthur but all the heralds from the Office of Arms.

MacDonnell's report had given King Edward

more to worry about than Aberdeen ever imagined. As with most 'royals', Edward's world revolved about himself and other members of royalty. By 1907, his relations with his nephew, Kaiser Wilhelm II of Germany, had become virulently poisonous. International affairs has rarely seen the intense personal animosity played out by this uncle and nephew duet. If the historical consequences were not so calamitous, this bickering would appear comical.

Wilhelm suffered from emotional insecurity and many of his contemporaries thought he was mentally unstable. Lamar Cecil states:

By the 1890s, the concern in Germany was that the Empire was in the hands of a ruler not mentally normal. Even those within Wilhelm's family questioned if he was right in the head. Among the Kaiser's English relatives, the two who knew him best, Queen Victoria, and the Prince of Wales, were both sure that he was not quite lucid. The Queen wrote about her grandson's 'very unhealthy and unnatural state of mind', while Edward's gesture of a rap to his forehead indicated his views on the subject. As a child Wilhelm had frequently suffered from ear infections, which afflicted him well into his forties. There was anxiety that this infection may have spread to his brain and a German physician declared that the ailing prince would always be susceptible to 'sudden accesses of anger'. To those who knew him well, the Kaiser seemed to teeter on the edge of mental collapse.

English-speaking historians never fail to point out Wilhelm's failings, but they invariably portray Edward's long list of character flaws in a glamorous light. In reality, Edward was morally depraved and liberally indulged in the seven cardinal vices throughout his life. He suffered from intellectual sloth, and took pride in never reading books. His failure to curb his gluttony impaired his health and led to his premature demise. Of his vices, those that interest us are his jealousy, envy and anger towards Wilhelm. The problems between the two men began in earnest when Edward, languishing as Prince of Wales with nothing to do but wait for his mother to die, had to endure the galling sight of his young nephew ascend the German throne and rule as the Imperial Emperor. In a fleeting reference, Lamar Cecil states:

Edward VII's annoyance at his nephew had been long maturing and he resented the fact that a much younger nephew had become a sovereign long before he succeeded to his own throne.

The Kaiser complained: 'My uncle never seems to realise that I am a sovereign, but treats me as a little boy.' With all the maturity of a juvenile delinquent, Wilhelm reacted by competing with Edward, and in an unpleasant display of vindictiveness, turned on his mother, Vicki, simply because she was Edward's sister. By the time Edward ascended the English throne, the rift between uncle and nephew had become irreparable. Hough comments on Edward's attitude to the Kaiser:

Bertie's private feelings about his nephew were known within the foreign Office. Lansdowne had once written that the King 'talks and writes about [the Kaiser] in terms that make the flesh creep, and the official papers that go to him, whenever they refer to his Imperial Majesty, come back with all sorts of annotations of a most incendiary character.

The Kaiser's appalling relationship with King Edward VII all but broke down over Britain's policy of encircling Germany with alliances. In March 1907, the Kaiser, on learning that Edward had begun negotiating with the Russian Czar, described his uncle Edward thus: 'He's a Satan. You can hardly believe what a Satan he is!' Edward delighted in provoking Wilhelm. The two men had also developed the habit of sniping at each other through the medium of their courtiers. After the diplomatic débâcle at Algeciras, Edward described Wilhelm as 'the most brilliant failure in history.' This remark enraged the Kaiser to such an extent that he publicly derided Edward's morality and mocked his affair with his mistress Mrs Keppel. With some prodding from politicians, the two feuding monarchs met in Germany, and the Kaiser accepted an invitation to visit Britain in November 1907. However, neither had an ounce of goodwill for the other.

In the beginning of 1907, months before the Irish Crown jewel affair began, a homosexual scandal had come to light in Berlin. All of Europe's aristocrats and politicians watched as the German public reeled from revelations that homosexual influence reached to the highest levels of the Kaiser's court. By June 1907, Prince Philip Eulenburg, three Aide de Camps to Kaiser Wilhelm II and Count Kuno von Moltke, Commandant of Berlin, had resigned their positions following accusations that they belonged to a homosexual secret society. The close friendship between Eulenburg and Wilhelm made this scandal different to any other, and the suspicion that the German Emperor either tolerated 'unnatural vice', or even worse, participated in the same, made the story sensational. Kaiser Wilhelm had few friends in Europe, and the prospect or hope that he might lose his crown led the press in Vienna and Paris to cover the crisis in excruciating detail.

While still a Count, Eulenburg met Wilhelm in May 1886, when the latter was the Prince of Hohenzollern. Astonishingly, Wilhelm, a man who spent his life projecting his masculinity, immediately took to the effeminate Philip Eulenburg. One suspects that these two men were perfect alter egos.

The friendship between the two men blossomed instantly, and Wilhelm developed a greater intimacy with Philip than with any other person in his life. At the heart of the friendship lay a genuine empathy. Philip understood Wilhelm and had the rare ability to speak honestly to his powerful friend. For his part, Wilhelm understood Philip, and gave him his complete acceptance. Wilhelm confided in Philip, sought his advice, introduced him to the highest tier of German society, and within a short time described Philip as: 'my bosom friend, the only one I have.'

Eulenburg was a pragmatist. He realised that his growing influence with Wilhelm could create problems with the power brokers of German politics. To fend off trouble, he ingratiated himself with Chancellor Bismarck, and the Chancellor's sinister *eminence grise*, Fritz Holstein. This tac-tic would have served Eulenburg perfectly had Holstein not turned on his master. He engineered the removal of Bismarck from the Chancellor's post by the Kaiser, leaving 'faithful Fritz' a free hand in German foreign policy. Eulenburg crossed Holstein by persuading the Kaiser to make peace with Bismarck. After this 'betrayal' the paranoid Holstein never trusted Eulenburg.

Despite his difficulties with Holstein, Eulenburg exercised so much influence over the Kaiser that during the 1890s he became known as a maker and breaker of men in Imperial Germany. However, he had to restrain his personal ambitions. As with other prominent homosexuals, he knew that the police had included his name on their notorious list. Even worse, he knew how Holstein operated, and had witnessed how the man entrapped and blackmailed German ambassadors. The pragmatist in him realised that if he accepted high office, he would

154

simply fall into Holstein's clutches. Therefore, he rejected the offer of the Secretary of State's post, and he disbarred himself from becoming Chancellor in 1894. Nonetheless, he had power, and used this influence to advance his friend Von Bulow. By 1900 he had arranged for Von Bulow to become the new Chancellor. In the same year, the Kaiser rewarded his friend by elevating him to the rank of Prince. By now exhausted, Prince Eulenburg withdrew from active life at the court, though he maintained his friendship with the Kaiser.

In 1906, both Chancellor Von Bulow and the Kaiser had tired of Holstein's interference. When the chance came, Von Bulow advised the Emperor to accept Holstein's resignation, but in a strange quirk of history, Holstein never discovered which hand had felled him. Making inquiries, he discovered that the same day the Kaiser accepted his resignation he had dined with Eulenburg. For the paranoid Holstein this proved that Prince Eulenburg had orchestrated his downfall. Holstein always retaliated against his enemies — real or imaginary — and he wrote the following to Eulenburg;

My dear Phili — you needn't take this beginning as a compliment since nowadays to call someone 'Phili' means — well, nothing very flattering. You have now attained the object for which you have been intriguing for years — my retirement. And the general attacks on me are all that you can wish . . . I am now free to handle you as one handles such a contemptible person with your peculiarities.

Eulenburg had no delusions concerning Holstein's ability to ruin him. Cornered and desperate, he challenged Holstein to a duel to: 'exchange pistol shots until disablement or death.' When informed of the duel, the German Secretary of State collapsed in his chair and urged Eulenburg to withdraw the challenge for the sake of Germany and the Empire. The Secretary of State shuddered at the prospect of two ageing former high officials of the Empire shooting it out. Exerting all his influence, the Secretary of State forced Holstein to apologise for the insult and Eulenburg to withdraw his challenge. This enforced peace did not delude Eulenburg, for he knew that Holstein would never relent. He commented in his diary: 'I cannot say that I consider Holstein's attacks to be really disposed of. He will revenge himself in his wonted fashion.'

Eulenburg did know his enemy. Holstein made a pact with a former enemy of his, Maximilian Harden, the editor of the weekly publication *Zukunft*. Drawing on his so-called 'poison cupboard', Holstein provided the editor with the ammunition to destroy Eulenburg. Harden published a series of articles in the autumn of 1906 accusing Prince Eulenberg of being the moving spirit in a clique within the Kaiser's court. Eulenburg lived at Liebenberg, and Harden described the camarilla as the Liebenberg Round Table, a clique of effeminate men

156

which pushed through undesirable policies and encouraged the Emperor to act absolutely. He went on to suggest that the camarilla wanted to unseat Chancellor Von Bulow and replace him with a more pliable individual sympathetic to their interests.

Eulenburg reacted by speaking to Von Bulow and assuring him that the article was absolutely false. Displaying the typical fickleness of a politician, Von Bulow chose not to help the man who had made him. He had no desire to alert Holstein that he had engineered his removal from office, so he advised Prince Eulenburg to leave the country for a while.

Harden resumed his attack on Eulenburg in April 1907. He revealed that three Aide de Camps to the Kaiser were homosexuals and he alleged that they were members of Eulenburg's Liebenberg Round Table. He also implicated the commandant of Berlin, Count Kuno von Moltke in the so-called camarilla. In a devastating blow, Harden revealed that Moltke and Eulenburg referred to the Kaiser in their letters as 'Liebehen' (darling).

The Crown Prince of Germany brought the article to the Kaiser's attention. Wilhelm immediately ordered the three Aide de Camps and Count Moltke to resign. When Count Moltke resigned, and became a civilian once more, he challenged Harden to a duel, but the editor adroitly declined. Later, Wilhelm commanded Eulenburg to resign and return the Black Eagle, the highest honour in Imperial Germany, the Kaiser aroused enormous suspicion over the way he treated his closest friend. Without seeking any proof, he had demanded the resignation of his friend of twenty years, which amounted to a condemnation of the Prince. Although nobody in Germany would impugn the Kaiser directly, his actions led to the suspicion that he shared the 'proclivities' of his close friend.

Under pressure from the Kaiser, Moltke and Eulenburg took legal action against Harden, though the Prince acted more carefully than Moltke, who initiated a civil action against the editor. Moltke's action brought the scandal worldwide attention and Berlin was shocked. The German papers gave the scandal extensive coverage and interest in Vienna and Paris became intense. In June 1907, *The Times* published fourteen articles on the Berlin scandal.

Back in England, King Edward gloated over his difficult nephew's problems. When he heard that the Kaiser had forced Count von Moltke to take legal action he declared that 'Not even the Hohenzollerns had behaved as stupidly as this before'. However, considering the 'incendiary' comments he appended to Foreign Office documents, one can safely conclude that he derided his nephew's handling of the Berlin crisis. We know that Wilhelm tried to weasel out of his visit to England in November 1907 for fear of an unwelcome reception from the English public, causing Edward to comment that he dare not 'face the music'.

Given that Edward had mocked the Kaiser's handling of the Berlin crisis, one can see how he would never permit a full-blown homosexual crisis to develop in his own household and give his nephew the last laugh. No matter how much the King disliked his brother-in-law, he would stretch every sinew to protect the family name from any hint of scandal.

Back in Ireland, MacDonnell felt that Aberdeen had done well in his confrontation with His Majesty. The King, washing his hands of the affair, no longer pressed Dublin for a robust police probe, and no longer concerned himself with the recovery of his jewels. Under these circumstances, the Irish administration could keep Lord Haddo's name out of the investigation. Also, by command of His Majesty, Vicars had to go, and Aberdeen, even if he wished otherwise, had to obey. Sir Arthur could not blame the Lord Lieutenant for obeying a royal directive. MacDonnell, thinking the matter was all but closed, decided to continue with his scheduled visit to America. In his absence, he left his assistant, Sir James Dougherty, in charge.

10

THE GOVERNMENT PROCRASTINATES

In October, prior to his visit to America, MacDonnell travelled to England, confident that he had settled the 'little problem' in the Office of Arms. He suffered no qualms over the gross injustice he had inflicted on Sir Arthur with his insidious smears. As he left, the whispering in Dublin's drawing rooms accused Sir Arthur and his friends of ever more depraved and sordid acts. Little by little, the scathing slander ate at Sir Arthur's jealously guarded good name. Defenceless, Vicars looked on in anger as he saw old friends desert him, but his one haven remained the Kildare Street Club. Even with members who knew about Sir Arthur's secret life, the upper brass of the club stayed loyal to Vicars. Thus, unknown to MacDonnell, his plan to have the gossiping tongues of Dublin's 'quality' reduce Sir Arthur to a social pariah had somehow fallen short of the mark.

Before leaving, MacDonnell advised Aberdeen that he faced two possible scenarios. In the first case, the smear campaign would wreak havoc on Sir Arthur's reputation and pressure him to resign voluntarily and this would be the best result. In the second case, His Majesty would order Aberdeen to dismiss Vicars. MacDonnell impressed upon Aberdeen that if this should happen, he had to dismiss Sir Arthur 'peremptorily'. Either way, Sir Arthur should go quietly and Aberdeen could breathe easier.

Sir Arthur did not resign, and King Edward, good to his word, demanded results. His Majesty fully appreciated the need for firm action when dealing with scandal. Scarcely had MacDonnell left Ireland than Knollys wrote to Aberdeen, reminding him that the two weeks were up and he must now carry out the King's wishes and dismiss Sir Arthur and the other heralds.

All good plans rely on their performers playing their roles. Aberdeen knew his part exactly; he knew what he had to do, and he gave every indication he would follow through. However, after MacDonnell left Dublin, Aberdeen's nerve crumbled. He may have lacked the character to carry out the plan, or feared Vicars' powerful friends in the Kildare Street Club, but most probably he suffered nightmares of an enraged Vicars going mad and exposing everybody's secret life, including his own. From herein, the fear of scandal paralysed Aberdeen's every thought and action. Galloway suggests that Aberdeen's fear never abated:

Within eighteen months of his arrival in Dublin, Aberdeen's lieutenancy was overshadowed by an event that was to haunt the remainder of his time in Ireland, and in a sense worry him the rest of his life; the theft of the diamond insignia of the Grand Master of the Order of St. Patrick in the summer of 1907.

Armed with the royal command, the plan called for Aberdeen to cut down Sir Arthur with one swift, clean blow, but he did nothing of the kind. On 12 October, he instructed Dougherty to dismiss Stivey, the office messenger. Poor Stivey, a navy retiree, the most menial member of staff, was the only man the Lord Lieutenant had the nerve to dismiss outright. Later in the month, Aberdeen wrote to the three heralds, Mahony, Shackleton and Goldney, asking for their resignations. Shackleton and Goldney complied, but Peirce Mahony refused.

However, when dealing with Sir Arthur's dismissal, the hapless Aberdeen wavered with fear. He had no choice in the matter, yet took fifteen days before he summoned the courage to obey his Sovereign. Finally, on 23 October, Aberdeen ordered Dougherty to write to Vicars conveying the King's disregard for his services:

I am directed by the Lord Lieutenant to inform you that His Excellency has received from the King, His Majesty's approval for the reconstitution of the Office of Arms, Dublin Castle.

This will involve your being relieved of the office of Ulster which you now hold.

I am therefore to request you to make

immediate arrangements for relinquishing the duties of your office.

I am,

Sir,

Your obedient servant,

J.B. Dougherty

Sir Arthur might have gone quietly. He knew he had no support in the Government, and now, owing to MacDonnell's slanderous smears against his name, he had lost many allies among his Unionist friends. Yet, to his great delight, he still had support among powerful men in the Kildare Street Club. They urged him to stand his ground and to seek a full judicial inquiry into the theft. In this way he could clear his name and hold onto office. The men he had served so well, the Knights of St Patrick, rallied to his side. In particular, Lord Mayo promised to promote a petition to the King for a proper inquiry. More immediately, Sir Arthur waited on the arrival of his brother, The O'Mahony of Kerry, to help him fight off his dismissal.

The O'Mahony, rushing home from Bulgaria, telegraphed Sir Arthur to cling to his post until he returned. If he lost office before then, he had little hope of a remedy. For a homosexual in Edwardian Dublin, Sir Arthur chose what seemed a risky stalling tactic. All along he had spoken vaguely about an inquiry into the theft; now, inspired by Lord Mayo, he demanded a full judicial inquiry. He chose that course, even though he believed his former friend, Shackleton, had committed the theft, and knowing that he had brought the young herald into the Office of Arms without a reference. Worse still, by sharing his home with this young man, he had inadvertently given him access to the safe key. No matter what an inquiry might finally decide, he faced some hard questioning about his judgement and his associates. He also ran the risk that Shackleton's lack of discretion could result in a sexual scandal coming to light that could explode in his face. Despite these obvious risks, Sir Arthur signed an open letter to the Knights of St Patrick in which he asked for a full inquiry. Lord Mayo, Sir Arthur's great ally, spent the next three weeks canvassing his fellow peers to sign a petition to the King.

Sir Arthur tempted fate and gambled with his own reputation, his family's and that of his fellow heralds. He staked everything on Aberdeen's personal vulnerability and that of Lord Haddo. In a judicial inquiry or Royal Commission, Haddo's name would have to come out, and the Irish administration would have to release Kane's report. Thus Vicars stridently called for his judicial inquiry, utterly confident that the Lord Lieutenant would block it with all his power and influence. He held something over Aberdeen, possibly letters from Haddo, that turned Aberdeen into a mouse and himself into a lion.

However, Sir Arthur never discovered that the King had intervened personally to have him dismissed from office. Instead he based all his strategy on the belief that the Irish administration had initiated his dismissal, and that it lay

164

within the Lord Lieutenant's power to retain him in office. His Majesty had made his wishes regarding Vicars' fate clear to at least two of the Knights, Viscount Iveagh and Lord Enniskillen. These two gentlemen informed Lord Mayo how the King felt, but nobody told Sir Arthur. On 23 October, the same day he received his dismissal notice from Dougherty, Vicars wrote directly to the King asking for a judicial inquiry into the theft.

Vicars' demand for a public inquiry alerted the palace that cleaning up the royal household in Dublin might prove awkward. Sir Arthur might resort to legal action, and just the hint of a court case raised the spectre of a royal scandal. Experience had taught the King to distance himself from scandals at once, and to leave the details in the hands of his officials, but in the background he would insist that they must be rid of Sir Arthur and his heraldic court.

Promptly the next day, 24 October, Knollys replied to Sir Arthur, advising him to direct his request for an inquiry through the proper channels. By the same post, Knollys also wrote to Aberdeen, sternly directing him to keep the King's name out of the affair. His Majesty's abrupt turn greatly distressed Aberdeen. Now he had to obey the King's command to clean out the Office of Arms without invoking the royal command. For Aberdeen, losing the trump card of the royal command made an appalling nightmare much worse.

Sir Arthur, upset by Knollys' curt reply, then wrote to Aberdeen asking for a full inquiry into the loss of the jewels. The Lord Lieutenant had no desire to talk to or deal directly with Sir Arthur. He timidly replied that he should write instead to Dougherty. Wasting no time, Vicars wrote to Dougherty the same day. He began by complaining that his Lordship had refused him the chance to explain, in person, his side of the story and he ended by telling Dougherty that he was taking legal advice. Giving Dougherty no chance to reply to this letter, Sir Arthur wrote to him again the following day, 25 October. This time he argued at length that as Ulster King of Arms, he had served with distinction under several Grand Masters and listed three Lords Lieutenants, the Prince of Wales and the Duke of Connaught among the nobles who had praised his work. He then pointed out that the Board of Works bore much of the responsibility for the theft by refusing to provide him with a smaller safe which could have fitted into the strong room. Sir Arthur also stated that MacDonnell had written to him on 15 July, informing him that an inquiry would be held. Finally, he assailed Lord Aberdeen. He accused him of 'condemning a man behind his back', and he concluded by demanding a chance to clear his name 'to which the humblest subject of His Majesty is entitled'.

In MacDonnell's absence, Aberdeen, intimidated by Vicars' defiance, turned to Birrell for help. Naturally, Birrell's sharp political instincts told him to distance himself from the growing mess engulfing the Lord Lieutenant, a man whom he held in little regard. However, he was the Chief Secretary for Ireland and the minister in charge of the Irish administration, so he could hardly hope to walk away unscathed if a major scandal brought down the Lord Lieutenant. Realising that his fate was tied to that of the Lord Lieutenant's, the Chief Secretary prudently joined forces with Aberdeen but unlike Aberdeen, Birrell agreed to meet Vicars in person.

Consequently, Dougherty replied to Vicars' letters on 25 October; 'His Excellency is advised that your office has been legally and properly terminated, and I am therefore to inform you that your request for an inquiry cannot be complied with.' However, he advised Vicars in the same communiqué that the Lord Lieutenant would meet him on 28 October.

Birrell studied the reports on the theft, and talked to Dougherty privately about the more sensitive issues. After this briefing, he realised how great a mess had developed, and how dangerous the whole issue had become. At the start the King had pushed Aberdeen to catch the thief, but when the threat of scandal surfaced His Majesty withdrew behind the palace walls. The King still wanted to dismiss Sir Arthur but he had no notion of soiling his own royal hands. Aberdeen now had to handle things in a way pleasing to the King but without involving him directly.

As a member of the cabinet, Birrell had to humour the King. Although the Liberals held a huge majority in the Commons, they could not pass their bills into law. Each time a bill went to the Lords, it was cut to pieces by the Tory majority. Ultimately they wanted to curtail the Lords, and they anticipated a time when they would ask His Majesty to approve the creation of hundreds of Liberal peers to offset the hereditary Tory majority. This constitutional battle weighed more with the cabinet than a squabble in Ireland, and thus the Liberals wanted to avoid offending the King at any cost. In deference to the King's wishes to avoid scandal, Birrell concluded that his administration dare not raise the issue of Sir Arthur's homosexuality, or 'the graver charge' as it was called. He decided they had to dismiss Sir Arthur solely on the grounds of negligence in his custody of the jewels.

While Birrell came to Aberdeen's aid, Lord Mayo worked at mustering his fellow Knights in support of Vicars. Mayo knew Sir Arthur well; they had a mutual interest in historical matters and served together on the committee of the Kildare Historical Society. Nonetheless, Mayo's decision to champion Sir Arthur's cause was out of character, because as a rule he kept out of politics, and held little influence over his more politically inclined peers. Also, Vicars was only the hired help of the Order of St Patrick, and as such, his fate counted little to each of the Knights. Despite these difficulties, Mayo exuded supreme confidence that he could persuade the Knights to sign Vicars' petition to the King.

In light of Sir Arthur's tenuous hold on office, one would have expected Mayo to rush the petition to all the Knights at the same time, but Mayo took 25 days to contact nineteen men — despite the urgency of Sir Arthur's plight. All the record shows is that over a span of three and a half weeks, Mayo secured the support and the signatures of sixteen out of nineteen available Knights, a remarkable feat for a man who professed to be non-political.

Mayo's success was more remarkable because he worked in opposition to the King, who personally discouraged the Knights from signing the petition. Viscount Iveagh replied to Mayo, 'It is impossible for me to sign the petition as I happen to be told by Lord Knollys that the presentation of this petition would be distasteful to the King'. The Earl of Enniskillen echoed this by replying that, 'The King spoke to me about the case and told me that Sir Arthur was going to be dismissed and seemed to think it was necessary to do so'. However, despite his Sovereign's clear wishes, Enniskillen signed. His Majesty chastised Field-Marshal Lord Roberts so badly that the Field-Marshal telegraphed Mayo to withdraw his name from the petition. The King even persuaded the Earl of Kilmorey, a kinsman of Sir Arthur's, not to sign. Kilmorey informed Mayo that as the King's Aide de Camp he was in a most difficult position and replied, 'Do not imagine from this that I am in any way hostile or wanting in sympathy or support for my unfortunate relative. Far from it. I am doing all I can quietly, and hope through advantageous courses.'

How Mayo overcame the rumours of Sir Arthur's sexual misconduct remains a complete mystery. He persuaded sixteen men from the highest tier of Irish society to put the prestige of their Order behind an alleged homosexual. Any of these men could have asked Assistant Commissioner Harrel or any other high official in Dublin Castle for the truth about the rumours. We surmise that Harrel gave them a rundown on Chief Inspector Kane's theory of the case without mentioning Sir Arthur's homosexuality. The prospect of causing acute embarrassment to the Aberdeens would have appealed to the Knights, because the entire Unionist establishment of Ireland had boycotted the Vice-Regal court on account of Aberdeen's unwavering support for Irish home rule. The petition preserved in the Home office reads:

To The King's Most Excellent Majesty

The Humble Petition of The Knights of the Most Illustrious Order of St Patrick Sheweth.

That it has been brought to the notice of the Companions of your Majesty's Most Illustrious Order of St Patrick that his Excellency the Grand Master has received Your Majesty's approval of the reconstitution of the Offices of Arms, Dublin Castle, which will involve Ulster King of Arms being relieved of the Office which he now holds.

That having regard to the fact that Ulster King of Arms, as Executive Officer of the Order, in addition to his other heraldic duties, has invariably discharged his functions for the last fifteen years in a manner which has called forth the special approbation of the various Grand Masters of the Order under whom he served, and has received the signal

1. Sir Arthur Vicars,
Ulster King of Arms.

2. Kilmorna House, County Kerry.

3. Mrs Mary Farrell, cleaning lady at the Office of Arms.

4. Lord Ronald Gower, the Duke of Argyll's uncle and lifelong friend.

5. The Marquess of Lorne, (later ninth Duke of Argyll) in formal uniform.

6. Francis Bennett-Goldney (Mayor of Canterbury) and Athlone Pursuivant.

7. The insignia of the Order of St Patrick (commonly known as the Irish Crown Jewels).

8. Other valuables stored in the strong room at the Office of Arms.

9. Michael Galvin, a volunteer, who was fatally shot by British forces in the Kilmorna ambush, April 1921.

10. Left to right, Michael Murphy Jnr (Sir Arthur Vicars' valet), Michael Murphy Snr, and Billeen Murphy, who also worked on the Kilmorna estate.

11. The Crypt in Chichester, where Frank Shackleton operated an antique shop under the name of Frank Mellor.

12. Frank Shackleton (right, with umbrella) arriving in Liverpool, January 1913, with Detective Inspector Albert Cooper (in bowler).

13. Chief Inspector John Kane of Scotland Yard.

14. Lord MacDonnell, Under-Secretary for Ireland at the time of the theft.

15. 'The' O'Mahony, half-brother of Sir Arthur
Vicars, at Grange Con.

16. The Royal party bids farewell to Lord Aberdeen at the end of their visit to Dublin in July 1907.

17. The hoax stone found near the ruins of Kilmorna House in 1997.

commendation of Their Royal Highnesses The Prince of Wales, and the Duke of Connaught.

That Your Petitioners feel that an inquiry into all the circumstances connected with the recent disappearance of the Insignia of the Order, at which Vicars may be given an opportunity of being heard before any steps be taken to relieve him from office, would be only fair and just.

Your Petitioners therefore humbly pray that Your Majesty may be graciously pleased to direct such an inquiry to be held.

The signatories were the marquesses of Ormonde and Waterford, the earls of Gosford, Carysfort, Erne, Bandon, Mayo, Listowel, Dunraven, Rosse, Lucan, Longford, Enniskillen and Meath, F.M. Earl Roberts and Lord Monteagle of Brandon.

Meanwhile, Birrell and Aberdeen asked Sir Arthur and his solicitor, Meredith, to come to the Chief Secretary's Lodge on 28 October. At the meeting, Aberdeen sat silent throughout. In a formal, deadpan voice, Birrell read from a typed brief, and told Sir Arthur that he had to be removed from office because he had been lax in his custody of the jewels. Meredith, fearing this might be the last word, asked for a short adjournment. He told Birrell that Sir Arthur's brother, The O'Mahony, was on his way from Bulgaria and argued that the fair course of action was to wait until he arrived. Meredith earned his fee, because Birrell agreed to stay his hand until he met The O'Mahony. In fact Meredith's reasonable manner had impressed Birrell and hatched a bizarre plan.

Birrell knew he should have taken firm action and dismissed Sir Arthur on the spot. He had read the damning report on Sir Arthur's sexual mores, and he had to obey the King, but, always the intellectual, he decided to work more subtly. When his visitors left, Birrell sent for Dougherty. Together they went through the details of the police report on Sir Arthur and agreed that no man could survive a public inquiry with this amount of scandal hanging over his head. Birrell grilled Dougherty on the accuracy of the report and Dougherty stood by the police information. Then Birrell instructed Dougherty to discuss, in strictest confidence, the police report with Meredith!

Since arriving in Dublin twelve years earlier, Sir James Dougherty, Assistant Under-Secretary for Ireland, had achieved great respect in Dublin's legal circles. Drawing on this standing, he sent a letter to Meredith's home. In the letter, Dougherty asked the solicitor to come alone to the Castle for a private meeting on 30 October to discuss Sir Arthur's case. At the meeting, Dougherty bound Meredith to silence and insisted that their conversation should be kept confidential — even from his client. As a solicitor acting for Sir Arthur, he had a professional duty to inform his client of all relevant facts. Yet, he respected Dougherty, and despite the impropriety, Meredith judged that he could best serve his client by listening to Dougherty.

We can only guess at what Dougherty told the solicitor. Almost certainly he showed him the police report on Sir Arthur, but we can only speculate at how much he disclosed on the extent of the homosexual affair. We suspect that Dougherty may have shown Meredith an affidavit from Arthur Phillips, Sir Arthur's former coachman. Shortly after the theft Sir Arthur had dismissed him. Phillips, who had been employed by Sir Arthur for seven years, knew a great deal about his master's private life, and we can be sure he did not hesitate to reveal what he knew to the police.

At the time the theft was discovered, Sir Arthur mentioned Phillips' name to Inspector Lowe as a possible suspect. After questioning Phillips, the police established his innocence at an early stage of their investigation. However, evidence emerged later that the police inter-viewed Phillips again, in September, just after Horse Show Week.

At the end of their meeting, Dougherty suggested to Meredith that his client could not face a public inquiry, and to demonstrate the Irish administration's goodwill, they wanted to offer Vicars a pension for his services. Meredith was so influenced by Dougherty's information that he advised Sir Arthur to accept the pension offered and resign.

11

ENTER THE O'MAHONY — CHAMPION OF CAUSES

Peirce Charles de Lacy O'Mahony, self styled 'The O'Mahony of Kerry', was at this time charging home from Bulgaria to champion his brother's cause. Although The O'Mahony was almost 60, he still made for a 'bonnie fighter' and a formidable foe.

The O'Mahony claimed ancestry to Mahony, Lord of Kinealmeaky, under the law of the great High King of Ireland, Brian Boru. Born in 1850, to a wealthy barrister in Kilmorna, The O'Mahony had inherited the liberal views of his grandfather, who had served Daniel O'Connell as his solicitor. As a young man, The O'Mahony came under the influence of Parnell, who his father entertained at Kilmorna, and these encounters with 'the uncrowned king of Ireland' drew him to politics. In 1886, he won the seat of North Meath, and entered parliament as a member of Parnell's Irish Nationalist Party.

After Gladstone split the Irish Party over Parnell's adultery with 'Kitty' O'Shea, The O'Mahony loyally stood behind his leader. In the fierce feuding that followed, The O'Mahony emerged as a ferocious combatant. When the general election came, the anti-Parnellites persuaded Michael Davitt to contest the North Meath seat. The resulting savage battle between these Titans proved to be a fierce political confrontation. Davitt at first won by a slim margin, but The O'Mahony appealed and had the result overturned. Davitt withdrew and threw his support behind James Gibney who subsequently defeated The O'Mahony by 258 votes in a subsequent election.

The O'Mahony, tired of the Irish infighting, decided to lay claim to a kinsman's fortune in Russia. His ancestor, Count Peter de Lacy, had risen to the rank of a General in the Tsar's army and had amassed a great fortune. Apparently the Count left no heir, leaving his Irish kinsmen free to claim his estate if they had the gumption to make their claim. Timidity never being one of his qualities, The O'Mahony accepted the challenge. He travelled to Russia, and battling his way through the various courts, is said to have inherited the sum of £300,000 in 1905. This inheritance made him one of the wealthiest men in Ireland. On his travels, he passed through Bulgaria, where he witnessed the inspiring Bulgarian fight for independence from the Turks. Warming to the Bulgars who found themselves locked in a difficult struggle, he took up their cause in the true spirit of the 'Wild Geese' of Ireland. After financing an orphanage in Sofia, the Bulgarians, in gratitude, named a street there after 'the Great Irishman'. Now on his way back to Ireland, he intended to champion Sir Arthur's cause with equal zeal.

The O'Mahony arrived in Dublin on 1

November ready for a fight. No sooner had he landed than he went to Sir Arthur's home to hear the latest news. Sir Arthur's account of his curt dismissal drove him into a rage. However, his brother conveniently omitted any mention of a sexual scandal. Unaware of the moral slurs circulating in Dublin, The O'Mahony declared that the authorities had wronged his brother, and family honour demanded that he right this wrong. With his warring spirit fully aroused, The O'Mahony set out to confront the Irish administration.

Instinctively, The O'Mahony turned to his Nationalist friends for assistance, and arranged to meet John Redmond, the leader of the Irish Party. Although Redmond and The O'Mahony had stood together as allies with Parnell, in recent times they had clashed over MacDonnell's scheme for devolution. Despite these political differences, the O'Mahony thought that old loyalties entitled him to ask Redmond, as a personal favour, to help Sir Arthur.

Unknown to The O'Mahony, Redmond had already reviewed the situation. He knew Sir Arthur's politics and considered him no friend of Irish Nationalism. In particular, he discovered that Vicars had enthusiastically embraced the Kildare Street Club and the powerful landlords who had turned the club into the headquarters of Irish Unionism. Vicars' love of the Kildare Street Club had clinched the matter for Redmond. In reality, he shared power in the party with John Dillon, the deputy leader. If one were to search the whole of Ireland for the man who most loathed, hated and despised the Kildare Street Club and all that it stood for, John Dillon would surely be that man. With the best will in the world, Redmond would never dare ask Dillon to stand up in the Commons and speak for a staunch member of the Club.

Ironically, The O'Mahony had long resented his brother's association with the Kildare Street Club, but he thought that because this involved his family, Redmond might help as a personal favour. When they met, he found Redmond unusually evasive. The O'Mahony suggested a series of parliamentary ploys that would fluster the British Government, but Redmond refused the bait. From the nature of The O'Mahony's suggestions, Redmond realised that his old friend had no idea about the 'graver charge' clouding the whole affair. As their meeting ended, Redmond gave The O'Mahony a brief account of the unwholesome accusations levelled at his brother, mentioning in the process the police reports and the vicious slurs swirling about Dublin. Finally, abandoning all attempts at evasion, he bluntly told The O'Mahony that he could not risk the position of the Irish Party by defending a homosexual, even worse, one who belonged to the Kildare Street Club. Perhaps old loyalties stirred in Redmond's heart, because, before they parted, he told The O'Mahony to contact Birrell regarding the 'graver charge' against his brother.

The O'Mahony left the meeting shocked. Redmond's attitude had jolted him, and he knew his old comrade far too well to fall for his excuses. The Irish Party felt disenchanted with the Liberals, yet when presented with this chance to make mischief on the floor of the Commons, Redmond seemed strangely shy about pressing his advantage. The O'Mahony construed that Birrell had struck a deal with Redmond to secure his silence. This unexpected turn of events alerted The O'Mahony that the Irish administration intended to use all its political power to oust Sir Arthur from office. Always a man to confront his adversary in person, he arranged to meet the Chief Secretary the next day.

'Shocked' probably wildly understates how The O'Mahony reacted to the 'graver charge'. As one would anticipate in light of such serious charges, the historical record is silent about the subsequent 'showdown' between the two brothers. After analysing The O'Mahony's statements and letters, we have concluded that Sir Arthur confessed to him all about his secret life. How The O'Mahony reacted, when informed that his son and heir, Peirce, practised the same lifestyle as Sir Arthur, we do not know but he must have endured deep disgust on hearing how the 'incontinent tongues' of Dublin's 'quality' had feasted on the squalid rumours and sordid sagas supposedly describing his brother's behaviour. Sir Arthur denied all allegations of perversion and impressed upon his brother that he had led a most discreet life.

However, Sir Arthur had other secrets to lay before The O'Mahony, and these revelations gave the 'bonnie fighter' new heart. He revealed to him the lifestyles of Haddo, Shackleton, Gower, and the Duke of Argyll. He convinced him that Shackleton had stolen the jewels and that Aberdeen and the Irish administration had as much to hide as he had. The O'Mahony returned to the battle utterly convinced that Lord Aberdeen would never permit the 'graver charge' to surface. The O'Mahony's subsequent actions only make sense if he fully believed that the entire administration would act to quash any mention of a homosexual scandal in Sir Arthur's heraldic court. He believed that he and Sir Arthur had a great chance of fending off his dismissal if they could prevent Aberdeen and Birrell from holding a private inquiry. He would play out a mammoth bluff, fraught with peril, by calling for a public inquiry — all the more so because he was unaware that His Majesty had already decided Vicars' fate.

When The O'Mahony met Birrell on the morning of 2 November he was game for a fight, but so was the Chief Secretary. The O'Mahony took the offensive. With typical gusto and force, he presented the case for retaining his brother in office. However, Birrell remained unimpressed. This forced The O'Mahony to challenge the Chief Secretary to explain his reasons for dismissing Vicars. Birrell replied that Sir Arthur had been lax in his care of the jewels. He went on to accuse Vicars of befriending Shackleton, a man whom he described as having a low character. Worse still, Vicars had introduced this man into the Office of Arms solely on the strength of his own commendation. Now that Sir

Arthur himself suspected Shackleton of taking part in the theft, he must also take the blame for giving this 'abandoned ruffian' the means to steal the jewels. Birrell also mentioned Shackleton's notorious friend, Captain Gorges, and in the same breath described him as 'even more abandoned'.

The O'Mahony countered these charges by noting that Shackleton had close ties with the Duke of Argyll, Lord Gower and the Bishop of Peterborough, and these exalted men thought the Dublin Herald was a man of good character. Therefore, he argued, the administration should not hold Vicars to a higher standard than those men. Birrell continued stating that those good men had not had the Crown Jewels stolen from their safe with their own key. Then Birrell compared Vicars to 'a butler in charge of the keys to his wine cellar', and said that it was Sir Arthur's gross negligence to allow these keys to slip into the hands of the thief. This point inflamed The O'Mahony, who seized on the chance to make the legal argument that 'one pays a butler to care for the wine cellar, but Sir Arthur never received 'a salary for the custody of the tainted baubles of the mistress of an English King, presented to the most Noble Order Of St Patrick, because the virtuous queen of his successor refused to wear them.'

Finally, The O'Mahony pressed Birrell for a full and open inquiry. Birrell, borrowing from MacDonnell's tactics, issued a threat, though in an urbane and polished style. He told The O'Mahony that if he insisted on having an inquiry then he should have one. However, he also noted that an open inquiry might delve into questions of character, and pointed out that even blameless men might become tainted with the wide brush of scandal.

After his bruising battle with Birrell, The O'Mahony arranged to see Aberdeen later that afternoon. He found to his surprise that the Lord Lieutenant had also asked Birrell to attend. The O'Mahony considered Birrell's presence a sure sign of Aberdeen's weakness. During the meeting, The O'Mahony covered much the same ground as he had done that morning with Birrell, and went on to argue that the 'real charge' laid against his brother to the King was that of befriending an undesirable man. He wanted to test how far the administration would press the 'graver charge'. Birrell answered that they had laid two charges against his brother before the King. They had impugned Sir Arthur for consorting with a man of undesirable character and they had charged him of being negligent in his custody of the Crown Jewels.

Birrell shied clear of even hinting of a 'graver charge' against Sir Arthur. This reluctance boosted The O'Mahony's confidence, and confirmed his theory that the Irish administration were loath to open the Pandora's box of scandal. He felt Sir Arthur had been right in his assessment of Aberdeen. The Lord Lieutenant had no stomach to face an open inquiry, because he too had much to lose if certain private matters came to the surface. The O'Mahony seized the moment and pressed hard for just that

— a full public inquiry. Bewildered and aghast, Aberdeen advised The O'Mahony to consider the terrible nature of the scandal that would result from airing the case in public. With the Lord Lieutenant visibly shaken, The O'Mahony left the meeting feeling he had exposed Aberdeen's Achilles heel. He would concentrate all his efforts on exploiting this weakness and he determined to deal only with the Lord Lieutenant.

Finishing a whirlwind of talks, The O'Mahony called on Meredith, whom he had retained to act as Sir Arthur's solicitor. Meredith recounted his meeting with Birrell and Aberdeen, and how he strongly advised Sir Arthur to accept the offer of a pension and resign. After demanding Meredith explain himself, The O'Mahony sat in disbelief as Meredith described his meeting with Dougherty. At first he flew into a rage when the solicitor, refusing to give details, only hinted at having found out something of great importance. He hurled abuse at the solicitor, saying that in all his life he had never heard of such unethical conduct. Meredith agreed that his meeting with Dougherty had no parallel in Irish legal history, at least he had never heard of a client's solicitor being bound over to confidentiality by the authorities. Despite The O'Mahony's fury, Meredith held his ground, and as the confrontation progressed, The O'Mahony discerned that he must unearth the solicitor's secret. Although Meredith insisted on keeping his oath of secrecy, he still had a duty to give advice, and considered that he served his client's best interests if he did just that. Thus began an irritating game of 'guess'. The O'Mahony posed the questions while Meredith gave advice on each one. The effort proved worthwhile. Slowly, The O'Mahony came to grasp that the administration had a damning affidavit from a man who knew much about Sir Arthur's private life. Although Meredith would not name the man, he hinted that Sir Arthur could identify him with ease.

Returning to Clonskeagh, The O'Mahony briefed his brother on his meeting with Birrell and Aberdeen, and then described his meeting with Meredith. Sir Arthur became indignant that his own solicitor had had a secret meeting without his consent, but The O'Mahony silenced him. He told him that Meredith had found out that a man close to Sir Arthur had given the police an affidavit concerning the nightly 'goings-on' in Sir Arthur's home. As they went through a list of possible names, Sir Arthur realised that the police witness had to be Phillips, his former coachman. He explained to The O'Mahony that at the time of the theft, he had given Phillips notice, as he initially suspected him of taking his keys. He told the police about his suspicions, but after they interrogated Phillips, the police became satisfied that he had no part in the crime.

The O'Mahony now grasped the full gravity of Meredith's information, and why the solicitor had advised Sir Arthur to resign and take a pension. Unlike Sir Arthur, he realised how much the servants knew of the goings on in any household. Knowing that Vicars had much to hide, The O'Mahony tracked down Phillips. Just as he feared, the coachman knew far too much about his brother's secret life, and admitted that he had spoken freely to the police. Phillips would make a devastating witness in an inquiry, and though much damage had already been done by his affidavit, The O'Mahony knew he had to persuade Phillips to leave the country. He offered Phillips and his family a free passage to America and perhaps a sum of money to start him off in the new country. Delighted with this offer, Phillips, his wife and four children left Ireland within the week. To explain the situation, The O'Mahony concocted the story that Sir Arthur had paid the passage for Phillips out of remorse for having accused him of the crime. However, at the time, Sir Arthur suffered severe financial straits and could not afford to pay his own bills let alone Phillips' passage to America.

Meanwhile, Birrell and Aberdeen, reeling from the first onslaught of The O'Mahony, took him seriously when he threatened to raise a commotion in the press. They decided that their best interests lay in hushing up the case, even if that meant leaving Vicars in office. Unfortunately His Majesty had made clear his wish to have Sir Arthur dismissed. Their one hope of persuading the King to leave Sir Arthur in office lay in proving that Shackleton stole the jewels. Birrell asked the Home Secretary, Herbert Gladstone, to instigate a detailed probe into Shackleton. Gladstone agreed, and the Home Office launched a new inquiry. This investigation proved much more thorough and intense than the previous half-hearted work. They found and checked the herald's telegrams, and delved deep into his financial and personal affairs.

On 6 November, officials in the Home Office brought Chief Inspector Kane back on the case. They had found twelve telegrams from Shackleton, and they asked Kane to review their contents. Kane examined the telegrams, but 'could find nothing bearing in any way on the robbery'. This concluded the probe by the Home Office into Shackleton's part in the theft.

As Birrell's hopes for a solution from the Home Office inquiry faded, he thought it was in everyone's best interest to offer Sir Arthur another deal. He felt great concern that The O'Mahony would go to the press and incite public feelings to such an extent that the Government would be forced to order a public inquiry. Common sense told him that this could bring ruin on all the parties involved. Birrell, aware of Sir Arthur's financial plight, issued him with an ultimatum regarding the pension.

Birrell's dart found its mark. Having terminated his co-tenancy agreement with Shackleton, Sir Arthur now found that he could not afford the house in Clonskeagh on his own. The debts he had previously incurred compounded his financial circumstances, forcing him to ask his family for assistance. Facing a bleak and penniless future, Sir Arthur felt tempted by the pension and discussed the offer with The O'Mahony and Meredith. The O'Mahony thought the pressure on the pension issue only indicated the administration's weakness, adding

185

that it did nothing to salvage Sir Arthur's reputation, and he would have to leave Dublin under a cloud of suspicion. Meredith strongly disagreed with The O'Mahony, arguing that under the circumstances Sir Arthur had secured a far better deal than he had anticipated, and he urged his client to accept the pension and resign.

Sir Arthur felt he had no choice but to agree with Meredith, because at his age he had no desire to face the future without an income. Though he had no wish to give up his post, armed with a pension he could set up his genealogical practice in London where he had contacts. If he lost both his job and pension, he faced financial ruin. Realising that the Government's pressure had badly weakened his brother's resolve, The O'Mahony made Sir Arthur a counter offer he could not refuse. He promised to pay Sir Arthur the equivalent amount, if he spurned the pension and continued the fight. Financially secure, Sir Arthur now sprang back into the struggle with renewed hope that he might stave off his dismissal and remain Ulster King of Arms.

Sir Arthur haughtily rejected the pension, and in the process utterly dismayed Aberdeen. The Lord Lieutenant had no choice but to obey the King's wishes and thus no matter what else happened, Vicars would lose his post, whilst Vicars continued to insist on having a public inquiry. The thought of an open forum digging out the family skeletons made Aberdeen shudder, yet The O'Mahony and Sir Arthur appeared to care little about possible disclosures that might tarnish their own family's reputation.

Aberdeen could not understand Sir Arthur's stance, and tried to reason with him, but he only exposed his own vulnerability. Sir Arthur, coached by his brother, construed each overture from Aberdeen as a further sign of weakness. Thus, even when Aberdeen improved his pension offer with a stipulation of Sir Arthur's innocence in the theft, Vicars still refused. Aberdeen had no experience in waging a public fight with a man of The O'Mahony's feisty spirit. In the end, Aberdeen subverted his own cause so badly that Sir Arthur's camp lost all fear of a scandal. They believed that the Lord Lieutenant, fearing public humiliation, would never agree to a public inquiry. This knowledge of Aberdeen's fear drove The O'Mahony to continue with his demands. He campaigned in the press for justice and a full public inquiry with all his vigour and theatre.

At the end of November, Aberdeen tried one last time to reason with Sir Arthur in person. Vicars attended the meeting with Meredith at his side, but this time the solicitor took a back seat. Sir Arthur threw caution to the winds, and from the start he railed at Aberdeen. He charged him with grave injustices, and accused him and his administration of shielding the real culprit to protect the Duke of Argyll. Again and again Sir Arthur demanded an inquiry as his right; again Aberdeen ducked the issue by saying he had to consult with Birrell first. These weak excuses drove Sir Arthur into a frenzy, and he pounded the desk, venting his pent-up rage. The scene slid into a full-blown farce when Sir Arthur, rising from his chair, started shouting and screaming, and chased the Viceroy round the office.

After lambasting the Lord Lieutenant, Sir Arthur, spirits soaring, consulted The O'Mahony on their next move. They taxed their minds over whether or not they should give some ground. Sir Arthur felt he should keep his post as Ulster King of Arms, and leave the Irish administration to solve its own problems. Thrown into the rare role of conciliator, The O'Mahony felt they had to leave the Lord Lieutenant some room to save face, so he cast about for a compromise. The O'Mahony's 'concession' was as follows: Sir Arthur would stay on in a modified post in the Office of Arms. He would resign as Knight Registrar to the Order of St Patrick, but would remain as the chief genealogist. Such was the feeling of triumph in Clonskeagh that The O'Mahony chose to let the Lord Lieutenant suffer a few more days before he presented his proposal. However, unknown to the jubilant men in Clonskeagh, MacDonnell had returned from America and was now on his way to Dublin.

12

MacDonnell Takes Charge

Returning to Dublin in early December, MacDonnell threatened to resign after he saw the sheer scale of the stupidity that had taken place in his absence. Wide eyed with disbelief, he could not accept that Sir Arthur, who served at the King's pleasure, and whom the King had commanded to be dismissed, still remained in office. To add to the folly, Birrell, bowing to pressure from The O'Mahony, had decided to hold some sort of formal inquiry. Then came the final straw when the Lord Lieutenant asked MacDonnell for his advice about The O'Mahony's proposal for a modified post for Sir Arthur. That Aberdeen should even consider the proposal frustrated MacDonnell, because they both knew that it was out of the question. The Lord Lieutenant had a clear command from the King to dismiss Vicars and 'to reconstitute' the Office of Arms. Instead of obeying his Sovereign, Aberdeen had caved in to the threats and taunts of The O'Mahony, and allowed the man to run him round in circles.

We have no information on who persuaded MacDonnell to remain in office. Birrell would have been more than happy to see the end of his difficult Under-Secretary. Aberdeen, having

189

created the mess, was in no position to persuade MacDonnell to do anything. Only two other candidates come to mind, the King or Lady Aberdeen. The King could easily have persuaded MacDonnell, but subsequent developments lead us to conclude that His Majesty became involved with MacDonnell later. This leaves only Ishbel, Lady Aberdeen. Ishbel's modus operandi in the male-dominated world of her time was elegantly simple: whenever necessary, she recruited strong-willed men to do her bidding, as she had done in setting up the Victorian Order of Nurses in Canada. Whatever happened, MacDonnell did not resign: instead he set out to put an end to Aberdeen's dithering.

Discussing the situation with Aberdeen, MacDonnell insisted that the Lord Lieutenant take a stand, the King's Viceroy. He urged Aberdeen to reply personally to The O'Mahony, and state firmly, without hedging or dodging, his Government's position. Thus with a renewed sense of confidence, Lord Aberdeen wrote to The O'Mahony on 7 December:

Dear Mr O'Mahony,
    With deep regret I have to inform you that I find it impossible to arrange for Sir Arthur Vicars to occupy a modified position (as suggested) in the Office of Arms.
    Under these circumstances I must ask you to inform him that the position of the matter is still that which was stated in Sir James Dougherty's last letter to him, viz. That it has been decided to reconstitute the Office of

Arms; & that this involves the resignation of Ulster & all the Heralds.

The decision has reference solely to the fact that the insignia of the Order of St Patrick have disappeared.

I am very sorry that I must add that the resignation must take effect not later than Monday evening the 9th, Inst., otherwise I fear it would be necessary on Tuesday to announce that the Office of Ulster is vacant.

I remain,
Very truly yours,
Aberdeen

Aberdeen's firmness and new-found sense of purpose caught The O'Mahony off guard. The following day, he replied to Aberdeen with a long letter, which started as follows: 'As I informed Your Excellency early last week, I had an engagement to speak at a meeting in Salisbury tomorrow, December 9th, I was therefore surprised when I found Your Excellency's letter awaiting me ... ' Clearly The O'Mahony thought he could control the agenda to the extent that he could dictate when the Lord Lieutenant might reply to him. Thus he found the 'peremptory tone' in Aberdeen's letter irritating.

In his letter, The O'Mahony, seeking to put the Lord Lieutenant back in his place, emphasised the issues of scandal, and the need for the fullest public inquiry. He knew that somebody had stiffened the back of the Lord Lieutenant, but he still calculated that Aberdeen feared, above all else, the shame of a public scandal:

. . . On the 5th November I wrote to your Excellency pointing out how grossly unfair it was to keep my brother in absolute ignorance of the charges against him and I asked Your Excellency that the substance at least of the charges against my brother in the report laid before His Majesty should be given to me.

To this letter Your Excellency did not reply.

To this day neither I nor my brother know of what he is really accused!

I have however reason to believe that in the report laid before Your Excellency by the Police grave but unfounded charges have been made against my brother and matters within their knowledge which would exculpate him have been deliberately kept back.

I also am aware that owing to the incontinence of Official tongues of which I have previously warned Your Excellency, scandalous matters are being gossiped about in Dublin to my brother's detriment.

Your Excellency is apparently now anxious to confine the charge against my brother to the charge of negligence, but I feel bound to inform Your Excellency that my brother and his friends will not allow the graver charge to be withdrawn now that it has done its deadly work unless Your Excellency is prepared to put on record the fact that you have enquired into my brother's moral character and that you are fully satisfied that it is without stain, and will so inform His Majesty.

Your Excellency and Mr Birrell at the interview with my brother and Mr Meredith offered to put in writing that there was no question of my brother's integrity regarding the Jewels. If Your Excellency will now add to that the above declaration regarding his moral character, I shall be happy to lay the matter before my brother and his friends with a view to considering how far such a letter would vindicate my brother's character.

My brother has nothing to fear from the fullest public inquiry, which he has always desired. If Your Excellency objects to a public inquiry it is for your Excellency to find a means of satisfying my brother's most reasonable demands.

Aberdeen, unable to cope with this reply, asked MacDonnell to take charge and deal directly with The O'Mahony. On reading the letter, MacDonnell chuckled in admiration at The O'Mahony's gall. He knew that Sir Arthur, and the O'Mahony clan, could no more survive a public hearing than Oscar Wilde could have, yet they continued to insist on their right to a judicial inquiry. He realised that The O'Mahony was gambling that the Irish administration would never agree to hold one.

MacDonnell decided to signal his adversary that the administration's days of waffling had come to an end, and he replied sternly to The O'Mahony on 9 December:

Sir,

I am directed to acknowledge the receipt of your letter dated 8th. instant, addressed to His Excellency the Lord Lieutenant.

The reconstitution of the Office of Arms, which involves the retirement of Sir Arthur Vicars, was decided upon by the Irish Government solely in consequence of the loss of the regalia of the Order of St Patrick, of which Sir Arthur Vicars was the responsible custodian. To that decision, which was communicated to Sir Arthur Vicars in Sir James Dougherty's letter of 23rd October last, the Lord Lieutenant must adhere.

Upon the intention you express of publishing your letter under reply, I am to offer no comment: but I am directed to point out to you that the statement you make in it as to what passed at your private interview with Mr Birrell at the Chief Secretary's Lodge is quite inaccurate.

The whole responsibility for the decision rests with the Irish Government, and with the Irish Government alone: and, therefore the introduction of the King's name into your letter is out of place and improper.

I am,
Sir,
Your obedient servant,
A.P. MacDonnell

The O'Mahony now realised that he had run into a stone wall; MacDonnell was fearless. This man had taken on the entire Unionist establishment single handedly, and had written an open letter to *The Times* with veiled threats against Balfour, the former Prime Minister. He had also taken on his Nationalist friends with equal ferocity. The O'Mahony knew that he could not bend this man to his will as he had done with Aberdeen and Birrell. In a desperate ploy, he wrote to Aberdeen the same day stating that he would only deal directly with him:

My Lord,
An official reply to the letter I addressed yesterday to your Excellency has been sent to me from the Chief Secretary's Department.
At my first interview with Mr Birrell he informed me that the matter was one for your Excellency to deal with and since then all my correspondence has been with your Excellency. I therefore send my answer to you . . .

Less than flattered and shuddering at the thought of confronting The O'Mahony again, Aberdeen quickly handed over the letter to MacDonnell. Seeing no reason to humour the O'Mahony further, MacDonnell curtly replied:

Sir,
I am directed to acknowledge the receipt of your letter, dated 9th. instant addressed to His excellency the Lord Lieutenant.
I am,
Sir,
Your obedient servant
A. P. MacDonnell

The O'Mahony's strategy in handling the Irish administration had unravelled. MacDonnell, with his brutally terse reply, had simply slammed the door in his face, indicating that the Government would no longer discuss the matter. Having lost access to the Lord Lieutenant, he had to forgo both the hope of a modified post for his brother and the offer of a good pension. Pride prevented him from going to MacDonnell to retrieve the pension offer, so he elected to continue fighting.

As The O'Mahony brooded over MacDonnell's hard line, he also looked back with regret on how he had failed to win over the Nationalists of Sinn Féin. In November, he had invited Arthur Griffith, Bulmer Hobson and J.W. O'Beirne to his estate at Grange Con in County Wicklow. Over a lavish meal, The O'Mahony tried to persuade his guests that Shackleton had stolen the jewels. The O'Mahony presented them with his theory that Shackleton had removed Sir Arthur's spare key to the safe and made a copy. Then, while he established a firm alibi in England with high-society friends, his despicable accomplice, Captain Richard Gorges, stole the jewels from the safe. Shackleton and Gorges found the inspiration for their scheme from the juvenile prank played by Lord Haddo at Christmas. Gorges, an odious and mean-spirited creature, had removed the blue ribbon from the diamond star as a cruel taunt to Sir Arthur. Furthermore, Gorges compounded Sir Arthur's sorrow and suffering by stealing his late mother's jewels. Hoping that his guests would seize the chance to attack the symbols of British rule, he coloured his story with sordid details of Captain Gorges' lifestyle, reminding them that this unwholesome man still 'graced the British army'. In hindsight, The O'Mahony wished he had held his fire on the vile Gorges. With all his smears on the man, he had only raised suspicions among his guests that the entire Office of Arms, including both his brother and son, led immoral lifestyles. After the dinner, the Sinn Féin men politely thanked their host but declined to take up Sir Arthur's cause.

Now The O'Mahony had only two cards to play. He could continue creating an uproar in the press, and simultaneously he could expedite the Knights' petition to the King. By mid-November, Lord Mayo had persuaded fifteen of the nineteen available Knights to sign Sir Arthur's petition. However, Mayo faced one last hurdle — how was he to present the petition to the King? Protocol demanded that either a minister of the Crown or the Grand Master of the Order should present the petition. This posed obvious problems on both counts. Birrell, anxious not to upset His Majesty, refused even to read the document, let alone present it to the King. As for Aberdeen, the Grand Master of the Order, the Knights had violated protocol by not consulting him first on the petition, and therefore he need not co-operate with Mayo. Lord Mayo related these difficulties to The O'Mahony and suggested an unusual remedy. He thought they could bypass the Irish authorities altogether by sending the petition directly to the Home Secretary, Herbert Gladstone, where he felt it would get a sympathetic hearing. At the time, The O'Mahony still had Aberdeen under his thumb, so he elected to torment him further by sending him the petition on 26 November with a request that he forward the document to the King. After MacDonnell slammed the door in his face, The O'Mahony wrote to Aberdeen demanding to know if he had forwarded the petition to the King.

Simultaneously, The O'Mahony also followed up on Mayo's original suggestion. At best, the move was a long shot. The case fell within the domain of the Irish Office, and Gladstone would have to respect Birrell's jurisdiction. Also, Gladstone's officials would warn him that it was an 'ugly business' and advise him to stay out of a no-win Irish feud. However, The O'Mahony, feeling that he had nothing to lose, sent the petition to Gladstone on 11 December with an accompanying letter. In this first letter he argued that Sir Arthur belonged to the royal household and that they should grant him an inquiry as is the right of the 'meanest criminal in British law'. He also protested that the Lord Lieutenant had not seen fit to forward the petition to the King, and with his usual nerve threatened to publish in the press that Sir Arthur was being made a scapegoat to protect others who were close to His Majesty.

Around the same time, Birrell informed Aberdeen that some sort of inquiry must be held. Horrified, but without options, Aberdeen had written to the King asking him to sanction this course of action. His Majesty, even though he was reluctant to give into his renegade Knights for having signed a petition against his express wishes, grudgingly consented to the inquiry, saying he did so for the good of the Order. Aberdeen, MacDonnell and Birrell got together to plan their strategy so as to avoid any scandal arising. MacDonnell, a seasoned bureaucrat, quickly pointed out that all such inquiries have strict terms of reference. He suggested that they could avoid the scandal issue completely by limiting the powers of the Commissioners to enquire solely into the negligence of Sir Arthur. However, Aberdeen harboured grave doubts. He felt that The O'Mahony was determined to raise the 'graver charge' in a public forum, and with the press in attendance, who knew what unpleasant exposés would come out. MacDonnell calmed Aberdeen, assuring him that The O'Mahony was just bluffing and that Sir Arthur would not dare raise the 'graver charge' in public as its disclosure would also incriminate both himself and The O'Mahony's son.

Aberdeen then discussed the Knights' petition with MacDonnell, as The O'Mahony had inquired if it had been forwarded to the King. After reading the petition MacDonnell advised Aberdeen to refuse to forward it, because doing so might convince His Majesty to sanction a Royal Commission of Inquiry. They could not restrict the terms of reference of a Royal Commission in the same manner that they could a local inquiry. Counsel for Sir Arthur would have a freer hand in raising issues that the Irish administration would prefer to suppress. If Aberdeen, as the Grand Master of the Order, refused to forward the petition, then the King had a perfect excuse for doing nothing. This course of action also complied with the King's wishes that he be kept out of the whole affair. Aberdeen agreed with MacDonnell's suggestion, and on 14 December, Dougherty returned the petition to The O'Mahony advising that the Lord Lieutenant could not agree to forward it to His Majesty.

Meanwhile, The O'Mahony's attempts to circumvent the Irish authorities proved singularly successful. The Home Secretary, Herbert Gladstone, and his advisors saw the petition as the needed pretext to intervene in Birrell's jurisdiction. They argued that The O'Mahony's threat to publish in the press posed a graver risk to the Government than the inquiry. Fifteen Irish nobles had signed Sir Arthur's petition, and it was sheer folly to snub their wishes. Also, the King had mentioned to Gladstone his desire to have this mess cleared up and had made hostile comments over Aberdeen's handling of the 'Vicars business'. His Majesty, taking the high ground, told Gladstone that any inquiry must be held in public. The Home Office advisers took the King's posturing at face value and advised Gladstone that the King truly wanted to 'clear the air'.

Though Herbert Gladstone was the son of a great Prime Minister, he lacked the political shrewdness of his father. Holding his own abilities in the highest esteem, he felt that he was the right man to sort out the Dublin mess, and he jumped into the affair unreservedly. He invited Birrell to the Home Office to discuss the case. Birrell, bowing to his senior cabinet colleague, reviewed the 'Vicars' business' at length with Gladstone and they both agreed:

1) they must set up an inquiry; 2) this inquiry would be a small Royal Commission; 3) the proceedings of the Commission must be completely transparent and open to the press.

After meeting with Birrell, Gladstone then informed the King about their decision to hold a Royal Commission. His Majesty, faced with the 'public airing' of the case that he himself had demanded, had no choice but to give his sanction. Gladstone, pleased with his progress, informed Aberdeen. Of course, this news left Aberdeen aghast, and in despair he again turned to MacDonnell for help against this new threat. MacDonnell reacted quickly. He advised Aberdeen to alert the King to the danger of holding a Royal Commission. Such a course would inevitably involve taking evidence over a wide range of issues, and they must expect scrutiny of the 'graver charge'. MacDonnell could not have calculated his move with greater effect, for this was the one issue that His Majesty had determined to suppress.

Meanwhile, the Home Office went ahead and drew up the terms of reference for a Royal Commission. Feeling confident, Gladstone went in person to the palace and asked the King to sign the warrant. His confidence proved short lived, as the King had changed his mind, and now rigidly refused to put his name to a Royal Commission. Gladstone persisted, but His Majesty would not budge. The Home Secretary became deeply puzzled as His Majesty vented venomous vitriol on his Irish Knights for signing the petition. Gladstone endured a royal tirade on the nobles who worked behind their King's back, and against his wishes. Naïvely, Gladstone thought that the King misread the situation, so he tried valiantly to persuade him to change his mind. His efforts proved futile and the King obdurately refused to sanction a Royal Commission.

Gladstone went back to the Home Office bewildered by his Sovereign's change of heart. After conferring with his officials on his dismal failure at the palace they suggested that he ask The O'Mahony to provide more details. The O'Mahony was more than pleased to have the ear of the Home Secretary, and he wrote back with a detailed summary of his dealings with the Irish administration, including these points in support of Sir Arthur:

Gladstone should ascertain Lord Aberdeen's private opinion about the case as distinct from that of the Irish Government as officially expressed . . .

That Ulster now holds 'during good behaviour' and that it is without precedent to remove anyone so holding without a public and judicial inquiry . . .

That the report which led to the proposal to

reconstitute the Office of Arms was the product of a secret inquiry, held behind Ulster's back and that he was given no proper opportunity of defending himself at that inquiry, nor since . . .

That he has never been informed of the nature of the charges brought against him . . .

That from the position of the safe it is quite clear that the robbery could not have taken place during office hours . . .

That it was not part of Ulster's original duty to have the custody of the jewels . . .

That under the new Statutes in 1905 they were consigned to Ulster, who never received any pay for this onerous duty, and therefore ought to be regarded as a voluntary trustee.

That a trustee is never regarded by law to take better care of his trust property than an ordinary man takes of his own property.

That if the authorities required Ulster to take expert care of the jewels, such as is required from a bank manager, they should have laid down regulations to that effect.

Apparently The O'Mahony's arguments so impressed Gladstone and his advisors that they felt compelled to hold some sort of inquiry. To compromise with the King, Gladstone reduced his request from a Royal Commission to a public Vice-Regal Commission, to which his Majesty consented.

By 20 December 1907, the official position regarding the Commission of Inquiry had been settled. The King, together with three senior cabinet ministers, Augustine Birrell, Herbert Gladstone and John Morley had agreed to hold a public Vice-Regal Inquiry in Dublin. Campbell-Bannerman, the Prime Minister, having suffered two heart attacks, played no part in this decision. Who intervened over the next ten days is not recorded, but we can infer that somebody with authority changed the plan.

We know MacDonnell set stringent terms of reference for the Commission of Inquiry. However, contrary to the Home Office request, the Irish administration decided to conduct the inquiry in private. As a civil servant, MacDonnell did not have the authority to oppose his political masters, nor for that matter the King of England. Aberdeen may have wanted to hold the inquiry in private, but he had no power to authorise MacDonnell to do so.

Two other pieces of evidence support the inference that a man of great authority intervened. First, MacDonnell maintained a home in London, and his only child, a daughter, lived in England. We know that he went to London just days before Christmas either to be with his daughter for the holidays or on business. On his return from America, he had visited the Irish Office in London just twenty days earlier. Thus, one can assume that he would have dealt with any pressing business in London then, before he crossed over to Dublin. What makes MacDonnell's pre-Christmas trip to London of such great interest is that he returned to Dublin on Christmas eve. Presumably he desired to spend Christmas with his wife and daughter. If his family were in Dublin, only a matter of great importance would have prompted him to abandon them for five days in Dublin, a city where they had no relatives. On the other hand, if the women were in London as we suspect, then only something extremely urgent would compel him to travel back to Dublin to arrive on Christmas eve. Either way his trip to London must have been of great importance and we believe that during this trip he received orders to ensure that the Commission of Inquiry went satisfactorily.

MacDonnell wrote the following extraordinary letter to Gladstone on 4 January:

Confidential
4 Jan 1908

Dear Mr Gladstone

I enclose the copy of the letters of the Knights of St Patrick to Lord Mayo as desired by you. We are keeping our notes and comments for the present.

Very Truly Yours
A.P. MacDonnell

Although short, this letter is one of the most suggestive pieces of evidence to be unearthed. Clearly MacDonnell possessed the letters of the Knights but we can only speculate on how he obtained them. Lord Mayo would have viewed the Under-Secretary as an opponent, especially in light of the way he treated The O'Mahony. Thus, there is every reason to believe that his Lordship would have resisted handing over his private correspondence to Vicars' enemy. Also, it is unlikely that MacDonnell, a civil servant, could have browbeaten Lord Mayo into handing them over. However, an important person whom MacDonnell met in London somehow arranged for him to get the papers. Equally intriguing is the evidence that MacDonnell and Gladstone were discussing the letters of the Knights just six days before the inquiry began. The obvious suggestion is that the Irish administration, represented by MacDonnell, had become suspicious of the action of the Knights.

The man of authority whom MacDonnell obeyed can be none other than the King himself. MacDonnell would never have countermanded the instructions of the Chief Secretary of Ireland on his own or Aberdeen's authority. Also, only the King had the ability to browbeat Lord Mayo into handing over his correspondence with the Knights, and the King had apparently become deeply suspicious that so many of his Knights had defied him in favour of Sir Arthur Vicars.

13

THE INQUIRY

On 6 January 1908, Lord Aberdeen issued the following notice to the press:

> Whereas we have deemed it expedient that a Committee should issue forthwith to investigate the circumstances of the loss of the Regalia of the Order of St Patrick and to inquire whether Sir Arthur Vicars exercised due vigilance and proper care as the custodian thereof.
>
> Now We, John Campbell, Earl of Aberdeen, Lord Lieutenant General and General Governor of Ireland, nominate, constitute and appoint you, His Honour James Johnston Shaw, Robert Fitzwilliam Starkie, Esquire, and Chester Jones, Esquire, to be Commissioners for the purpose of the said Inquiry.
>
> We do by these presents authorise and empower you to inquire of and concerning the premises, and to examine witnesses, and call for and examine all such books and documents as you shall judge likely to afford you the fullest information and to report to us what you shall find touching and concerning the premises.

Given at His Majesty's Castle in Dublin this 6th day of January, 1908.

MacDonnell had insisted on appointing his own man, Starkie, a resident magistrate in County Cork, to the Commission. On the basis of his unqualified loyalty, the Irish administration selected Shaw, a County Court Judge of Kerry, to chair the Commission. Birrell felt that an independent man was needed and therefore asked Gladstone to appoint the third Commissioner. The Home Office selected Chester Jones, a London police magistrate.

On 10 January the Commission met in the library of the Office of Arms, where the empty Ratner safe stood as a mute reminder of the theft. Mr J.C. Campbell, K.C. MP, and Mr T. Healy K.C. MP, instructed by Meredith & Co. appeared as counsel on behalf of Sir Arthur Vicars and the Solicitor-General, Mr Redmond Barry, K.C. MP instructed by Mr Malachi Kelly, Chief Crown Solicitor appeared on behalf of the Government.

The Inquiry almost floundered at the beginning. Sir Arthur attended accompanied by his nephew, Peirce Mahony, Campbell, Healy and Meredith. From the start they vigorously attacked the private nature of the inquiry and its restricted terms of reference. Campbell called on the Commission to honour the request for a 'full public inquiry'. Replying, Chairman Shaw dismissed Campbell's request, saying that they had decided to sit in private. Taking another tack, Campbell tried testing the terms of reference of the Commission. He stated that his client had suffered severe slander to his reputation from shocking suggestions and slurs spread by high Government officials regarding his moral character. Further, he told the Commissioners that the Government accused Sir Arthur of knowingly introducing persons of low character into his office. Campbell then stated that the theft had thwarted the police from the start, and seemingly they still had no suspect for the crime. This attempt to broaden the scope of the inquiry provoked Chairman Shaw to exclaim: 'But we are not investigating crime.' Supporting this stunning statement, Commissioner Jones added: 'We are not here to find out who the thief was. That is a job for the police.' The Chairman, Mr Justice Shaw, immediately confirmed that Mr Chester Jones had interpreted their terms of reference correctly.

Campbell then asked that the Inquiry be held in public and that it be granted powers to compel the attendance of witnesses under oath. Chairman Shaw replied that the objections to the terms of reference by the defence were inapplicable as the same terms applied to any commission held under a Vice-Regal Warrant, whether it be public or private. In a prepared act of drama, Campbell asked to confer with his client. After a short pause, Campbell addressed the Commission saying 'that under no circumstances could Sir Arthur Vicars or his counsel take any part in an Inquiry held under Your Excellency's warrant, and withdrew his application for a public inquiry'. Upon which, Sir Arthur and his nephew rose, and flanked by his counsel and solicitor, marched out of the library to speak to the throng of waiting press outside. The Commissioners, stunned by Sir Arthur's withdrawal, recessed in the belief that in the absence of the principal witness, their inquiry had come to an end.

Later in the afternoon Sir Arthur's legal advisors issued a statement to the press explaining their reason for withdrawing. 'They were of the opinion that the scope of the Inquiry was limited to an investigation into the loss of the jewels so far only as the negligence, if any, of Sir Arthur Vicars was involved and that they were precluded under the very terms of his Excellency's warrant from any inquiry by them in reference to other matters of a serious and grave character which had been insinuated by the Irish administration and which he believed, had influenced the decision to reconstitute the Office of Arms and remove Sir Arthur.' The statement also mentioned that Sir Arthur objected strongly to the Commission's inability to compel witnesses to attend, to take evidence under oath, and to subpoena documents.

Meanwhile, the Government's lawyers conferred with MacDonnell and Birrell to decide the official response to Vicars' manoeuvring. Barry, the Solicitor-General, believed that Sir Arthur would not willingly assist any court of Inquiry whether judicial or otherwise. He advised Birrell to continue the proceedings, because to dismiss Sir Arthur legally, they had to have an inquiry of some kind. If they agreed with the Commissioners and terminated the process, Sir Arthur had recourse to the courts. Agreeing with this argument, Birrell instructed the Solicitor-General to persuade the Commissioners to proceed. Later that evening, MacDonnell probably alerted Starkie and Shaw of their decision.

The next morning, the Solicitor-General Barry asked the Commissioners to hear the evidence that he could present to the inquiry. Despite having lost their principal witness and central character, the Commissioners agreed to proceed. In their report they explained their decision as follows: ' . . . we felt that we could not refuse to receive and record the evidence thus tendered, and that we must leave the responsibility for any deficiencies in the evidence on those who refused to take part in our proceedings.'

Over the next five days, a deluge of bad press and hostile public comment fell on the Irish administration. Sir Arthur had become Dublin's hero of the hour, and enjoyed a sympathetic hearing from the press, while the administration became the laughing stock of the country, as the press pilloried and harangued Birrell and Aberdeen for conducting a secret inquiry. Even His Majesty, King Edward, found it expedient to criticise the nature of the inquiry. Considering Birrell's allergy to bad publicity, one would anticipate that the Chief Secretary would have severely reprimanded MacDonnell for disobeying him and for leading his administration into this political nightmare. Birrell had returned to Dublin on 10 January, in time to countermand any orders given by MacDonnell. Thus, bearing in mind this dreadful public relations débâcle, we digress to discuss the correspondence between Birrell and Gladstone after the third day of the inquiry. These letters indicate that Birrell had come under the same influence as MacDonnell, but Gladstone had not.

Commissioner Jones, the London police magistrate and nominee of the Home Office, wrote to M.L. Waller of the Home Office, informing him of the state of the proceedings. He told Waller that from the beginning he had pushed for a public Inquiry, and that by the second day the Inquiry had become a 'secret Inquiry'. Jones attached a copy of the days proceedings with his letter. This communiqué caused consternation in the Home Office, prompting Gladstone to write to Birrell the following day:

Confidential
Secretary of State
Home Department
Jan. 13. 1908

My dear Birrell,

When we met that Saturday at the H.O. we came unanimously to the conclusion as regards the Vicars business (1) that there should be enquiry (2) by a small R. Comm. and (3) that the inquiry should be public.

At that time H.M. had personally to me expressed approval of this course, and I wrote fully to Aberdeen on the whole matter.

When H.M. received the petition he objected to the R.C. My belief is that he became angry with the signatories and objected to the appearance of surrender involved by his personal connection with the constitution of a R. Comm. I tried in vain to show him that the dignity of his body was necessary to give it the right impetus in this unlucky business. But in vain. Then, in communication with Aberdeen I compromised, and to H.M's satisfaction, on a Vice-Regal Commission. But all along publicity so far as Morley and I were concerned — and surely you also — was insisted on as essential. For as the Irish Govt had been pecking in private at this matter for some months, what on earth was the good of more private inquiry by three men of such lower official status than the Lord Lieutenant, the Chief Secretary, the . . . and the Attorney General of Ireland?

On Sat. to my astonishment I read what occurred. You will remember that we discussed the scandal side, which is one of the two chief difficulties in this matter. Our view was that the Irish Govt — through some official witness should state to the commission that no charge, excepting negligence, was brought against V(icars), and that the Irish Govt had absolutely nothing to do with any rumour or allegations which might have been circulated to V(icars)'s prejudice; that so far as the Irish Govt was concerned Ulster King of Arms was entirely free from any suspicion of a graver charge than negligence. That left the ground free for Vicars to meet the simple charge of negligence, if he could.

Now as I understand, the Commission has barred out any statement on the graver charge and at the insistence of the Irish Govt has decided for privacy.

I have discussed the matter with John Morley, and we are absolutely agreed that this course has made the appointment of the Commission entirely futile. Knollys writes that H.M 'insists' on publicity, and we think he is right. And we adhere to the necessity that the Irish Govt should make a statement on the graver charge.

Of course it is not within our responsibility. But the petition brought me, in a sense, into the business, and now H.M. presses me on the whole case. So I state my view to you. I have telegraphed the position to Aberdeen who does not appear to have had a full grasp of the situation. Morley and I thought that you as head of the Irish Executive would see that the Commission was properly started.

If there is no publicity you will have to face an awkward position with the King, and a real flare up when the House meets. It may be too late to undo all the mischief. But I think in any case you must make the whole thing public. Publish the evidence already given and admit the press.

If I was responsible I should go frankly to Vicars' representatives and come to an agreement on the lines we set forth at the

H.O. If they won't accept, at any rate make the whole inquiry public and show you have nothing to hide. If you don't do this I fail to see what defence you can make in the H of C. Adjourn the inquiry for a day or two to enable an agreement with the other side at least to be attempted.

I am afraid Aberdeen has not seen how far this matter will go. But after our meeting I thought you would intervene and see that everything went straight.

I had neither the authority nor the opportunity to give effect to what we all agreed was the best course to pursue under the circumstances. It's a very ugly business, and you will have, as things are Nationalists and Unionists against you.

Yours always,

H.T.G.

Recalling that MacDonnell, on 4 January, had sent Gladstone a copy of the replies from the Knights to Lord Mayo, we are puzzled that Gladstone continued to believe that the King wanted a public inquiry. Lords Iveagh, Enniskillen and Kilmorey informed Mayo that the palace opposed the petition and the King desired Vicars' dismissal. We can only conclude that the official in the Home Office who read these letters never saw fit to inform Gladstone of the King's true wishes regarding Vicars.

While Gladstone remained resolute in pushing for a public inquiry, Birrell's reply indicates that he had completely changed his mind. He wrote back assertively, bordering on the defiant, and he defended fully the proceedings of the Commission since this would appear to contradict what was said earlier about Birrell's position on the matter, two letters follow that Birrell wrote to Gladstone. These letters are just fourteen days apart, but they underscore how dramatically he had changed his mind about the inquiry. Though he was Ireland's Chief Executive and the Commission fell under his jurisdiction, the first letter on 30 December 1907, demonstrates that he had all but abdicated his authority to Gladstone:

The Pightle,
Sheringham
Norfolk
Dec. 30. 1907

My dear Gladstone

I think you ought to nominate/appoint the Third Man — Everybody in Ireland is suspect — a good man of Business is I think what's wanted. Somebody accustomed to giving orders and see them obeyed and manage a staff. Not a policeman —

It has been a mismanaged business from the first to last. When is the Inquiry going to be held? Are you proposing to consult Ulster's friends about details? I can't see what good he expects to get out of it if it's to be in camera?

We are having beastly weather here, but as it is not Ireland — it seems paradise.

Yours

A. Birrell

Bearing in mind that Gladstone had intruded on Birrell's jurisdiction, it can only be concluded that on 30 December, the Home Secretary had taken control. Birrell allowed Gladstone to appoint his own man (Chester Jones) to the inquiry, and permitted him to set the date, and left him free to consult The O'Mahony about his demand for a public inquiry. In startling contrast, fourteen days after writing the obsequious letter above, Birrell replied to Gladstone's letter of 13 January:

> Private and Confidential.
> Jan. 14. 1908
>
> My dear Gladstone,
> I have consulted with the law officers and particularly with the S.G. [Solicitor-General] who has charge of the inquiry and a statement will be forwarded by this post telling you exactly what has happened and the present position of the inquiry.
> But I want to say a word or two on my own account. You do not and cannot appreciate the situation which exists here in Dublin.
> The man ought to have been dismissed long ago, peremptorily. If he felt aggrieved he might have sought an inquiry. However, he was allowed to remain on. I did not know him, had never seen him, and did not feel either qualified or concerned to take the matter up. The Order, some of the Knights at all events, petitioned H.M. and in the result a Vice-Regal Commission was approved with a carefully considered reference. Following the usual

practice, the Warrant said nothing about the proceedings being held either in private or public, I assumed it would be in public — secret of course it was never intended to be as Vicars was to be attended by counsel and his friends but I thought the press also would attend, and so no doubt it would have done if Campbell and Healy (knowing their man and his case) had not thought it fit to withdraw because of the narrowness of the reference.

This Commission then had to proceed in the absence of Vicars and having regard to the fact — which must not be overlooked that criminal investigations are still being made and that names of persons were likely to be introduced, the Commissioners (and in this respect the law officer were in accord with them) thought it proper to proceed without the public or the press.

A full shorthand note of the evidence has been taken.

Today the Commission on their own accord entirely, decided an intimation to be made to Vicars that they thought he ought to have another opportunity, if he chose to avail himself of it, of learning of the case made against him and of replying to it. The S.G. then stated that if Vicars thought fit to respond, the Government desired that his evidence and any other evidence he might call should be taken in public. The Court then adjourned.

I don't suppose for a moment Vicars will come. The S.G. entertains a very strong opinion as to his fault. I mean in respect of the jewels.

When the commission has made their report, when that report has been published and the evidence also, I don't think anybody need be frightened of a debate in the House of Commons. I certainly shall not be.

I have just heard Vicars has refused to attend and give any explanation on the ground not of want of publicity, but of the restricted nature of the inquiry.

To approach Vicars and his advisers any further than has been done would be impossible. They are not bent on vindicating the character of one honest man but are raising false issue to obscure the true one. I could not personally consent to any such course. It is our weakness and delay in action that has occasioned almost all the trouble.

Nothing will satisfy 'the other side' as you call it but a General Inquiry of a police character as to the stories and rumours affecting a number of persons more or less closely associated with Vicars. With these stories and rumours I refuse to be identified — whether if it came to the point, Vicars would ever appear before such an inquiry I feel at liberty to entertain grave doubts.

Yours Always,
A. Birrell

The contrast in the tone and thrust of these two letters testifies to a tremendous turnabout for Birrell, over a period of fourteen days. The

Chief Secretary for Ireland had switched from abdicating abjectly to asserting actively his authority. Three points in Birrell's letter need emphasising:

He states, 'You do not and cannot appreciate the situation which exists here in Dublin'. This extraordinary assertion has nothing to do with the workings of the Commission as Gladstone's man, Chester Jones, faithfully reported the proceedings to the Home Office. Nor can the statement refer to Lord Haddo or the issue of scandal, because Gladstone already had the Kane report and he mentioned the scandal issue in his letter to Birrell. Thus, something new has arisen that Gladstone knows nothing about, and it seems logical to infer that this is the reason for Birrell's new-found confidence that things are under control — despite the appalling condemnation that the Irish administration received in the press.

He states, 'The Order, some of the Knights at all events, petitioned H.M. and in the result a Vice-Regal Commission was approved with a carefully considered reference'. Historically this is inaccurate. Birrell had agreed to an inquiry before the petition got into Gladstone's hands, yet he attributes the inquiry to the influence of the Knights.

Throughout their discussions, Gladstone had emphasised the difficulties Birrell might face in the House of Commons. This was a sore point for Birrell. His calamitous handling of the Education portfolio a year earlier had resulted in his demotion to the undesirable Irish post. He had no desire to go through another débâcle in the House, yet he wrote: 'I don't think anybody need be frightened of a debate in the House of Commons. I certainly shall not be.' Birrell does not fear either the Unionists or the Nationalists in the slightest, as Gladstone suggested he should. We already know that Birrell had concocted some deal with Redmond and his Nationalists not to raise the matter in the House. Thus, when he dismisses any concern regarding the Unionists, we presume that he had put in place a political pact to procure their silence.

Thus, Aberdeen, Birrell and MacDonnell rode out the storm of negative publicity secure in the knowledge that their political foes would remain quiet. Having explained the political indifference in Dublin to the bad press, we now return to the evidence heard by the Commission of Inquiry.

On day two of the Inquiry, Saturday 11 January, the Commissioners accepted Solicitor-General Barry's urging to continue the proceedings and hear the evidence that the government wanted to present. They took evidence for five days, interviewed almost all the staff in the Office of Arms, the Heralds and the police. Mr Horlick, Sir Arthur's Secretary, and Miss Gibbons, his typist, refused to give evidence, stating that Sir Arthur 'was not getting fair play'. As the Commissioners had decided to work in private, they barred the press from attending the proceedings. This limited the ability of the press to report on the evidence and findings of the Commission except when they obtained information through official channels.

An array of Irish police officers testified, and their evidence paints the picture of a confused, lacklustre, and uncoordinated investigation. Although the Commissioner and the Assistant-Commissioner of the police testified at the inquiry, we cannot determine who, if anybody, they had put in charge of the investigation. This absence of a leading Irish investigator is evident both before Chief Inspector Kane of Scotland Yard arrived and after he left. Consequently, no Irish officer offered a theory on any aspect of the case, nor did any Commissioner request him to do so.

Mr M.V. Harrel, the Assistant-Commissioner of Police, gave evidence concerning the security arrangements in the Castle:

Yes there are three gates, the Main Gate, the Lower Castle Yard Gate and the Ship Street Gate. There is a military guard and policeman at the Main Gate, but at each of the other gates there is only there a policeman on duty throughout the 24 hours every day. The military are responsible for the closing of the gates to wheeled traffic which they do at sundown every evening. When that is done the gates are locked, and a constable has charge of the wicket gates . . . As I have stated there is a policeman on duty at the gates by day and night; and I should mention that these mens' duties are not defined as are the duties of a sentry. The police have a responsibility of their own; and they are most particular not to allow anyone to pass after dark without knowing what their business is; and they never leave their posts, because there is always another constable in the Upper and Lower Yards . . . so that, as far as the police regulations can ensure it, no person can enter the precincts of the Castle and the offices without being observed. There is no reason to think that anyone could enter the gates without being observed and the police knowing all about them.

Despite having heard evidence that a thief had twice broken into the Office of Arms, unseen, and unobserved, this remarkable confidence about the Castle's security arrangements went unchallenged by the Commissioners. In particular they ignored the evidence that a policeman patrolled the Upper Castle Yard when the offices were shut, and this man had instructions to identify individuals entering or leaving the offices. Compounding their omission, the Commissioners did not interrogate the night-constable in person, the man who it is believed held the key to the case. From all that has been said and written, we believe that this man would have testified that, other than Detective Kerr, he never saw anybody entering or leaving the Office of Arms, either on the nights of 2 July or 5 July. However, because the Commissioners declined to probe any further, they left forever unanswered the mystery of how the thief entered the Office of Arms without being seen.

Francis Bennett-Goldney, the Mayor of Canterbury, then gave evidence. He said he was appointed Athlone Persuivant to the Office of

Arms in 1907 and went to Dublin in May, for the opening of the Exhibition, as Sir Arthur's guest at St James' Terrace. Mr Shackleton also stayed in the house during this time. He understood that Sir Arthur and Mr Shackleton held the house as co-tenants. Critically, Goldney testified that he stayed in Dublin for three days, and during that three-day period he twice saw the Crown Jewels. The first occasion occurred when Sir Arthur showed them to Lady Donegall, Lady Orford and an American lady, who accompanied Lady Donegall. The second occasion occurred the following day, when Sir Arthur showed the jewels to a sister or cousin of Lady Fairbairn. He then said that he returned to England and did not come back to Dublin until the Monday following the robbery. (Sir Arthur, in his letters to Fuller, corroborated Goldney's account of events. Thus, although Goldney later proved to be a 'compulsive collector', he had to be removed from the list of suspects because he could not have taken the safe key. Goldney did not copy the key at the time, because no locksmith in Dublin recalled seeing him. Likewise, he could not have taken the spare key, because Sir Arthur found that key in its hiding place before Goldney returned to Dublin.)

Goldney then proceeded to inform the spellbound Commissioners about Sir Arthur's and Shackleton's financial difficulties.

'There had been a little friction . . . between members in the Office of Arms owing to money difficulties, and it has always been over this question. I helped these people honestly

224

believing it was Sir Arthur Vicars' wish that I should do so.' He elaborated that during his visit in May, Sir Arthur had confided in him that 'he had entered into financial commitments that he could not afford'. Goldney, feeling that he owed Sir Arthur a favour for appointing him to the Office, asked if he could help out in any way. Sir Arthur, aware of Goldney's wealth, explained that he had guaranteed two bills for Shackleton — one for £600, the other for £750, and he asked Goldney to accept responsibility for these.

Although the witness had wandered well beyond the scope of their inquiry, the Commissioners happily allowed Goldney to elaborate on these colourful financial arrangements. Goldney agreed to sign the lower of the two bills. He said that on his return to his mother's house in Abbots Barton, he received an unsigned telegram announcing that 'I am coming down by the eight train'. That evening, Shackleton arrived at Goldney's home.

'I am in a great hole,' Shackleton told his reluctant host. 'I cannot go over to Ireland to see Sir Arthur, who has requested me to help him in this matter. It is merely a question of shares, and it must be done at once. I must have the money by Monday morning, and unless I can get somebody to do it I shall be in the greatest of difficulty.' He then asked Goldney to sign a bill for £1,500.

Shackleton, anticipating Goldney's reluctance to sign the bill, had arranged for his money-lender to come to Canterbury to help him exert pressure on his reluctant host. Posing as the 'family solicitor', the money lender helped Shackleton coerce Goldney into signing the bill. Goldney protested and said to the 'family solicitor', 'I do not like it, but as it is to please Sir Arthur Vicars and I am to be in his office, I will do it'. The Commissioners then listened attentively to Goldney's disclosures about Sir Arthur's dealings with the same money lender. This avid attention contrasted greatly to his previous testimony, when Goldney had volunteered his opinions as to the identity of the thief — the Commissioners on that occasion struck out his statement.

In the midst of this questioning, the Solicitor-General appeared to wander into the irrelevant topic of the identity of Sir Arthur's household staff. Barry asked Goldney, 'Was there a manservant named Phillips in the house?' Goldney replied, 'Yes, but that was on another occasion that I came to Dublin, during Horse Show Week.' (27 – 30 August 1907). If all Barry wanted was the information regarding the names of the employees, he could have asked Mahony who had testified earlier, or Shackleton, who would take the stand later. We believe that he wanted Goldney to confirm a statement that Phillips had made about seeing Goldney in Sir Arthur's drawing room. The police had two statements from Phillips, the first, given in July, concerned the theft; however, we believe the second statement given after the Horse Show Week, revealed details of Sir Arthur's private life.

The most important police witness called by the Commission was Chief Inspector John Kane of Scotland Yard. Questioned by Solicitor-General Barry, he said he arrived in Dublin on 11 July, and proceeded to Dublin Castle, where Sir Arthur showed him a red morocco case in which he had kept the jewels.

Barry: And did you open it?
Kane: No, he opened it.
Barry: And when it was open what did you observe inside?

Kane said he saw a small ribbon inside that he recollected distinctly, because Sir Arthur had described the ribbon to him before he had opened the safe. Sir Arthur then remarked that the thief could not have been in any hurry, as the removal of the ribbon from the jewels would have necessitated the use of a small screwdriver and would have taken some time. Continuing, Kane said Sir Arthur then demonstrated to him how awkward an amateur or any other person not acquainted with regalia would have found moving the ornament over the frayed portion of the ribbon. Kane then remarked to the Commissioners that he could not understand why an 'outside' thief should waste time taking off the ribbon. He also said that Sir Arthur had suggested to him that somebody had taken impressions of his keys.

The Commission then questioned Kane about the strong room key:

Kane: . . . that if the thief came in predetermined to rob the strong room, he would have done so because he had opened it; and before he had forged a key for the strong room he must have made up his mind to rob it, otherwise one could not see any object in his forging of the key of the strong room at all, for the mere curiosity of opening it and looking at the articles there . . . I said that it was clear that the strong room door was opened and we must reasonably assume that whoever opened it went inside, and then I said if an outside thief did that will you please suggest why he did not secure some of the property there, such as the gold crown and the collection of valuable articles up on the shelf on an ordinary press with ordinary glass in it, and I understand that even the key of the press was kept in the drawer of the table in the middle of the room.

Later Kane said, in relation to the leisurely manner in which the theft had occurred that 'the thief had more right on these premises than I have'.

Shaw: Have you any theory as to why an inside thief should wish to take it (the ribbon) off?

Kane: Well the only theory I have is that this theft was not committed on the fifth of July.

Shaw: Why should any thief do that?

Kane: Well he would not want to encumber himself with the ribbon. We will assume that some person conversant with the place — I am not making a suggestion against any person, I have no right to express an opinion at all about persons, I can only state facts — my theory is that he would be a person who would have to remove it and would remove it at his leisure. It would be useless to an ordinary thief or housebreaker, or burglar coming in, to take that trouble. To me it is incomprehensible that any ordinary burglar should do so ... No sir, I cannot believe a burglar did this. You might say that the burglar would not want to run any risk, but I may suggest, with great respect, that the burglar would run as great a risk of being caught with the diamonds alone as with the ribbon attached. I do not see why the burglar should want to detach it. He would roll it up and put it in his pocket, and clear off as quickly as possible.

Barry: Might it not happen that it might have been left in the hope that at some time the jewels might be restored by a person who took it for a temporary purpose?

Kane: Well that suggestion will hardly apply to an outside thief.

Shaw: interrupted with 'Oh no'.

Undeterred, Barry continued: Would that be a possible explanation of it, supposing that the jewels were taken for a temporary purpose?'

Kane: Certainly, of course that would be an explanation.

Somewhat later Kane related that 'Sir Arthur said of his staff 'I have implicit confidence in every member of my staff' repeating this over and over again.' Kane later stated that 'Sir Arthur had changed his mind by August second and he accused Francis Richard Shackleton of the theft and that he acted in collusion with another person.'

In reply to the question as to whether he thought the robbery occurred on the night the thief left the strong room open,

Kane: No I did not.

S-G Barry: On what did you form that opinion?
Kane: There I must object to expressing an opinion. I shall express no opinion, because if I expressed an opinion, that would lead up possibly to involving of persons, and that I must not do. It would be the natural consequence, if I was to express an opinion that I should have to explain how I associated the opening of the strong room door that night with the robbery, but my opinion is that the robbery did not take place that night . . . the theory I formed at the time and the theory I maintain up to the present moment was that the strong room door was purposely opened that night for the purpose of bringing about an investigation that would lead to the discovery of a robbery that had taken place before Friday night, the fifth of July. That impression I formed at the time and that is the impression I still maintain . . . to my mind the same object was intended to be achieved on the night of the third which was intended on the fifth. We know that the persons who found those doors opened did not do what one would have expected they would have done, rush off to the police and report it.
Shaw: Why do you think that the person who opened the front door wished to precipitate an investigation?
Kane: There was a certain high personage coming here, and possibly certain people thought that when these jewels had disappeared it would be necessary that some explanation of that should be forthcoming before their arrival.
Shaw: But how was the thief interested in that?

230

Kane: That was just the very thing that I objected to at first, expressing an opinion about this matter at all, because it leads from one thing onto another. This will all possibly be in blue book form and, therefore, I want to be very guarded, besides I am not here under the protection of my superiors. I am certain that my superiors would, in the most positive terms, object to my expressing an opinion. A police officer has no right to express an opinion at all with regard to persons. I must only state facts . . .

Starkie: Have you formed an opinion as to whether that safe there was locked or not from the date of the robbery up to the night of the fifth?

Kane: No; I have not formed an opinion about that, but I pointed out at the safe to Sir Arthur Vicars that it seemed to me so utterly impossible that any outside thief would have done all these things, putting back the cases, and I particularly noticed that this is a very large safe and I said 'Just imagine an outside thief doing the very thing that might attract the attention of the sentry outside by closing a door which is very thick, in this front room, by shutting-to a strong room door in the silence of the night.' I said he would have gone off and left the cases on the floor and the door wide open. And I specified the shutting of the door and the turning of the handle downwards giving to the observer the appearance of a locked safe. I said an outside thief never did that.

Starkie: Have you any theory as to why the thief

231

did not proceed further and lock the safe?

Kane: Possibly he was under the impression he had done so.

Starkie: That is assuming that the robbery took place some time before the night of the fifth.

Kane: Some time, yes.

Starkie: He could have locked the safe and opened it in the same way as the strong room?

Kane: The same way as the strong room. But I think there must have been an intention, Sir, to impress the observer with the idea that the safe was locked by turning the handle right down to give it the appearance of a locked safe.

Starkie: But if the jewels were taken for a temporary purpose and the safe left unlocked, anyone who turned the handle would discover that the jewels were gone and the thief would have no opportunity of retuning them undiscovered?

Kane: Yes; if it was left open for some time, but in my mind the safe was left unlocked the same night as the strong room door.

Barry: Do I understand you to say that it was unlocked the same night the strong room door was opened?

Kane: That is the impression I have formed.

Barry: Although it is your impression that the jewels had been taken on a prior occasion?

Kane: Oh, yes, because I cannot understand opening the strong room door and touching nothing at all, because before the key was made, if an outsider did it there must have been a predetermination to rob the strong room, otherwise there is no sense in forging the key.

Kane was never asked or volunteered who he had named as the thief in his report.

On the second last day of the Inquiry, the Commissioners proposed a compromise to Sir Arthur. They wrote to him, offering to hold their inquiry in public and to call whatever witnesses he requested if he would assist them with their investigation. After consulting with his solicitor, Sir Arthur declined the offer as it still did not address his objections concerning the inquiry's narrow terms of reference. He then forwarded both the Commission's letter and his reply to the press, who, the following day attacked both the Irish administration and the Commissioners for the way in which they had handled the case.

Frank Shackleton, living the high life, had travelled to a villa in San Remo to holiday with his friends, Lord Ronald Gower and Frank Hird, when he read about the inquiry in the English papers on 10 January. He contacted Dougherty to ask him if the Commissioners needed his testimony. Dougherty told him that he had sent a summons to his club three days earlier. Shackleton, displaying his worldly wisdom, feared that some people might infer guilt from his absence, so he hurried back to Dublin to give evidence on the second last day of the inquiry. Barry questioned him about his housing arrangements with Sir Arthur. He said that even though he spent only two months a year in Dublin, he paid half the rent and half the servants' wages. He said that when in London he lived at the fashionable address of 44 Park Lane. During the early part of 1907 he was also heavily involved in raising funds from friends in the City to help finance his brother, Ernest, who planned to make another Antarctic expedition. Any scandal or hint of financial difficulties could cause concern among Ernest's backers. When the Commissioners quizzed Shackleton about his dealings with moneylenders, he protested strongly, saying that his financial difficulties had no bearing on the inquiry and that if these leaked out to the press, his reputation could suffer greatly.

Shackleton was then queried about the remark he had made at Lady Ormonde's luncheon party where he had said that 'I would not be surprised some day if the jewels are stolen'. Shackleton replied that it was just an innocent remark and that he had no reason to say it except that he thought that the jewels were unsafe. The Chairman then asked him, 'Why did you think they were unsafe?' — 'Well for many reasons. I considered there were too many keys for the door . . . of the outer door.'

Shackleton also mentioned the existence of a skylight in the Office of Arms, saying that a potential thief could get into the building from the rooftops of adjoining buildings. Also, he suggested that a thief could enter the premises in broad daylight unnoticed while the office messenger went upstairs to attend on Sir Arthur. This person could then closet himself in the cellar downstairs until evening. When all had gone home, one would have free reign of the offices and could then walk out of the office next day undetected. Shackleton said he had often walked into the office during the working day and found that Stivey had gone upstairs leaving the strong room unlocked while visitors waited in the library. On such occasions, Shackleton showed a strong sense of security, because he would pretend to have something to do, walk over to the strong room without attracting attention, and remove the grille key.

The Commissioners questioned Shackleton about the keys to the safe.

Barry: Had you yourself access at any time to the keys in Sir Arthur Vicars' house?

Shackleton: 'I might have access to this extent, but I have never had occasion to use them. Certainly I could have gone into his room when he was in the bath and taken these keys. I think he did not take them into the bathroom, and when I went in to speak to him, when he was in bed, they were under his pillow, and I could have very easily, had I so wished gone to his room and taken an impression of his key, or taken the original key off if I had known it and walked away with that key and replaced it quite easily, because I was in and out talking. I don't say that I was always going into his room, because he used to grumble that I got up so early. He said that I was like a Donegal peasant getting up at cock-crow; but I used to go to bed early, which was one of his grievances, because he had no companion.

With such forthright candour about having possible access to the safe key on Sir Arthur's ring, one has to wonder why he made no mention of the spare key that Sir Arthur hid in his drawer. Through his previous testimony, Shackleton had already demonstrated a keen eye for detail in matters of security. Thus, one has to calculate a high probability that such a man learned of the whereabouts of this key over the previous two years — especially in the light of the intimate friendship existing between himself and Sir Arthur.

Barry then asked: 'Mr Shackleton, do you remember anything about Sir Arthur losing his latch key to the outer door of the Office?' 'No, I do not recollect that.' Sir Arthur had stated that on 28 June, which was the King's birthday, he had gone down to the Office and was not able to find his latch key to the outer door. Shackleton replied that he himself had not been in Ireland on 28 June. The Commissioner then explained that Sir Arthur did not find his key until 9 July, when it mysteriously reappeared on his dressing-table. Shackleton was asked again if he took the latch key. He replied, 'I did not, Sir, at any time. This is the first I have heard of it. I am perfectly willing to swear that I never took it.'

The Commissioners then questioned Shackleton about the mysterious Hadley Street telegrams, and he explained what had transpired in Kane's office at Scotland Yard. He told the Commission that he was upset that he had not been informed until much later that they had been sent by a man named Bullock Webster. He did not disclose who had told him that information. Shackleton was also queried about why he burnt his personal papers when he arrived in Dublin on 8 July, just days after the theft. He said he had burnt certain letters relating to money he had lent people and that if anything should happen to him he did not want his executors 'to come down on anybody he had lent money to'. He specifically mentioned a bank clerk who had stolen money and he had lent him the amount to put it right. He also said that he did not wish that letters from people who had absolutely taken him into their confidence should be found. Finally, Shackleton, when asked bluntly if he took the jewels, replied, 'No, I had no hand in it, nor do I know anybody that took them, nor have I the least suspicion who might have.'

After this Peirce Mahony was recalled to clear up some questions about a letter Shackleton sent to him. Then the Commission recalled Chief Inspector Kane.

On recall, Kane was questioned about the Hadley Street telegrams and the accusations against Shackleton.

Barry: With regard to the telegram which was sent to Lord Aberdeen that the jewels were in 9 Hadley Street, I should like to ask Inspector Kane a question on that.
Shaw: Very well, but I thought that had already been cleared up.
Barry: Mention was made today about the telegram that came from Great Malvern to say 'jewels in box, 9 Hadley Street, Dublin?'
Kane: Yes.

Barry: That telegram was unsigned?

Kane: Yes.

Barry: And I think Mr Shackleton on seeing the word 'Dublin', stated to you that the word 'Dublin' was, as he thought, in his handwriting.

Kane: Yes.

Barry: And then when the telegram was opened out he said that it was not?

Kane: Yes.

Barry: Have you investigated that matter?

Kane: I have.

Barry: And a further telegram sent from the same place by Mr. Bullock Webster?

Kane: Yes.

Barry: And have you satisfied yourself that they were sent by Mr Bullock Webster?

Kane: Absolutely.

Barry: That is Mr Bullock Webster says they were?

Kane: Absolutely.

Barry: And is he a gentleman of high position?

Kane: Of the highest repute, and he wrote them absolutely bona fide in consequence of a communication made to him of his wife.

Later the Commissioners questioned Kane about the accusations against Shackleton.

Starkie: Did you ever trace any fact that would tend to throw suspicion on Mr. Shackleton?

Kane: Never.

Starkie: Not a shred of evidence against him?

Kane: I have repeated to Sir Arthur Vicars and his friends, over and over again, and I desire to say now that when they pestered me with not only suggestion, but direct accusations of Mr

238

Shackleton, that they might as well accuse me so far as the evidence they produced went to justify them.

★ ★ ★

Although the Kane report has never been made public (Scotland Yard to this day denies its existence), we can glean important inferences from his testimony. Kane suggested that the thief was a Castle insider with more right to be in the Office of Arms than himself. The thief 'forged' the keys and stole the jewels well before 5 July. The thief's motive was to create a great embarrassment prior to the King's visit and then return the jewels. By mentioning a forged key, Kane implies that Sir Arthur was not the thief. He also vouched for the innocence of Shackleton. We know that the Irish administration was most distressed over the suspect named in Kane's report, and dismissed the Chief Inspector. Thus the person he named in his report must have had considerable stature in Ireland. Mahony was not a man of any stature, nor was Goldney, who was just an English Mayor. Only one remaining person associated with Sir Arthur had the stature and prestige to compel the Irish administration and the Lord Lieutenant to go to such extreme lengths to shield him — that person was Lord Haddo.

Of interest here is the persistence of the Irish administration's representatives in prodding Kane to reveal the details of his report. Both Commissioner Starkie, (MacDonnell's man), and Solicitor-General Barry introduced the suggestion that the jewels were stolen on a temporary basis. Each time Kane had to dodge the question and said he would not name individuals. Their questioning of Kane reveals a surprising lack of fear that he might go too far and disclose the person he named in his report.

The confidence of the Irish Commissioners contrasts completely with that of Commissioner Jones, the man Gladstone appointed. Jones, a London police magistrate, had the qualifications and the experience to question Kane profession-ally, yet he did not ask the Chief Inspector a significant question throughout his testimony. This omission is even more puzzling considering that the Home Secretary insisted on a complete airing of the details. Similarly we draw attention to the fact that Jones took no part in the questioning of Shackleton.

We are astonished that Jones, an experienced police magistrate, did not question Kane's police methods at all. Surely he would have liked to have seen the original telegram form, and asked Kane if he had consulted with a handwriting expert. Jones must have had serious reservations about Kane's unorthodox methods when he asked Sir Arthur to identify the handwriting while Shackleton was still present in the office. We have concluded that Jones received specific instructions from the Home Office not to press either Kane or Shackleton — a stark contrast to the attitude of the Irish representatives.

Detective Sergeant Murphy in the course of his evidence said that he went on one occasion with Sir Arthur and Mahony to Mulhuddart and Clonsilla.

Barry: What was the date?
Murphy: On July the fifteenth.
Barry: Did Sir Arthur tell you why you were going there?
Murphy: Yes; to search for the jewels in consequence of a statement that had been made to him by a clairvoyant at his residence the previous evening.
Barry: Did you go to the churchyard?
Murphy: We did, Sir, we searched among the tombstones in both churchyards and found nothing.
Barry: The clairvoyant did not go with you?
Murphy: No.

After hearing this bit of absurdity, the Commissioners then concluded their inquiry and retired to consider the evidence and to issue their report.

We note that the Commissioners elected not to call an important witness, Mr McEnnery, Sir Arthur's friend, who, accused Shackleton of the theft.

On the first day of the Inquiry, the Commissioners informed Sir Arthur's counsel that they had no mandate to investigate the crime, and that their terms of reference restricted them solely to considering Sir Arthur's negligence. The Commissioners went far beyond that frame of reference when they issued the following statement about Shackleton:

Although it was no part of our duty under your Excellency's warrant to conduct a criminal investigation into the robbery of the jewels, or to take evidence with a view to the ascertainment of the thief, yet as, on the evidence given before us and now in print, it appears that the name of Mr Francis Richard Shackleton was more than once named as that of the probable or possible author of this great crime, we think it only due to that gentleman to say that he came from San Remo at great inconvenience to give evidence before us, that he appeared to us to be a perfectly truthful witness and that there was no evidence whatever before us which would support the suggestion that he was the person that stole the jewels.

The Commissioners followed this unusual affirmation of Shackleton by the following condemnation of Sir Arthur:

Having fully investigated all the circumstances connected with the loss of the Regalia of the Order of St Patrick, and having examined and considered carefully the arrangements of the Office of Arms in which the Regalia were deposited, and the provisions made by Sir Arthur Vicars, or under his direction for their safe keeping, and having regard especially to the inactivity of Sir Arthur Vicars on the occasion immediately preceding the disappearance of the Jewels, when he knew that the

242

Office and the Strong Room had been opened at night by unauthorised persons, we feel bound to report to Your Excellency that, in our opinion, Sir Arthur Vicars did not exercise due vigilance or proper care as the custodian of the Regalia.

On 30 January, MacDonnell's assistant, Sir James Dougherty, sent the following letter dismissing Sir Arthur:

I am to request you to arrange, either by attendance at the Office or otherwise, as may be most convenient to you, to hand over your keys . . . by 12 o'clock on Saturday next, February the 1st.

Dougherty then announced Sir Arthur's successor in the *Dublin Gazette*:

Dublin Castle Jan 30
His Majesty's Letters Patent have passed the Great Seal of Ireland appointing Captain Neville Rodwell Wilkinson to be Ulster King of Arms in the room of Sir Arthur Vicars.

This appointment came as a cruel blow to Sir Arthur, because Wilkinson had no experience whatsoever of heraldry. However, Wilkinson had proved himself a man's man as a Captain in the Coldstream Guards, and far more importantly he carried no hint of scandal. Bamford and Bankes record His Majesty's approval as follows:

King Edward was delighted; and, when one

Privy Councillor ventured to ask if Captain Wilkinson knew anything about heraldry, His Majesty swept such considerations aside. 'That doesn't matter,' he declared, 'so long as he's honest.'

Whatever other accusation has been levelled at Sir Arthur, nobody questioned his honesty. Thus, we have to conclude that King Edward meant heterosexual when he used the word 'honest'.

However, Wilkinson still had a defiant predecessor to contend with. Sir Arthur would not surrender his key to the strong room, which contained the silver maces and the Irish Sword of State as well as some of the remaining gold collars of the Order. These were needed for an upcoming ceremony, and Wilkinson broke into the strong room, with the aid of crowbars wielded by two hardy labourers supplied by the Board of Works. 'Then,' the new Ulster reported, 'my quest accomplished, I quietly joined the guests as they sat over their coffee, and pointed out the recovered symbols of state to His Excellency as we passed through the Throne Room on our way to join the ladies.'

14

TIDYING UP

The Commission of Inquiry, while not illuminating the mystery of the disappearance of the Irish Crown Jewels nor quenching the rumours that circulated in its wake, did fulfil its intended purpose. King Edward got his wish. The Irish administration succeeded in suppressing all mention of scandal during the inquiry. It ousted Sir Arthur from office, and imposed a blanket silence over the affair. Those who took part, politicians, lawyers, policemen, and civil servants, took their secrets to the grave. Kane's report disappeared from the Chief Secretary's files, while in London it disappeared from Scotland Yard and the Home Office, completing the official silence that has engulfed the incident. Even 90 years after the affair, the Home Office has not opened its files on the subject. Considering the wall of secrecy surrounding the affair, we had hoped the Robert Brennan papers, housed in the special collections department of the University of Delaware, may have some clues. Sadly they only confirmed how thoroughly the affair had been sanitised.

Robert Brennan, born in 1881, worked for the Wexford County Council and then joined the *Enniscorthy Echo* as a journalist. As a young man, he joined Arthur Griffith's Republican movement, took an active part in the Easter rising of 1916, and spent time in jail for his efforts. He became the Under-Secretary for External Affairs in the Free State Government until the Irish Civil War broke out, when Brennan, siding with De Valera, became the director of publicity for the Republicans.

Brennan helped De Valera fulfil his ambition of having a national newspaper sympathetic to the Republican cause when he helped found *The Irish Press*, and served as its general manager from 1930 – 1934. In 1934, De Valera, now the head of the Irish Government, sent Brennan to Washington as the Secretary of the Irish Legation, and in 1938 he became the Irish Minister in Washington, a post he held until 1947. He returned to Ireland to become the Director of Broadcasting for Radio Eireann and retired in 1948. A colleague of his mentioned the possibility of making a film of Brennan's play, *Goodnight Mr O'Donnell*, a farce about the theft of the Irish Crown Jewels. He wrote the play over twenty years before, and the Irish language version, translated by Professor Liam O'Briain, enjoyed great success. Having been approached with a film offer, Brennan began researching the theft in earnest. In October 1948, he published an abbreviated account of the theft of the Irish Crown jewels in *The Irish Press*.

Brennan's unpublished account of the theft, entitled 'Where Are the Crown Jewels? A Dublin Castle Mystery' unfortunately offered no great insights into the mystery. Brennan is the only Irishman to have written extensively about the theft, and with his superb contacts in the Irish Government, the civil service and the press he would have had access to files and information unavailable to others. This, however, proved untrue. His only original information came from Seamus O'Farrell, the eldest son of Mrs Farrell.

Seamus O'Farrell, like Brennan, had taken part in the Easter Rising, and became a member of the first Irish Senate. He moved in the same political circles as Brennan, but did not have the extensive contacts of the latter. During the quarter of a century that elapsed from the formation of the Free State Government, Seamus O'Farrell had uncovered no new evidence about the theft, though he had an avid interest in the subject. When Brennan published his article in *The Irish Press*, O'Farrell contacted him and told him what he knew.

On Sunday 7 July, the day after the discovery of the theft, Detective Kerr and two officers arrived unannounced at the Farrell home in Mary's Abbey. Without a warrant, Kerr and his men tore the place apart, apparently looking for the Crown Jewels. Kerr questioned Mrs Farrell, and she told him about the open front door, the open strong room, and about seeing Lord Haddo in the Office early one morning. O'Farrell told Brennan that later, as the inquiry was set to get underway, the police again interviewed his mother and browbeat her into retracting her story about seeing Lord Haddo.

Seamus O'Farrell told the same story to the

authors Bamford and Bankes more than ten years later. However, was most intriguing was Detective Kerr's attitude. From the start the police had determined that this was no ordinary theft — normal burglars are not in the habit of tidying up after themselves and removing ribbons from jewels. Thus, they hardly suspected Mrs Farrell or her sons were involved, yet Kerr took the place apart. Detective Kerr appears to have been extremely angry with Mrs Farrell.

Brennan also related how during his research in 1950 he contacted William Harrel, the Assistant Commissioner of the Dublin Metropolitan Police at the time of the theft. During the Great War, Harrel tried to recruit Brennan to engage in counter espionage against the Germans. Having met Harrel 30 years earlier, Brennan phoned him, but in response to the requested interview Harrel said: 'I'm sorry to say that that is a subject I feel I should not discuss with anyone.'

Brennan's main sources turned out to be the newspapers and the minutes of evidence from the Vice-Regal inquiry. Apparently, Brennan had run afoul of the mysterious silence that blanketed the case on both sides of the Irish Sea. Bamford and Bankes researching the theft in the 1960s note their frustration as follows:

Even now, after more than 50 years, the mere mention of the case retains the power of afflicting reputedly intelligent persons with a kind of mass amnesia, rendering them unable to remember anything of events in which they

248

themselves, or their close relatives, were personally involved.

This pervasive silence ranks as one of the great mysteries of the affair. Dublin drowned in disclosures, leaks and rumours right up to the time of the Commission of Inquiry, but afterwards the leaks fizzled out in unison, suggesting that despite their apparent diversity, they all had shared a common source that had abruptly dried up. The Unionist papers, the Nationalist papers and the Ultra Nationalist paper *The Gaelic American* all ran out of new information at much the same time. This silence has continued to the present, and points to a concerted and co-ordinated effort by normally opposed parties, who, for some reason, discovered they shared a common cause in suppressing the details.

KING EDWARD VII

King Edward died of heart failure in 1910. During his last hours, his spirits soared on hearing that his horse had won at Kempton Park. Conscious of the prying appetites of historians, His Majesty, in his will, ordered his personal papers to be burnt. Lord Knollys, loyal to the end, carried out these wishes. Most biographers of the King concentrate on his personal brushes with scandal and pay no heed to the theft of the Irish Crown Jewels or Edward's visit to Dublin in 1907. However, Edward Legge's, *More About King Edward*

(Boston, Small Maynard and Company, 1913) devotes a full chapter to the story, and discusses the significance of the affair in his preface:

> The theft of the Crown Regalia from Dublin Castle is narrated . . . I regard this episode as one of the leading events of the nine years' reign. I am sure the King so considered it; I am equally certain . . . that this ugly business caused the Sovereign the utmost exasperation and dismay. It was not merely the material loss of the jewels . . . environing circumstances, the nature of which I am not disposed to describe explicitly for reasons of public policy, added fuel to the flame. I believe this story of a crime has not its parallel . . .

Legge, a contemporary of the King, states that he had privileged information, leading him to appraise the theft of the Crown Jewels as an unparalelled crime. Even if we grant the author some poetic licence in this matter, the mere abduction of the Irish Crown Jewels could never rise to this level. Is this pompous bluster or does Legge ache to tell us something that loyalty to his late King has forbidden him to disclose? He mentions the material loss associated with the theft, but implies that this was insignificant compared to the 'environing circumstances' he would not disclose 'for reasons of public policy'.

In his chapter on the theft, Legge refers to the account of Filson Young, published in *The Saturday Review* of 12 July 1913:

At this point King Edward held up his hand, and the whole traffic of detectives, police officers, Crown officials and Ministers was held up. 'I will not have a scandal,' he said. 'I will not have mud stirred up and thrown about; the matter must be dropped.' And dropped it was like a hot potato. A scapegoat had to be found to satisfy the public opinion, and Sir Arthur Vicars, as officially responsible for the disappearance of the jewels, was told he had better resign.

While covering much of the ground already described, Filson Young has omitted all mention of the part played by the Knights of St Patrick. In approving of Young's theory, Legge has committed himself to the same course. Legge never mentions the Knights and their petition although he claims to have had knowledgeable Irish sources and knew some of the Knights associated with the royal household. Thus, Legge deliberately omitted the role of the Knights, and it must be more than coincidence that Birrell, in his letter of 14 January 1907, to Gladstone, laid the blame for holding the inquiry squarely on the shoulders of the same men.

THE ORDER OF ST PATRICK AND THE JEWELS
The theft of the Crown Jewels struck a severe blow to the Order of St Patrick, but not as severe as the emergence of the Irish Free State in 1922. From then on, the Order went into uninterrupted decline, and is now in abeyance.

Unknown to the Irish Government, investitures continued until that of King George VI in 1936. The last surviving Knight, the Duke of Gloucester, died in 1974. Besides the current Sovereign who is still the Head of the Order, there is an Ulster King of Arms at the College of Arms in London, who is the Order's Registrar and Knight Attendant. The British Government made a number of efforts to revive the Order, the most important attempt occurring in 1927. Lord Granard, a Knight of St Patrick, a member of the Irish Senate, and a trusted go-between for the Irish and British Governments, believed a good chance existed of getting Free State approval to revive the Order.

Of particular interest to us is memorandum S.3926 in the Irish Archives. This states that in 1927 Lord Granard wrote to W.T. Cosgrave, the Irish Prime Minister, with a proposal to revive the Order. Granard told Cosgrave that the Irish government could buy back the Crown Jewels for the bargain price of £2000-£3000, but only if Cosgrave permitted the rebirth of the Order. Cosgrave declined the offer for political reasons. No doubt Granard made his offer with the full support of the British Government, and therefore the offer was authentic and the jewels were available at that time.

We can infer three facts from this memorandum. First, the jewels were intact in 1927, and therefore had not been broken up for sale on the black market. This implies that there was no monetary motive to the theft. Secondly, if the Irish declined to recover the jewels, then the

British Government would do so, especially at this price. Thirdly, the historical value of the jewels at the time was put at £50,000, and the break up value amounted to at least £10,000. Thus, the recovery price of £2,000-£3,000 makes no commercial sense. To take the memorandum at face value, we would have to believe that a jewel fence, after hoarding the gems for twenty years, was prepared to forego nearly £7,000.

The implications of the memorandum are: Granard made a genuine offer of the jewels to the Irish Government. However, the notion of a jewel dealer in Amsterdam is a smoke screen. The palace had already recovered the jewels prior to 1927, but for the same reasons, that a blanket of silence covers the entire case, they had to find a way to reintroduce them into the public domain. The palace and the British Government decided it best not to inform the public how they came to possess the jewels. Awkward questions, such as when did they get them back and why did they keep it secret, were best left unasked rather than unanswered. In allowing the Irish Government to 'officially' recover the jewels, the British authorities would have no explaining to do. Instead they could simply offer their congratulations to Mr Cosgrave and his colleagues for a job well done.

Lord Jenkins, in his biography of Asquith, relates how the Prime Minister liked to write to the King on matters which he thought interested His Majesty. After a cabinet meeting in March of 1908, he wrote to inform His Majesty that the cabinet had decided not to increase the reward for the return of the Crown Jewels. Clearly Asquith thought the King would be pleased that they had not increased the reward, but why? Surely the King would welcome the return of his treasure? To make sense of this, it is possible that the Crown had already recovered the jewels. Asquith's note to the King leads us to suggest that his Majesty recovered his jewels early in 1908.

During the course of our research, a 'high official' in London confirmed, off the record, that this was the case. However, the official position has not changed. The Central Chancery of the Orders of Knighthood in London and wrote the following:

Central Chancery of
The Orders of Knighthood
St. James' Palace, SW1A 1BH
Telephone 020 7930 4832
Fax 020 7839 2983
11th April, 2001
Reference: 3/1/01

Dear Mr Hannafin,

Thank you for your letter dated 6th April, 2001.

The case of the theft of the 'Irish Crown Jewels' from Dublin in 1907 has been considered closed for many decades and there is no reward on offer for their recovery. It is widely thought that the jewels were taken to the Netherlands shortly after their removal and broken up. If this was the case then it would not be possible to identify any components of the jewels now. There are various other theories as to what may have happened to the jewels but there is no longer any expectation that they may be recovered.

You may like to read chapter 6 of Peter Galloway's book *The Most Illustrious Order* published by the Unicorn Press, 21 Afghan Road, London SW11 0QD, which contains what is probably the most detailed account of the circumstances surrounding the theft.

Yours sincerely,
Jeremy Bagwell Purefoy, MVO.

Therefore, Mr Purefoy's theory fails to explain how Lord Granard was in a position to offer the jewels to the Irish government in 1927.

Many of the characters involved directly or indirectly in the events surrounding the theft subsequently met with untimely misfortune. It would appear that for some, King Edward's baubles were not only tainted by their origins, but also bore a curse.

PEIRCE MAHONY, THE CORK HERALD,
AND THE O'MAHONY

Sir Arthur lost his post after the inquiry, Goldney and Shackleton had resigned earlier, yet Peirce Mahony, the Cork Herald, surprisingly remained. Why the Irish administration allowed him to stay on after the inquiry is puzzling. Possibly they feared another confrontation with his tenacious father, The O'Mahony, or more probably, everybody, including the King, had had enough of this dreadful affair, so wishing to avoid rekindling the flames, they left him in office. Sir Arthur strongly believed that his Unionist friends would reinstate him as Ulster, and Mahony waited for his uncle's return. However, when the Liberals were re-elected in 1910, Mahony resigned.

After the Cork Herald resigned, he was called to the Bar in Dublin. Returning to County Kerry, he lived with his wife, Ethel, in Kilmurry House, just twenty miles from Kilmorna House where Sir Arthur now lived. In April 1914 he assisted Sir Arthur with legal advice on an upcoming confrontation with the Attorney-General, when Sir Arthur planned to reveal 'certain facts'.

In July 1914, Mahony spent three weeks visiting his father at Grange Con, County Wicklow, and on Saturday 26 July, Charles McAuley, the estate manager, saw Mahony put on a coat and depart in the direction of the lake bordering his father's estate. McAuley had reminded Mahony earlier in the morning to have his luggage brought to the station for his departure the following day. The estate manager recalled that Mahony seemed in fine spirits, and while he often took his shotgun on the lake to shoot pigeons and rabbits, he had not seen him take the gun that evening.

While out boating on the lake, Mahony called out to Joe Dunne, a twelve-year-old local boy, to request the ladies of the house to join him for a row. Young Joe obeyed and went to tell the ladies.

Afterwards, the boy said he also did not recall seeing a gun. The four ladies went in search of Mahony but not finding him, they sent for McAuley. After searching, they discovered Mahony's body partly submerged in the lake about three yards from the bank close to the locked boathouse. Atlantas Blagoff, one of The O'Mahony's Bulgarian orphans, helped McAuley drag the body into the boat. At the time, Blagoff said he saw a shotgun resting on a low barbed-wire fence that skirted the lake, quite near to the boathouse. Picking it up, he noticed that both barrels had been discharged. Both blasts had hit Mahony in the chest, blowing his heart apart.

The coroner called an inquest into Mahony's death. Doctors who carried out an autopsy testified that the body had moved between the first and second discharge of the shotgun and that the wounds were not deliberately self inflicted. Strangely, the coroner did not call a police officer to explain how the shotgun remained resting on the barbed wire after it had discharged both barrels. The Jury at the inquest returned a verdict of 'accidental death' through gun-shot wounds, with no blame being attached to any person. They advanced the following theory: Mahony had rested the shotgun on the barbed wire fence before crossing over it, and while in the boat he attempted to lift the gun over the fence by catching the muzzle, then with the boat possibly receding, a protruding piece of barbed wire snapped the triggers. A mark on the stock of the gun and near the triggers supported this theory.

Since Mahony was an experienced hunter, he would hardly have lifted the loaded gun with its two barrels aimed straight at his chest. Also, McAuley said he saw him leave the great hall without a firearm. Atlantas Blagoff saw the gun by the fence but when he examined it, he saw no marks on the stock. There are grave doubts that a shotgun discharging its two barrels in sequence could recoil in such a way that it again came to rest on the wire fence. However, the motive for foul play remains the same but if so, the motive remains obscure. Peirce Mahony's will, made in 1912, gives us no clue. We note that the authors Bamford and Bankes also found the official account of Mahony's death unacceptable. In the course of their review, they advanced a number of possible theories to explain his death, the most intriguing being that Mahony had discovered the identity of the thief of the Crown Jewels. Unfortunately, they had no supporting evidence.

The battling exploits of The O'Mahony deserve a book in their own right, but we leave this to others. As an ardent Nationalist, he strongly disapproved of his son serving the British Crown, but in truth, he never enjoyed a particularly warm relationship with him. In 1900, he conceived the idea of adopting a boy who had a beautiful singing voice and of giving him the O'Mahony name. Incensed by this threat to their future, his two sons, Peirce and Dermot, plotted to kidnap the boy. A furious row ensued that threatened the family's stability, but

Sir Arthur intervened to restore the peace. The boy was adopted and later became an officer in the British Army. The O'Mahony, disappointed with all his sons, departed for Bulgaria to espouse their struggle for independence from the Turks. Though he did much for Bulgaria, he eventually had a falling out with King Ferdinand, and never returned. Even in his last years, The O'Mahony proved game for a fight. Although he belonged to the Greek Orthodox Church for many years, he had arranged with a Church of Ireland rector to receive communion according to the Anglican rite. In 1927, a new rector put a stop to the practice, and The O'Mahony fought the decision with all his old zeal. The rector won the battle, prompting The O'Mahony to join the Catholic Church before he died in 1930. In death, however, The O'Mahony and his son Peirce achieved what eluded them in life, for they rest in peace, side by side, in Ballynure Graveyard.

For no recorded reason, The O'Mahony reneged on his pledge to give a pension to Sir Arthur Vicars. Everything we have learnt about the man leads us to assert that he was a man of his word. Thus, he must have had extraordinary reasons for not fulfilling his promise. Whatever these reasons were, Sir Arthur knew nothing about them, and he remained resentful about the pension for the rest of his life. Sir Arthur in his will bitterly recounted his brother's broken promise.

FRANCIS BENNETT-GOLDNEY

Francis Bennett-Goldney, the Athlone Pursuivant, had never been a suspect in the theft. He was a man of means and had little opportunity to access the key of the safe. However, he had only held the position of Athlone for five months when the jewels were stolen. In hindsight, maybe he should have been a suspect, for after his death, some items from the Canterbury Archives were traced to his estate. Vicars at least thought Goldney to be innocent and said so in a letter he wrote to Fuller on 6 July 1909:

I do not suspect Goldney for he had no opportunity of access to the safe or any key as S. had — and was only once in Dublin (for 3 days in May) in the year of the robbery. Besides Goldney has money and is a wealthy fellow . . .

Goldney had applied for the post of Athlone Pursuivant in November 1905; however, it was not until February 1907 that a vacancy arose and he was appointed.

The scandal in Dublin hardly touched Goldney at all, and he continued on as Mayor of Canterbury until 1911. In the 1910 General Election he won a seat as an independent Unionist and held it until he died in a car crash in France in 1918. A year earlier, he had been appointed Honorary Military Attaché at the British Embassy in Paris.

CAPTAIN RICHARD GORGES

Captain Richard Howard Gorges, the infamous companion of Frank Shackleton, had a most distinguished Norman pedigree. Settling in Ireland, centuries ago, the Gorges had occupied many important posts. One of his ancestors, Sir Ferdinand de Gorges, had discovered the Province of Maine. However, Captain Gorges, failing to live up to the exalted standards of his ancestors, suffered the ignominy of having his name deleted from the family tree.

Gorges has the rare distinction in the Crown Jewels affair of being the only person claiming to have stolen the jewels. He had little loyalty to any cause and after leaving the British Army offered his services to the Irish Republican cause. It was during a meeting with the Republican, Bulmer Hobson, that Gorges claimed that he and Shackleton stole the jewels and pawned them in Amsterdam, stipulating that they were not to be broken up for a period of three years. During our research a member of the Gorges family told us that Captain Gorges had boasted to family members about his part in the theft. Although Sir Arthur considered Gorges morally depraved, he falls short of calling him a thief. In a letter to Fuller, Sir Arthur gives his estimation of Gorges:

Capt. Gorges was in Dublin on 30th June and was a great friend of S's and hand in glove with him. I had refused to let Gorges into my house for fully a year before the robbery and warned S. that I considered him morally a bad lot and to have nothing to say to him. Gorges was never in the Office to my knowledge for over a year before the robbery and I don't see how he could have got in to do the job after office hours. Shackleton, of course, could have gone there any time and, if seen could have said that he had come only for his letters . . . Of course it is easy to be wise after the event, but who on earth would have guessed that Shackleton or Gorges were perhaps plotting a robbery?

After the disappearance of the jewels, the British Army dismissed Gorges, and he drifted into the shadowy world of chronic alcoholism. With the outbreak of the War in 1914, the Army, overlooking his appalling record, commissioned him as a Captain, but this was short lived and he was discharged in 1915. Returning to London, he rented rooms at Holly Hill in Hampstead and soon became well known in the area as a notorious and violent drunk.

On the morning of 14 July 1915, a warrant was issued for his arrest after he created a disturbance by shooting off a revolver in the night. Detective Young and Detective Sargent Askew arrived at his lodging to arrest him. As the detectives went upstairs to his room, Gorges spotted them from the landing and discharged his revolver, fatally wounding Detective Young. However, the other detective, with the help of a lodger, managed to disarm Gorges and arrest him. Even while in custody at the police station Gorges boasted that he had enough rounds to shoot the whole police force.

At his trial on 18 September 1915, he was found guilty of the lesser crime of manslaughter and sentenced to twelve years penal servitude. In defence, his counsel stated that Gorges had enlisted in the army at the impressionable age of fourteen and while on duty in South Africa had suffered a severe attack of sunstroke. From that time onwards he was subject to violent headaches and when under the influence of drink suffered a condition of extreme elation. During the trial, Gorges stated that when he drank whisky it made him practically mad. On the day of the shooting he said that he had drunk whisky, brandy, stout and ale. Major Ritchie, his D.S.O., said he knew the prisoner in 1896 as a volunteer in the Matabele War and at that time he seemed normal, but when he met him again during the Boer war, he noticed a marked change in his condition. Dr Seymour of Hampstead testified that the prisoner was a patient of his and that he was suffering from chronic alcoholism.

On 29 December 1916, an Inspector Sanders, C.I.D. applied for reimbursement of £7 13s 7d in regard to expenses he incurred in interviewing two prisoners. We believe the explanation he gave below must refer to Gorges:

A convict now undergoing sentence made a statement to the effect that a fellow convict had often spoken to him regarding the larceny of the Dublin Crown Jewels, intimating that he was concerned in the theft and could assist in their recovery . . . As the convicted criminal had been associated with certain persons in Dublin at the time of the larceny I communicated with the Dublin Metropolitan Police, and Chief Inspector Murphy of that force, who was employed in the original investigation, came to London and, with Inspector Sanders of this Department, interviewed both convicts and other persons, both in and out of London, and made very careful and thorough enquiry without I regret to say, any very good result. Inspector Murphy was engaged in the original enquiry with the late Chief Inspector Kane and was acquainted with the facts.

Gorges' claims that he stole the jewels are probably false. Had he been involved in the theft, he would have used the information, either selling it to a newspaper or writing a book. On his release from prison, he survived on the reluctant generosity of his family, and lived on until the 1950s. In the end, life became unbearable for him and he decided to end it all, by throwing himself under a train at Edgeware Road station. His family, however, were not too distraught by his decision, one member of the family remarked that 'the least he could have done was to do it at a decent address like South Kensington Station.'

CHIEF INSPECTOR JOHN KANE
Chief Inspector John Kane remained at Scotland Yard until he retired in December 1911, after 37

years service. Apparently he never disclosed the identity of the individual named in his report.

SIR ANTONY PATRICK MACDONNELL

Officially, MacDonnell did not escape censure for the disastrous press emanating from his 'secret Inquiry'. King Edward's public reaction to the Commission of Inquiry was scathing. His Majesty's biographer, Sir Sidney Lee, sums it up as follows:

> The whole episode showed extreme incapacity on the part of the Irish Government. Neither the Irish Secretary, Mr Birrell, nor the Under-Secretary, Sir Antony MacDonnell, nor above all, the Lord-Lieutenant, came well out of the matter. The King's anger was fully justified.

Ever since the failure of the second Irish Council Bill, MacDonnell had found his relationship with Birrell less and less satisfactory. In February 1908, *The Irish Times* reported that MacDonnell had tendered his resignation and only stayed on until his replacement could be found. The newspaper said that the two men had reached a state of 'incompatibility'. Disappointed with his achievements in Ireland, MacDonnell retired in the summer of 1908. However, before he left, there was a welcome surprise when the following letter arrived at his official residence from the Prime Minister:

> Under-Secretary's Lodge in Phoenix Park
> Downing Street
> Whitehall
> June 11 1908

My dear Sir Antony,

It gives me great pleasure to propose to you that with the King's approval, that on the occasion of His Majesty's approaching birthday, you should be raised to the peerage. It is a matter of sincere satisfaction to me to be the medium of conveying to you this well-deserved tribute to your long and valued services to the crown.

Yours Sincerely
H.H. Asquith

MacDonnell replied to the Prime Minister the following day:

My dear Mr Asquith,

Your letter of the 11th reached me this morning. I am very greatly honoured by the proposal you make which I accept . . .

In the end, MacDonnell's five unsuccessful years as Permanent Under-Secretary had ended with the greatest triumph of his career. He took the title Lord Swinford after a town near where he was born and reared. In the previous 300 years, no other Irish Catholic of humble origins, who openly favoured some form of home rule had received such an honour. (Lord O'Hagan, another Catholic, had a much more prestigious pedigree, and as a jurist he turned against his former home rule allies.) It is a mystery that MacDonnell should be so honoured, considering the resentment that the Unionists, the Irish Nationalists, his superior, Mr Birrell, and the Home Secretary held towards him at the time, and it is not known who suggested his name to the King. Prime Minister Asquith scarcely knew him and had been chastised by His Majesty for wanting to appoint too many Liberal peers. Birrell resented MacDonnell; Gladstone thought that he had mishandled the inquiry, while Lord Aberdeen could not recommend him as he himself was out of favour with the King. One can only conclude that despite His Majesty's public comments on the inquiry, MacDonnell had somehow found favour in the palace. *The Irish Times*, which two years earlier had tried to have him run out of the country, now commented that this was an honour MacDonnell richly deserved.

In retirement, he became an advisor to the British Government on Irish affairs and after the Republican Easter Rising, played an active role in the treaty negotiations. When the Irish Free State was formed he was offered a seat in the Irish Senate but declined it.

SIR JAMES DOUGHERTY

After MacDonnell resigned, his assistant, Sir James Dougherty, overcoming considerable competition, became the new Permanent Under-Secretary for Ireland. However, he had a most undistinguished career in this role. One fascinating incident that happened during his tenure concerned the Howth gun-running in July 1914. The Irish administration, having learnt that the Republicans intended to import guns at Howth, dispatched troops to intercept them. The troops dispersed the volunteers but found few of the guns. As a detachment of the Scottish Borderers turned into Bachelor's Walk on their way back to the barracks, an angry crowd of Dubliners confronted them. The soldiers opened fire, killing three and wounding 32 others.

In the Castle, the two men in overall charge of the operation were none other than Dougherty and Harrel. The Liberal Irish administration and Lord Aberdeen repudiated the actions of the soldiers and held their superiors responsible. However, they declined to punish Dougherty, the man ultimately responsible for policing Ireland, and instead dismissed his subordinate, William Harrel. The willingness of Lord Aberdeen and his Liberals to distinguish between the superior and his subordinate in this fashion implies that the Irish administration feared dismissing Dougherty.

THE ABERDEENS
Surviving the fallout from the theft, the Aberdeens completed a nine-year tour of duty in Ireland. Disliked by Chief Secretary Birrell, they were eventually pushed out of office. However, this unpleasant termination came as a blessing in disguise, because they left Ireland just before the

1916 Easter Rising. In his papers, Lord Aberdeen makes no mention of the Crown Jewels affair, and in his memoirs he makes only a passing reference. Of all the Viceroys to govern Ireland, the Aberdeens are remembered as being by far the most popular. Lady Aberdeen is still remembered fondly for her empathy and compassion. After leaving Ireland, Lord Aberdeen had ambitions of becoming a Duke; however, he had to settle for the title Marquess of Aberdeen and Temair. Despite the rumours, their son, Lord Haddo, generally escaped the Crown Jewel fiasco unscathed. He became an elder of the Church of Scotland and when the Liberals prepared to nominate hundreds of peers in the constitutional battles of 1910, Haddo's name was among them. He succeeded to the title and in his latter years devoted his life to a multitude of local issues, outlived his two wives and died in 1965, a much-respected Scottish nobleman. He had no heir and was succeeded by his younger brother.

FRANK SHACKLETON

The shadow of suspicion stalked Frank Shackleton for the rest of his life. At Lord Aberdeen's request he resigned his post as Dublin Herald. The Commission of Inquiry made a specific point of exonerating him of any part in the theft of the Crown Jewels. Despite the fact that Chief Inspector Kane, in his testimony, declared Shackleton to be innocent, Sir Arthur went to his grave convinced of his erstwhile friend's guilt.

Ambition drove the Shackleton brothers, Ernest and Frank, the one destined to earn enduring distinction for his daring and determination, and the other destined to disappear in disgrace for his disreputable dealings. Ernest, the renowned explorer, won an honoured place in history for his heroic efforts to reach the South Pole, and his herculean struggle to save his stranded crew. Frank continued his predatory ways, lightening the pockets of those unfortunate homosexuals who befriended him, and borrowing £1,000 from a Miss Browne. Although he hurt many influential friends, it was his defrauding of Miss Browne that eventually brought him down, compelling him to drift into oblivion.

After the Inquiry, Shackleton, 31 and still in his prime, continued living the high life. He maintained his close friendship with Lord Gower and Frank Hird. When Gower's financial adviser died, he gave power of attorney to Shackleton. Thus, the wolf found himself guarding the sheep. Never particularly strong in the face of temptation, Shackleton milked Gower dry, mortgaged his properties and left him almost bankrupt. In the middle of February, 1910, Lord Gower first became aware of his financial ruin when his stockbrokers, Rowe and Pitman, sued him for £10,000 owing on some shares. Shackleton, as his financial advisor, had exhausted Gower's wealth, leaving him with worthless shares. The court heard that Shackleton had even stooped to intercepting Gower's mail while visiting his home at Penhurst in Kent.

In stark contrast to the clean bill given to Shackleton by the Commissioners and Kane, the trial judge commented: 'If 'foozle' meant getting all of someone else's property for oneself', referring to Lord Ronald's nickname for Shackleton, 'Mr. Shackleton deserved the title.'

Frank Shackleton seems to have enjoyed the protection of King Edward. However, when His Majesty died on 6 May 1910, Shackleton's world began to decline. He received a letter from Mr Alden, a stockbroker in the City, whose firm had agreed to underwrite his latest venture — The North Mexico Land and Timber Company. Mr Alden told him that his firm could no longer underwrite the shares of his company 'owing to a variety of circumstances, of which the death of King Edward was by no means least.' Whatever protection Shackleton had secured with the King, it ended with His Majesty's death. On 6 August, Shackleton applied for bankruptcy. The Court, declaring him bankrupt, estimated that he had debts amounting to £85,000, a staggering amount of money at the time for a man without the backing of property.

At the proceedings, Shackleton revealed his darker side to those whose trust he had betrayed. Lord Gower, embittered with Shackleton, wished to attend the proceedings but illness prevented him from travelling. He sent Frank Hird, his adopted son, in his place. Hird accompanied Miss Browne to the courthouse, and during the proceedings Shackleton approached his two victims to give them a hideously callous grin. Utterly inflamed, Hird waited outside the courthouse, and confronted Frank, his brother Ernest, and one of his sisters. He accused Shackleton of being a thief, and later wrote postcards to Ernest accusing him of taking part in his brother's deceptions.

Ernest Shackleton countered with a libel suit. Meanwhile, Sir Arthur heard all the news from his friends, Lord Gower and Frank Hird. All three were ecstatic that the Shackletons were now getting their due deserts causing Sir Arthur to express his delight and expectations in a letter to his friend Fuller:

I hear there is a libel action coming on of Sir E. Shackleton against a man — and the defendant tells me that my affair is bound to come up and that he will help me as far as possible. He promises revelations . . . unless E.S. funks an exposure . . .

In the end it was Hird who evaded the issue and wrote a letter of apology to Ernest and the matter was dropped.

Frank took a strange course of action during the public examination of his bankruptcy. He persuaded the court to postpone the hearing until 4 May 1911, but when the time came he absconded to Portuguese West Africa. Why he did so is puzzling, because at the time he faced no criminal charges, and the court had already declared him bankrupt. We suspect an official might have suggested to Shackleton that he take up residence elsewhere to forestall further charges.

However, Miss Browne had not been party to any arrangement, and a year later she charged Shackleton with fraud, obtaining a warrant for his arrest in September 1912. The charges against him stated that together with an accountant, Thomas John Garlick, he had been entrusted with £12,778 of Miss Browne's funds for the purpose of investing and had fraudulently converted £5,778 of this to their own use. Acting on the British warrant, the Portuguese authorities arrested him in October, and jailed him in Benguela. In December, Detective Inspector Cooper arrived from Scotland Yard to extradite him and on his arrival, found Shackleton in poor health. He had contracted malaria and the prison conditions were so appalling that Shackleton, rather then wait for an extradition hearing, volunteered to go back to England to stand trial.

Upon Frank Shackleton's arrival in London, his father posted £1,000 surety for his son and secured his release. On 21 October both Shackleton and Garlick were brought before the Central Criminal Court on a charge of defrauding Miss Browne. In summing up, Mr Justice Horridge gave a radically different appraisal of Shackleton's character from that given by the three Commissioners in 1908. He stated that the defendant 'had violated all the rules of commercial morality and that he had further deluded and brought to comparative poverty a lady who treated him with affection and whose confidence he abused.' He then sentenced Francis Richard Shackleton, aged 36, and one-time Dublin Herald, to fifteen months hard labour and his accomplice, Garlick, to nine months. Probably the most interesting feature of the trial is that Shackleton faced no additional charges.

After his release from prison, Shackleton's star continued to wane. He changed his name to Mellor after a relative on his mother's side, Lydia Mellor. Then pretending he had returned from foreign parts, he obtained a position in the City through his brother's influence. However, in due course, Ernest repudiated him.

In 1934 he moved to Chichester, where he opened an antique shop in a building belonging to the Cathedral. His interest in heraldry continued and as a sideline he offered genealogical services and produced Coats of Arms. Residents in Chichester recall him as being 'slightly built and with grey hair and a moustache, always neatly suited and hatted. A certain air of dignity about him — in fact, gentlemanly.' Living in more modest circumstances than he wished, he died in June 1941, aged 64, in St Richard's Hospital. He is buried under the name Francis Richard Shackleton-Mellor along with a sister, Amy Violet Shackleton, in Chichester Cemetery. The simple epitaph on his humble tombstone seems very much at variance with his former lifestyle: It reads 'He lived for others'.

However, even 60 years after his death, the name Frank Shackleton is still able to grab the attention of the media: on 9 September 2000, a headline in *The Irish Times* read: 'Medal belonged to suspect in Crown Jewel Case.' The article was in relation to an auction of collectables and militaria at Adams' salesrooms and mentions:

> Among the most curious is that attached to lot 153, a Queen's South Africa Medal presented to a member of the Royal Irish Fusiliers in 1901. The recipient was Lieutenant Frank Shackleton, brother of the Antarctic explorer . . . but a somewhat less reputable character, described in the catalogue as 'an avaricious, unscrupulous rogue, he was one of the chief suspects after the theft of the Irish Crown Jewels'.

Accompanying the medal was a twenty-page transcript of his evidence given to the Commission of Inquiry. The sale caused some family controversy as a member of the Shackleton family thought that he possessed Frank's medal and that the one for auction was a fake. However, upon examination, it was proved that the medal that was up for auction was authentic as it had Frank's name engraved on the back. So whose medal did the relative possess? It appears that it was customary that if one lost or had his original medal stolen, a duplicate medal was issued, without the inscription. We can assume that this is the case here. Whether Frank lost it, had it stolen or pawned it is still anyone's guess. Interest in Frank is still strong as his medal made three times its pre-auction estimate.

Sir Arthur Vicars and the Press

Sir Arthur Vicars never resigned himself to the loss of his position as Ulster King of Arms, continuing his fight to regain office to the end. Two years after the theft, while on a visit to London, he met Herbert Gladstone by chance, and the Home Secretary concurred with him about Shackleton's guilt. After the meeting, Sir Arthur wrote an intriguing letter to his friend Fuller:

> . . . A cabinet minister the other day told me he suspected the thief and he was right — I would give you his name in confidence — he is the only gentleman in the govt of cads.

This was undoubtedly Herbert Gladstone, the Home Secretary. Gladstone's position is at great odds with that of Chief Inspector John Kane. If Gladstone had agreed with the Irish administration in 1907 that the prime suspect in the crime was Shackleton, then the insistence of the Home Office in bringing Chief Inspector John Kane back on the case was all the more remarkable and puzzling, since Kane would not hear of any suspicion falling on Shackleton.

After Edward VII died, Sir Arthur petitioned George V to grant a second Inquiry, but his efforts were blocked by Birrell and other cabinet ministers. Sir Arthur believed strongly that if the Tories (Unionists) returned to power he would get fair treatment. On 12 September 1909, Sir Arthur wrote to Fuller:

. . . I don't suppose I shall get any redress until the Unionists come in, when they can't well refuse me . . .

This confidence in his Unionist allies possibly persuaded his nephew Peirce Mahony to stay on until the elections of 1910. After the Unionists lost that election, the Cork Herald resigned his post without giving any explanation. Sir Arthur's confidence in his Unionist allies must have been severely tested when he again sought the support of the Knights who had signed the original petition. Of the twelve original signatories still living at the time, seven did not sign the second petition. Unlike his father, George V was sympathetic to the petition and even his private Secretary, Ponsonby, signed it. However, a surprising signatory to the second petition was Walter Long, the head of the Irish Unionists. Long had only stayed six months in Ireland as the Chief Secretary, and can have had little contact with Sir Arthur, yet he obligingly signed. It was possibly Long's support that gave Sir Arthur hope of regaining office if the Unionists were returned to power.

Although Sir Arthur's second petition was not entertained by George V, he did get the opportunity of having his day in court. On 11 November 1912, the *London Mail* published an article in which the following was stated:

What happened in Dublin Castle the night before the Crown Jewels were stolen? And why the lady who carried out such an elaborate

277

scheme of revenge against Sir Arthur Vicars was allowed to go unpunished . . . Why did Lord and Lady Aberdeen display such extraordinary vindictiveness against Sir Arthur Vicars when their son, Lord Haddo, did all he could to vindicate the accused man?

Sir Arthur issued a writ for libel and the paper chose to stand behind what they had published. In the article, the paper alleged that Sir Arthur had a mistress named Molly or Malone, and that he and Lady Haddo were on intimate terms. In a fit of jealousy, Molly stole the jewels, and Sir Arthur helped her to escape to France.

On 4 July 1913, the case was heard, but at the trial, the editor of the paper did an about-turn stating that no attempt would be made to justify their statements. Sir Arthur, Lord Haddo and Lady Haddo were present and gave evidence. It is fascinating that Sir Arthur always wanted to get into court to have his side of the story aired, yet when given the opportunity to blame Shackleton, who was by then a convicted felon, he declined. When questioned if he had any idea where the jewels were, he replied 'that he had not the slightest idea what become of them'. In light of this, one must conclude that Mr Birrell was correct in his assessment that Sir Arthur would not willingly take part in any inquiry.

Sir Arthur was awarded £5,000 in damages, equivalent to ten years his annual salary as Ulster King of Arms. Why the newspaper insisted on going on with the trial is a mystery, as they had no case. Despite the bitterness of Sir

Arthur's dismissal, his relationship with Lord Haddo remained strong enough for his Lordship to agree to testify in the case. This is a direct repudiation of the allegation in the *New York Times* of 19 January 1908. The article states:

I am sure that a certain Lord, who is the son of an Earl, is the person whom all Dublin believes could tell how they were taken from the safe and where they are now. The story runs that this Lord has a strong animosity toward Sir Arthur Vicars and would be glad to have him turned out of his office.

It is further said that politics figures distinctly in the regalia affair. Indeed, there is talk of a political vendetta in which the names of a number of persons of high titles are mentioned. All these names may be made public, but there is a strenuous effort going on to hush the affair, and it may prove successful.

The New York Times was not the only American paper interested in the Crown Jewels affair. We quote the following from *The Gaelic American*, well known for its anti-British stance.

Meanwhile as Shackleton was leaving the inquiry, he was called aside by a detective and led to another part of the Castle, where, Mr William V. Harrel, the Assistant Commissioner of the Dublin Metropolitan Police, was holding a secret inquiry. Here Mr Shackleton's whole private life was turned inside out — evidence of his disgusting misconduct was dragged to light and after having been cross examined by the detectives at great length he was let go with the admonition to leave the country as quickly as possible.

The Nationalist newspaper then went on to report under a bold heading; Argyll, the King's Brother-in-law:

The Chief Secretary Mr Birrell has described Shackleton as an 'abandoned ruffian' yet this abandoned ruffian has been the guest of Lord Aberdeen at Haddo House and on one occasion left there with the Duke of Argyll who is a brother-in-law of His Most Gracious Majesty, Edward VII, of England. The Duke of Argyll is a man of very bad reputation, to say the least of it, and it is to shield such 'abandoned aristocratic ruffians' that a public inquiry was refused, and that the men who stole the jewels were allowed by the police to escape. If Shackleton and Gorges were arrested they could tell a story about their titled associates that would make the rake Edward VII blush.

Both the English parties were anxious to oblige the King and for their own sake to have this whole matter silenced . . .

The paper then named all those concerned in this conspiracy of silence, giving Lord Haddo a prominent role. Rumours in Dublin pointed at Lord Haddo, and on 1 April 1908, Birrell had to defend the charge in the House of Commons:

Birrell: The robbery occurred between June eleventh and July sixth, 1907, and Lord Haddo had lived in Scotland, without intermission, from March seventh until December seventh.

Mr Ginnell, Nationalist MP and a thorn in Birrell's side, asked: On what grounds, except Inspector Kane's report, did the Chief Secretary ask Lord Haddo to say that he was absent from Dublin at the time?'

Mr. Birrell: I inquired about the movements of Lord Haddo because, I regret to say, in some infamous newspaper in this country his name was connected with the theft.

Mr. Ginnell: Why was not Lord Haddo produced before the Commission?

To which Mr Birrell, refused to reply.

HEALY AND CAMPBELL

One final curiosity in this whole business is the role of Tim Healy, the Nationalist MP, and one of Sir Arthur's two barristers at the Commission of Inquiry. We can find no evidence that Mr Healy pressed the Chief Secretary in the House of Commons. *The Gaelic American* laments on the fact in its issue of 11 April 1908:

It is only fair to say that Mr William O'Brien is hardly aware of the facts, but John Redmond, William Redmond and T. M. Healy know at least enough of them to embarrass the Government if any of them felt inclined to do so.

Equally intriguing was the silence of Sir Arthur's leading barrister, Mr Campbell, who held the seat of Trinity College Dublin as a Unionist.

The silence from Healy on the Nationalist benches and Campbell on the Unionist benches demands an explanation: possibly the two men chose to protect their client by not speaking out in the House of Commons. In short, their obligations as lawyers overrode their partisan political interests. Referring back to Birrell's correspondence to Gladstone on 14 January 1908, two short comments relating to this issue were made: 'if Campbell and Healy (knowing their man and his case) had not thought it fit to withdraw because of the narrowness of the reference' and 'Whether if it came to the point, Vicars would ever appear before such an inquiry I feel at liberty to entertain grave doubts'. Recall that it was Birrell who sent Dougherty to talk to Sir Arthur's solicitor, Mr Meredith, and after their meeting, Meredith advised Sir Arthur to accept the offer of a pension and resign. While Meredith had given an undertaking to Dougherty not to tell anyone about the substance of their discussions, this did not apply to the barristers he instructed on behalf of Sir Arthur. Meredith was obliged to tell the barristers about this discussion, although in the strictest confidence. Knowing what they did, Healy and Campbell had to remain silent.

SIR ARTHUR'S WILL

Finally Sir Arthur's will of 14 May 1920 deserves mention. The accusation contained within it reads:

[I might have had more to dispose of had it not been for the outrageous way in which I was treated by the Irish Govt over the loss of the Irish Crown Jewels in 1907 backed up by the late King Edward VII whom I had always loyally & faithfully served — When I was made a scapegoat to save other departments responsible and when they shielded the real culprit and thief, Francis R. Shackleton (brother of the explorer who didn't reach the South Pole) — My whole life and work was ruined by this cruel misfortune and by the wicked and blackguardly acts of the Irish Government — I had sunk my whole fortune in my profession and left without any means but for the magnanimous conduct of my dear brother George Gun Mahony — I am unconscious of having done anyone wrong and my very misfortune arose from my being unsuspicious and trusting to a one time friend and official of my former office — I had hoped to leave a legacy my dear little dog; Ronnie had he not been taken from me this year — Well we shall meet in the next world].

The Rt Honourable Justice Dodd excluded this section from probate on 20 March 1922. Perhaps the High Court made this decision to protect Shackleton, who was still alive. However,

Shackleton died in 1941, and in 1947 Diarmuid Coffey, Deputy Keeper of the Records wrote this unusual note and attached it to the will:

Not to be opened without the order of a High Court Judge or of the Principal Probate Registrar.

Amazingly the Government of the Irish Republic continued to suppress the document until 1976. Perhaps this is the reason that Robert Brennan, despite having the valuable contacts in the Irish Government, failed to uncover any information.

15

CONCLUSION

When you have eliminated the impossible, whatever remains, however improbable, must be the truth.
                    Sir Arthur Conan Doyle (1859 – 1930)

Having presented the facts of the case, we now present our explanation for the disappearance of the Irish Crown Jewels. In this chapter, endnotes are used to explain, expand and elaborate on points made in the text, to enable the reader to choose how much of the detail he or she wishes to read.

THE JEWELS
We believe that the Crown secretly recovered the jewels, shortly after the theft. Once one accepts that the jewels were not broken up on the black market, one must infer that the theft had no monetary motive. Thus, we exclude the principal suspect, Shackleton, as the mastermind in the theft, because he would have sold the jewels immediately, and they would never have surfaced again.

MOTIVE FOR THE THEFT

We believe a hard-line faction of Unionists conspired to steal the Irish Crown Jewels with the intention of undermining support for home rule within the Liberal party's ranks. They intended to ruin the reputations of Lord Haddo and his father with a homosexual scandal. Lord Aberdeen, the most committed supporter of home rule, would have to resign, fatally weakening the home rule faction within the Liberal party and the British cabinet. MacDonnell's devolutionary schemes proposed giving the Lord Lieutenant new powers such as chairing the Irish Council and appointing 24 members to the Council. If the Council ever materialised, the Unionists had no wish to see Lord Aberdeen appoint 24 home rulers to the Council.

PRECEDENTS

The conspirators did not have to originate the idea of using a homosexual scandal to impale the Irish administration, because they had lived through a similar incident. In 1884, twenty years before the theft, a previous Liberal Government had become embroiled in a homosexual scandal at Dublin Castle. At the time, William O'Brien, a Nationalist, wrote an article charging high officials in the Castle with homosexual misconduct. Although the Liberals knew O'Brien was correct, they coerced the officials to sue for libel. In a cliff-hanger court case, O'Brien, at the last minute, succeeded in persuading his witnesses to testify and won the case. The verdict cast a pall of moral suspicion over the Liberals, and scandalised the nonconformist ranks in their party.

The more widely publicised trial of Oscar Wilde in 1895 exposed the British public's deep-seated intolerance to homosexuality. His trial unleashed a backlash against homosexuals that forced many public figures to flee to the continent. The hard-line Unionists had first-hand experience with the Wilde case, because one of their champions, Sir Edward Carson, had precipitated Wilde's downfall. In 1907 this intolerance had not yet softened when the Kaiser became bogged down in the Berlin scandal. Prince Eulenburg, an extremely influential voice in Imperial Germany, was ruined by the accusations. Intemperate comments in the press and from the King at the time made the Kaiser almost cancel his official visit to England, for fear of hostility from the British people. With the Berlin crisis on everybody's mind during 1907, the conspirators required no great feat of imagination to exploit a similar situation in Dublin Castle.

The tactic of exploiting homosexual accusations to destroy a man's reputation is not unique. The British Government's treatment of Sir Roger Casement in 1916 is similar. The authorities arrested, convicted and hanged Casement for treason. In an effort to prevent him from becoming an Irish martyr, they continued to impugn his reputation by publishing the infamous 'Black Diaries', which described his homosexual lifestyle, and there is considerable doubt as to their authenticity.

The finest Irish example of gaining political advantage by ruining an opponent's moral reputation came with the downfall of Parnell. The destruction of just one man left the Irish Nationalists in complete disarray for ten years, and even when they reformed, they were only a shadow of Parnell's party — more to be scorned than feared.

UNIONIST REACTIONS TO HOME RULE

That Unionists conspired to steal the King's jewels may seem far fetched but one must take into account the depth of their animosity to home rule. They regarded themselves as the 'loyal minority' and under no circumstances would they accept the proposition that they should or could be governed by the 'disloyal majority'. Shuddering at this prospect, they adopted a policy of 'No Surrender'. MacDonnell personally felt their fury when they demanded his dismissal for helping Lord Dunraven publish his devolution scheme. He reacted to their animosity by describing it as 'bigotry' against a 'Catholic'. In 1906, when he introduced his Irish Council Bill under the Liberal Government, the Unionists, considered it a Trojan Horse for home rule, and held mass rallies in protest. Later, as home rule ground its way through parliament in the period 1911 – 1914, the Unionists rebelled. The Leader of His Majesty's loyal opposition, Bonar-Law, incited sedition. Of the élite British regiments stationed at the Curragh Military

Camp in County Kildare, 57 mutinied by refusing to coerce the Province of Ulster. The police and army turned a blind eye to the Larne gun running by Northern Unionists; and high officials in the British police and military committed treason by helping Sir Edward Carson escape to Northern Ireland. The passion that drove these 'loyalists' to rebel against home rule simmered in 1907.

REVENGE

The Aberdeens had made themselves prime targets for a conspiracy. Lady Aberdeen, during her husband's tenure as Governor General of Canada, conspired to pave the way for the Liberal victory of Wilfred Laurier. In doing so, she destroyed the political aspirations of Sir Charles Tupper, a Canadian Tory, who was extremely well liked by the English Tories. On the principle of 'he who lives by the sword shall die by the sword', some of Tupper's friends in England would have had no scruples about using a homosexual scandal to destroy the Aberdeens.

THE CAST OF CONSPIRATORS

Our theory calls for the following cast to pull off the conspiracy. It was spearheaded by a group of prominent Unionist politicians. The work of the conspiracy was carried out by at least one of the most senior Castle policemen, a high-ranking official in the Home Office, another high ranking officer in Scotland Yard, Chief Inspector John

Kane, and a junior Castle policeman who stole the jewels.

THE CONSPIRATOR'S PLAN

A senior Unionist officer in Scotland Yard had access to the confidential file on high society homosexuals. This report linked Sir Arthur and Lord Haddo, and included Lord Aberdeen's name. With the Kaiser's imbroglio in Berlin fresh in the conspirators' minds, Haddo's Christmas prank inspired them to exploit a similar scandal in Dublin.

Unionist police officers had free run of the Castle and could easily access the Office of Arms unnoticed, provided they could get hold of the necessary keys. Through their inquires in Dublin and London, they became aware of Shackleton's vulnerability to blackmail and bribery. Shackleton, living far beyond his means, led the life of a homosexual playboy. He was teetering on the edge of bankruptcy, while his famous brother tried to raise financing for his South Pole expedition. His business dealings were dishonest, and he suffered only the mildest moral scruples. Any whiff of scandal could have disastrous financial consequences for Frank Shackleton and his brother. Therefore, the conspirators had no trouble bribing or coercing him to borrow Sir Arthur's keys.

Lord Aberdeen had invited His Majesty to Dublin to open the International Exhibition in May, but the King declined, promising to come at a later date — this opportunity of highlighting a scandal during the King's visit galvanised the conspirators into action. When Shackleton came over for the opening of the Exhibition, they coerced or bribed him to borrow Sir Arthur's keys, from which they made perfect copies. Then they waited for the announcement of the King's visit.

On 6 June 1907, the palace announced that the King planned to visit Ireland on 10 July. Intending to exploit the national publicity of a royal visit to create a sensational uproar, the conspirators stole the jewels in mid June. In the midst of the excitement caused by the theft, they intended to expose Lord Haddo's association with Sir Arthur's homosexual court. To this end, they carefully mimicked Haddo's Christmas prank, taking care to make the theft as neat as possible, and give every appearance that it was an inside job. They removed the blue ribbon from the diamond star to make the theft appear as a temporary extraction, implying that the thief would return the jewels at a later date, just as Lord Haddo had done at Christmas. They even went so far as to lock the safe after they had extracted the jewels.

With the discovery of the theft, they planned to orchestrate an uproar, and sensationalise the event. In the midst of this uproar they would shock Dublin and embarrass the Government and the King with rumours of a homosexual court in the Castle, and contend that out of a jealous rage, one of Sir Arthur's lovers stole the jewels. They would then allege that Lord Haddo belonged to this circle of homosexuals. Further implicating Haddo, they would reveal how he had stolen the jewels at Christmas to embarrass Sir Arthur, and that he had returned them the following day. Meanwhile, while the public feasted on sordid rumours of high-society homosexuals romping about in the Office of Arms, the jewels would mysteriously reappear. With the jewels recovered, the conspirators would now spread the rumour that the authorities had caught the thief and given him immunity provided he returned the jewels, thereby preventing Lord Haddo's name and lifestyle being exposed in a trial. Then they would leak rumours that the Lord Lieutenant had much to hide in the matter.

Shell shocked, the Irish administration would be running around frantically trying to contain an exploding scandal over which it had no control. The politicians would find themselves in the invidious position of trying to convince the public that they were as mystified as anybody that the thief had returned the jewels. Egged on by further leaks form the conspirators, the public, disbelieving all protestations of inno-cence, would condemn the Irish administration for covering up another homosexual scandal in the Castle that included accusations against Lord Aberdeen.

In the midst of this, King Edward would arrive in Ireland to face a full-blown homosexual scandal in his household, similar to the problems his nephew, Kaiser Wilhelm, faced in Berlin. His Majesty, having intemperately condemned the Kaiser's handling of the German scandal, would demand to be informed of all the facts and whether the homosexual rumours were true. Conveniently, Scotland Yard would be in a position to tell His Majesty, in the strictest confidence, that Aberdeen, Haddo, and Sir Arthur belonged to the same clique of prominent homosexuals. In the process they would accuse Haddo of taking the jewels out of spite. The King would act decisively by demanding his Viceroy's resignation, and the Lord Lieutenant, a prime supporter of home rule, would have to leave Ireland a ruined man.

HOW THE PLAN WENT WRONG

Ironically, the conspirators did such a convincing job of making the theft look like the work of an insider that Sir Arthur believed the disappearance was another 'Christmas prank' by one of his friends. He discovered the jewels missing on 27 June, but when he saw the blue ribbon lying in the morocco case, and the tissue paper all neatly folded, he concluded that this was another hoax. Sir Arthur, a man described by contemporaries as a fussy, fastidious individual, full of his own importance, had no desire or intention of becoming the laughing stock of the Castle for the second time. With the King coming in two weeks, he thought the 'prankster' would have to return the jewels, so he decided to bide his time.

Thus began a nerve-wracking game of bluff; with on one side, the conspirators waiting anxiously for the theft to be discovered, and on the other, Sir Arthur waiting resolutely for the return of the jewels. With the arrival of the King in Dublin only a week away, the conspirators decided to act. They sent their man, a castle policeman, back into the Office of Arms on 2 July to leave the front door unlocked, with the intention of forcing the discovery of the theft. Chief Inspector Kane in his testimony suggested that any reasonable person who found the front door open should have reported the incident to the police. However, Sir Arthur's nerve held up. Though he knew that he was duty bound to report the incident of the unlocked front door, he did nothing.

The conspirators, fearing their actions might obscure the royal visit and leave them in a position of committing sedition directly against the Crown, became desperate and made a major blunder. Their accomplices within the Castle police told them that Sir Arthur had not reported, even informally, the first break-in. They then ordered their man back into the Office of Arms for the second time to leave another, but stronger calling card. Following his superiors' commands, this officer again entered the office and now left the strong room open and the safe unlocked. As Chief Inspector Kane stated, 'they went one up' on their first effort to precipitate the discovery of the theft.

On the morning of 6 July, Sir Arthur tried to ignore the news that the strong room had been found open, but by the afternoon, his nerve gave way and he began to panic. He then made the appalling mistake of giving Stivey the key to the safe to ensure that he had somebody in attendance when he officially discovered the theft.

THE IMPROVISED PLAN

With the discovery of the theft coming so late, the conspirators ran out of time to effect their plan and return the jewels before the King would arrive. As loyalists, they were loath to embroil His Majesty personally in a major scandal, so they postponed leaking rumours of the homosexual court and implicating Haddo until the King left the country. They realised that this delay gave the Irish administration some room to cover up the scandal but they thought they could force a judicial inquiry later that would expose the homosexual problem and force Aberdeen to resign.

THE CONSPIRATORS MANAGE EVENTS

Once the theft was reported, the conspirators had to avert a thorough police investigation that might expose their man within the Castle police. In a masterful stroke, they left the entire police probe directionless and confused by ensuring that it had no lead investigator. By the time the Commission sat six months later, the Dublin investigation still had no obvious officer in charge who represented the efforts of the Irish police. None of the Dublin police officers, or their superiors, Harrel and Ross, offered the Commissioners of the Inquiry a theory as to how they thought the crime had happened.

Because the conspirators had purposely arranged the theft to appear as an inside job, they had to prevent the police from compiling a list of people that were legitimately present in Upper Castle Yard after 8pm on 5 July. Obviously, the sentries or policemen on duty outside the Office of Arms must have seen the thief, but because he was known to them, they considered his presence legitimate. If detectives compiled a short list of those present after 8pm, they had an excellent chance of including the name of the thief. This list might also indicate that no member of Sir Arthur's staff was present at this time. They took care of this problem by asking the sentries if they had seen anybody suspicious, instead of compiling a list of all those that they had seen.

THE ENGLISH CONNECTION

A robbery within the royal household involving the theft of the Monarch's jewels must inevitably draw Scotland Yard into the investigation. The conspirators in the Home Office and Scotland Yard ensured that their man, Chief Inspector John Kane, was assigned to the case.

Kane's first contribution to the conspiracy was to delay getting over to Ireland or sending an advance party of detectives to interview the sentries. By doing so he allowed the memories of the sentries and guards to fade, and with all the excitement over the King's visit, they were unable to recall whom they had seen in the Upper Castle Yard six days earlier. Recall that some years later, Kane confided to a friend that he might have solved the case had it not been for all the amateur detectives working in Dublin. The lack of professionalism in Dublin can hardly have come as a surprise to Kane and his superiors. Scotland Yard had established the 'Murder Squad' precisely because provincial forces lacked professional detectives.

Unlike the Dublin police, Kane had to go through the motions of conducting a professional investigation. He took notes and got statements from the witnesses. However, Kane's investigation was just a formality as he had arrived in Dublin with his case already solved. In his report he exposed Sir Arthur's homosexual court, and included Lord Haddo as a member. Naturally, when he submitted his report, the Lord Lieutenant was horrified. The Irish administration dismissed Kane, sent him back to London immediately, and returned the case to the Dublin police.

One of Kane's key roles in the conspiracy was to shield Shackleton from investigation. While in Dublin, he dismissed McEnnery's accusations against Shackleton, and persuaded the Dublin police that they were groundless. Fortunately for Kane, the Dublin detectives, having no knowledge of the homosexual link, went along with his contention that Shackleton had airtight alibis and could not have taken part in the theft.

Back in London, Kane still had to shield Shackleton repeatedly. When Sir Arthur visited Goldney, he used McEnnery's information to persuade his host of Shackleton's guilt. Subsequently, Kane had to fend off Sir Arthur, Goldney and Sir Arthur's brother, Major Vicars, all of whom, he testified at the Inquiry, 'pestered' him repeatedly with their accusations.

Into this climate of accusation came the anonymous telegram to Lord Aberdeen. This caused some panic among the conspirators. Shackleton, feeling uncomfortable with Sir Arthur and McEnnery's accusations, was beginning to crack and sent a subtle message in the 'Hadley Street' telegram that Aberdeen instantly recognised. Despite there being no Hadley Street in Dublin, Aberdeen pursued the matter vigorously, going so far as to enlist the assistance of the Home Secretary to trace the anonymous telegram.

Fortunately for the conspirators, their man in the Home Office took care of things. Although the Dublin authorities had dismissed Kane, Gladstone sent for the Chief Inspector to investigate the telegram. Kane covered up the situation by threatening Shackleton to remain silent, and then sending Aberdeen another telegram, but this time it was signed by A. Bullock Webster.

During the Inquiry Kane had to come to Shackleton's defence once again, by telling the Commissioners that he had found no evidence whatsoever to incriminate the young man. Kane's strong assurances helped the Commissioners to go beyond their terms of reference and state explicitly that Shackleton was an innocent man. Rarely can men get things so wrong, for over the next five years, Shackleton misappropriated Lord Gower's fortune, bankrupted his own company, was convicted of fraud over his dealings with Miss Browne, and went to jail for fifteen months hard labour. We find that the comments of the judges in Shackleton's later cases contrast diametrically with the comments made by the Commissioners.

THE MAN IN THE HOME OFFICE

The conspirator's man in the Home Office played a crucial role in other parts of the plan. He persuaded the Home Secretary that a Royal Commission of Inquiry was needed to clear things up. Once Gladstone received the Knights' petition, this official persuaded him to get involved in the case and to press for a Royal Commission. When Birrell, and subsequently the King, agreed to the Royal Commission, the conspirators had all but won the day. A Royal Commission would have unearthed the homosexual ring in Dublin and brought Aberdeen down. However, the King, following Aberdeen's warning, scuttled the Royal Commission, and they had to settle for a public inquiry.

Birrell's offer to allow Gladstone to appoint the third Commissioner delighted the conspirators. They chose Chester Jones, a London police magistrate, to represent the Home Office. Jones would follow orders and they instructed him to see that the inquiry was fully public, just as the Home Secretary wanted. During the Inquiry, Jones could show off his professional expertise

299

by questioning the police witnesses fully. When Kane took the stand, Jones had his chance to shine. As a police magistrate, he knew the routines of professional police officers like Kane. He would lead Kane step by step through his investigation, pressuring him to reveal the contents of his report. As the other Commissioners listened, Jones would draw out all the details concerning Sir Arthur's homosexual ring. The press would feast on this sordid scandal, and before long the Aberdeens would be shamed into leaving Ireland.

Arriving in Dublin, Chester Jones, following Gladstone's instructions, pressed the other Commissioners for an open inquiry. During the Inquiry, Jones played a very active part in the questioning of the police officers. Yet during Chief Inspector Kane's testimony, Jones sat strangely silent as the Solicitor General and Commissioner Starkie peppered Kane with questions. Jones had received instructions from the conspirators to abort the questioning of Kane; the conspiracy had come to an abrupt end.

WHY WAS THE CONSPIRACY ABORTED?
The Petition
To understand what went wrong in the conspiracy, we have to return to Sir Arthur and his Unionist friends in the Kildare Street Club. From the outset, Sir Arthur had spoken of the need for an inquiry. Of course the conspirators, wanting a judicial inquiry to highlight the

scandal, encouraged, and egged him on in this direction. Meanwhile, the kindly and scholarly Lord Mayo supported him fully. Both men shared a greater passion for archaeology, antiques, and literary pursuits than political matters.

Then came Sir Arthur's dismissal on 23 October. If he accepted his summary dismissal and pension there would be no inquiry, and Haddo's reputation would remain intact. The conspirators, knowing Sir Arthur had a legal right to an inquiry, tried to strengthen his resolve by promising him the full support of the Unionists when they returned to power. They then suggested a petition to the King from the Knights. To suppress any hint of politics, they persuaded Lord Mayo to petition the Knights on behalf of his good friend Sir Arthur, promising to support him in his efforts. Mayo agreed and successfully persuaded sixteen Knights to sign the petition despite the following:

1. The anger of the Knights at the loss of their Order's jewels
2. The homosexual rumours about their Knight Registrar, Sir Arthur Vicars
3. The petition was distasteful to the King

The entry of The O'Mahony came as a godsend to the conspirators, for in him they had a perfect battering ram of unquestioned Nationalist allegiance. This reliance on The O'Mahony came in useful when the time came to hand the petition to the King. They could not risk having

301

a Unionist send the petition to Gladstone, as that would politicise the situation, particularly when one considered the anticipated outcome of the Royal Commission. Knowing their man in the Home Office could handle things if only they could get the petition to him, the conspirators convinced Lord Mayo to advise The O'Mahony to forward it to Gladstone. As the unwitting dupe of the conspiracy, The O'Mahony sent the petition to Gladstone, who, with the help of his officials, decided that the situation called for a Royal Commission.

THE IRON GLOVE FALLS.
'I'LL HAVE NO SCANDAL'
When Gladstone requested a Royal Commission, the King felt obliged to agree, because he had told Gladstone of his desire to 'clear the air'. However, he angrily changed his mind when Aberdeen warned him that the 'graver charge' must come up under such an inquiry. The King became more incensed upon learning that so many of his Knights had disregarded his clear wishes and signed the petition. When Gladstone asked the King for his signature on the Royal Commission, the King, angry over the petition from his Knights, sent him packing.

Furious at his Knights, the King set out to find why they had defied him. Some he met on a daily basis, and he leaned on them and pressured them for answers. Slowly King Edward learned of the influential Unionist pressure brought to bear on the Knights to sign the petition. Then the palace turned on the instigator of the petition, the hapless Lord Mayo. Apolitical all his life, Mayo had never before confronted extreme royal displeasure. He gave the palace a full account of the petition's history, and thoughtfully provided copies of the Knights' letters. Once in possession of Mayo's information, the palace realised that this political manoeuvring might precipitate a Berlin type crisis in England.

The King had to stop this madness, yet he was committed to an open inquiry to 'clear the air'. In better times he could have had a quiet word with the Prime Minister, but Campbell-Bannerman, having suffered two heart attacks, lay grievously ill. The Home Secretary, Gladstone, a thoroughly incompetent minister, pressed him for a public inquiry, and His Majesty had no desire to educate the man on the subtleties of what the King must say as against what the King actually wants. The Irish Secretary, Birrell, had abdicated his responsibility, while his Viceroy in Ireland could only wring his hands in despair. His Majesty thought that to involve himself with other politicians was only to risk being dragged further into the mess. The King turned to the one reliable man left in Ireland — MacDonnell. Arranging for MacDonnell to examine the petition letters between the Knights and Lord Mayo, the palace also briefed him on the Unionist plot, and commanded him to suppress any mention of scandal at the Inquiry.

Obeying the King's wishes, MacDonnell, true to his reputation, ruthlessly suppressed the conspiracy. He had faced these men before and he had no fear of doing so again. He confronted the conspirators with a brutal choice. If they ruined Lord Aberdeen he would expose their plot to the Nationalists, who would, and could, create a greater uproar than the conspirators ever imagined. To make matters worse, he informed the conspirators that he worked under the protection of His Majesty the King. If they continued with their plan, he would write a full official report to the King, charging the Loyalist conspirators with sedition, a far more serious crime than homosexual misconduct. MacDonnell insisted that the conspirators conclude the matter, allow the inquiry to proceed without incident and accept its findings. Finally, they would have to return the jewels secretly to His Majesty, and not to the Lord Lieutenant, and in return, the administration would not discipline any official, policeman or soldier.

From past confrontations, the conspirators knew well that MacDonnell did not bluff. In India, he was known as the Bengal Tiger and had proved to them repeatedly why he received that repute. The conspirators accepted MacDonnell's terms and terminated their plot.

Then MacDonnell briefed Birrell and Aberdeen, advising them against alerting Gladstone to the changed circumstances in Ireland. Once Birrell realised that he need no longer fear the Unionists, he reasserted his authority in Ireland

and allowed MacDonnell to conduct the inquiry as he saw fit. On 14 January Birrell replied haughtily to Gladstone that, 'You do not and cannot appreciate the situation which exists here in Dublin'.

The conspirators were as good as their word. They told Kane that they could not protect him if in his testimony he mentioned the subject of the 'graver charge'. Thus Commissioner Jones received instructions not to cross-examine Kane too vigorously, and leave the questioning to the Irish representatives. At the inquiry, Kane refused to give information on the grounds that he did not have the protection of his superiors.

During the Inquiry, MacDonnell told the Solicitor-General Barry and the Commissioner Starkie to give Kane every opportunity to introduce the contents of his report, knowing full well that Kane dare not say a word. MacDonnell wanted Kane to realise that the Irish administration did not fear him. They also wanted Kane's testimony on record about the Bullock Webster telegrams and the absence of evidence implicating Shackleton, whose exoneration would shield the Duke of Argyll and gratify His Majesty. As agreed, the Government's men questioned Kane on an issue that by right they should have tip-toed around. During five days of hearings, the Commissioners never heard a hint of the word scandal — MacDonnell delivered the King his wishes.

A short time later the conspirators secretly returned the jewels to the King, prompting Prime Minister Asquith to reject a suggestion in cabinet to increase the reward for the return of the jewels. Thus in 1927, the British Government was in a position to tell Lord Granard that the jewels could be bought for the bargain price of £2000 – £3000.

KEEPING THINGS QUIET

Within months of the Inquiry, MacDonnell announced his retirement. However, he knew far too much about the affair, and with his veiled threat to former Prime Minister Balfour in mind, the British Government and the King sought how best to ensure his perpetual silence. His Majesty suggested that a peerage would guarantee his loyalty, and both the Unionists and Liberals concurred. Thus, even before MacDonnell had left office, Prime Minister Asquith had offered him a peerage. MacDonnell accepted the offer and chose to become Lord Swinford. *The Irish Times* baffled their Unionist readers when, commenting on MacDonnell's peerage, they said that this was an honour he richly deserved. A strange turnaround, as only two years earlier, this voice of Irish Unionism had agitated to have MacDonnell dismissed from office.

With MacDonnell's resignation, Birrell came under great pressure from the Nationalists to fill the position with a person sympathetic to their cause. However, expediency demanded that Birrell promote MacDonnell's Assistant, Sir James Dougherty.

Before leaving Ireland, MacDonnell had one last piece of tidying up to do. The O'Mahony had published his correspondence with the Irish administration and wrote Birrell an insulting letter, leading the Chief Secretary to believe that this formidable opponent intended to continue the fight. MacDonnell met The O'Mahony and told him that his brother's so-called Unionist friends had nearly succeeded in having a Royal Commission appointed. These friends knew all about the homosexual court and, wanting to expose Lord Haddo, were fully prepared to sacrifice Sir Arthur and Peirce Mahony as well. Unwittingly, MacDonnell had just dealt Sir Arthur another cruel blow. Shocked at being duped by his brother's Unionist friends, The O'Mahony exacted his revenge on Sir Arthur by reneging on his offer of a pension. A short time later, the O'Mahony apologised to Birrell for his intemperate remarks.

One of the extraordinary features of this case is the silence of the principal characters. MacDonnell, Birrell, and Aberdeen left no papers that throw any light on the affair. After King Edward's death, Knollys, on his master's instruction, destroyed all the King's sensitive papers. The Kane report has disappeared from Scotland Yard and the Home Office files still remain closed to public scrutiny. The files in Ireland were completely sanitised before the British Government handed power over to the Irish Free State. Even the Irish Government kept quiet, and suppressed Sir Arthur's will for almost 60 years. Harrel, dismissed by Aberdeen and Birrell, refused to discuss the affair with Brennan, almost 40 years later.

Robert Brennan was the only Irish contemporary of the principal characters who chose to write about the case and who had access to the highest levels of the Irish Free State Government. Brennan publicised his interest in the case in his farcical play *Goodnight, Mr O'Donnell*. In 1947 he researched the theft in earnest, and in 1948 wrote an abridged version of the theft for the paper he helped found, *The Irish Press*. By so doing, he hoped to open up some closed mouths, but his only success was Seamus O'Farrell's recount of the police interrogation of his mother.

It is often what a writer does not say that offers the researcher fresh revelations. We carefully reviewed Brennan's unpublished manuscript but found that it contained no new insight into the case, which astonished us. Robert Brennan had great contacts. He could even call the Irish Prime Minister (the Taoiseach) or the Minister for Foreign Affairs directly.

Only two conclusions present themselves. The first explanation is that despite Brennan's excellent contacts, the Government of Eamon De Valera considered the theft of the Irish Crown Jewels such a sensitive matter that senior ministers declined to reveal what they knew. This scenario is the one we favour because, just a year before Brennan published his abbreviated account of the case in *The Irish Press*, the Government of the day reissued the directive to keep Sir Arthur's will suppressed, notwithstanding the fact that Shackleton had died six years earlier. Also, Brennan did not find out about

Lord Granard's offer of the Crown Jewels to W. T. Cosgrave. His close colleagues in the Department of Foreign Affairs must have known about the offer, but they kept it secret.

The alternative explanation is that the members of Brennan's circle, the politicians, Government officials and the press, knew so little about the case that they were not in a position to help their former colleague. If we believe this scenario then we must believe that the principal characters involved made amazing efforts to suppress all information about the case. King Edward's wishes alone could not have secured such a thorough sanitising of the affair. Many powerful people of the time had a lot to lose if the details became public, and they all co-operated in suppressing the information. Whichever interpretation one places on Brennan's failure to find out what happened to the Irish Crown Jewels we think that Harrel speaks for everybody involved, when he said: 'I'm sorry to say that that is a subject I feel I should not discuss with anyone.'

The story of the Crown Jewels is as much a story about Sir Arthur Vicars. While we would not espouse his politics, the man shines forth from the pages of history as a gentleman, more interested in scholarly pursuits than worldly affairs, and as often as not, willing to do a fellow human being a good turn. The final rebuke to all who deceived him came from his wife, Lady Vicars, who lies interred beside him: she added the inscription to her tombstone: 'Faithful to the end.'

16

EPILOGUE —
OUR INITIAL INVESTIGATION

Whilst researching Sir Arthur's life and the theft of the Irish Crown Jewels in 1996, with the intention of writing an article for the local newspaper, *The Kerryman*, the local organising committee of Listowel Writers Week wanted to display a short account of the Crown Jewels mystery in a vacant shopfront. Days later, a neighbour approached us with a receipt, dated 1917, made out to Sir Arthur Vicars for the purchase of a mirror at McKenna's hardware shop in Listowel. The neighbour wanted to remain anonymous, but also had three letters addressed to Sir Arthur Vicars which he had received from an old man living in the locality.

The old man's father had been one of the first looters of Kilmorna House and while rummaging through the ruins, found three letters in a gable compartment that had a strong bearing on the theft of the Crown Jewels. The arrangement was that he would allow us to examine the first letter for a week, and when it was returned, he would show us the next letter, and finally the third. The first letter read:

My dear Vicars,

Forgive the delay on my part, for not making correspondence earlier. However, on matters of this nature, discretion is often the better part of an endeavour such as ours.

Regarding the matter closest to our hearts, I have set in motion the mechanics. On this Friday evening, I expect a buyer from Amsterdam to arrive on the mail-packet at the North Wall, so let us hope for a calm crossing.

Under some pretext or other, we will arrive at Kilmorna the following week, where a scrutiny and examination can take place, so that this matter can be safely concluded, that we might have relief from this fruitful enterprise. Bear with the appalling writing, for I can scarce continue with a steady hand. I am sending this message by Castle messenger, the bearer can be trusted implicitly, he has been of use before in matters most secret.

So now my good and loyal friend we will shortly have an end to this matter. Remain staunch and we will finally emerge as men of great means.

Arthur, knowing your penchant for keeping memorabilia, I beg of you do not hesitate to destroy this note, as its contents or even proof of its very existence could constitute a great threat to our very lives.

Make no attempt at replying within the

Castle, where these walls have ears.
Remain Steadfast and Staunch
K.R.S.

If genuine, this astonishing document implicated Sir Arthur in the theft of the Crown Jewels.
However, he had maintained his innocence to his
dying day, insisting that the government had
covered up, and made him a scapegoat. In his
will, Sir Arthur bemoaned his financial plight
and insisted on his innocence in the whole affair.

We were not allowed to send the letter away
for an expert opinion. The writing paper looked
old, the ink was faded, and the language in the
letter was redolent of the Edwardian era
('mail-packet' and 'penchant'). We confirmed
that the mail-packet at that time did in fact berth
at the North Wall. That the buyer came from
Amsterdam, the centre of the world's diamond
trade, seemed reasonable. However, the initials
K.R.S. did not match Shackleton's (F.R.S.), the
man Sir Arthur accused in his will.

Three possible explanations for the letter came
to mind. One, it was a recent forgery; two, it was
an old forgery; and three, it was genuine. In the
first case, we saw no motive to incriminate Sir
Arthur some 80 years after the theft, nor was the
old man who had provided the letter hoping to
gain from its disclosure. We therefore doubted
that it was a recent forgery. In the second case,
considering that the high command of the IRA
stated that they had not sanctioned the shooting,
they may have planted the letter afterwards to
discredit Sir Arthur, thereby muting the outcry

following his murder. The British public would have lost their sympathy for Sir Arthur if they thought he was the thief. However, if the IRA had planted the letter, why did they not arrange for its discovery sooner and publicise its contents? In the third case, there was the possibility that the letter was genuine and therefore incriminated Sir Arthur. Without the benefit of scientific analysis or knowledge of the identity of the sender, we could not conclude one way or the other about the letter's authenticity.

It seemed most likely that the letter was an old IRA forgery, planted in the ruins to discredit Sir Arthur after the uproar following his murder. This would explain why the British army failed to discover the letters when they inspected the ruins just after the shooting. The old man's father probably arrived just afterwards to loot the house and found the letters, but, by keeping them to himself, he had inadvertently ruined the IRA's plans. If the letter was genuine then it opened a completely new chapter in the mystery surrounding the affair.

Since the old man who owned the letters would not allow us to get scientific analysis made, the best we could do was to try and get the background of how and when the old man's father got possession of them.

While waiting for the second letter, we obtained a sample of Francis Shackleton's handwriting from a member of the family but it did not match the writing in the letter, which is not surprising. Shackleton had resigned his post as Dublin Herald, and had no reason to be in Dublin Castle, let alone writing letters from within its walls. It would be difficult the guess the identity of K.R.S.

The text of the second letter read:

My dear Vicars,

Received last evening your letter by hand. Friend be assured our secret lies undisclosed. As for me forewarning that a search was imminent, how could I have done so. Please keep in mind had I done so, your demeanour would have been unable to mask the anticipation of their arrival, which in turn would have aroused suspicion. Do you not know of these three, one was the only man in the land with the authority to sanction the act. He! Coll, the other two are a blood relation of his . . . Please me further with your new found enthusiasm for gardening. There cannot be too many . . . capable of yielding such handsome returns. Aim to cover your efforts with produce that will be veritable jewels. The map . . . I cannot quite grasp it from the drawing as you omitted to show the Northern elevation and . . . relevant features . . . section me another map.

I will be able to keep abreast up here and you will know that I am with you, if only in spirit.

Arthur keep well . . . paper to the bank, so that it can be of some assistance.

Yours
K.S.G.

Unfortunately, parts of this letter (indicated by the gaps above) are illegible, but the text clearly indicated that Sir Arthur had buried the jewels on the Kilmorna estate. He also received an unexpected visit from members of the Coll family concerning the jewel affair. One of the visitors must have been Sir Patrick Coll, a retired Solicitor General at the time of the theft. Sir Patrick also had a nephew who had held a senior position with the Board of Works, the department responsible for the purchase of the safe at Dublin Castle, where the jewels were housed. We can only speculate that these are the Colls referred to in the letter and that they may have wanted to question Sir Arthur about the safe. There is no clue to the identity of the man referred to as 'one was the only man in the land with the authority to sanction the act'. Sir Arthur also apparently drew a map for his accomplice, revealing the hiding place of the jewels. Although the handwriting is identical to that of the first letter, the initials of the sender had now changed from K.R.S. to K.S.G. This change may indicate some sort of coding between Sir Arthur and his accomplice, thus the initials may not have referred to any particular man in the Castle. This letter did not have the word Dublin Castle on it, nor was there any bolding of letters as there had been in the first letter.

On the strength of our theory that this was probably an old IRA forgery, we thought that if we publicised the letters, others in the community might come forward with information. With this in mind, we approached Noel

Twomey, of *The Kerryman* newspaper to write a story on the letters, and he agreed.

Days after the newspaper article appeared, someone had anonymously placed a third letter in the reporter's mail box at his house.

Dublin Castle

Friday

Vicars,

What you contemplate is utter madness. The reverberations of such a disclosure would rock the Kingdom to it's very foundations.

We all understand the impossible strain under which you have had to labour these past years. We have grieved with you at the besmirching of your good name.

Preserve! For twas done for King, even for country, then for the Empire . . .

Mind how you heard expressed at first hand the heartfelt gratitude of your sovereign and you have witnessed the pain that the denial of your honour has caused. Lest you had been wrought of the finest steel, you could not have buttressed yourself better from the resulting events. Only true courage could have triumphed. Now you seek to set that victory aside. Extinguish that hope, for there lies ruin.

Did you not freely concur there could be no vindication for you in your lifetime. Arthur you will not be vindicated in yours or mine. Even K.G. allowed you must be given the reluctant option of refusal. Steadfastly you averred that the duty was yours and yours alone. Did you not reason in a childless marriage there would be no ignominy to fall upon your heirs?

Some day your part in all this will enter the public domain but old friend you and I will long have been fragments of earth. Vicars, when we started this venture, we were strangers, you Ulster King of Arms for our monarch, to ensure he dazzled and shone for the masses. I a shadowy figure, unelected, unknown, secret.

My power and loyalty foresworn in the blood that flows through K.G. and my own. I am that abomination, the secret arm of the monarch, connected by blood. I hold no office, yet freely access the highest in the land.

About the jewels, they are of no matter. It would have served better if you had allowed that shadowy buyer from Amsterdam to continue. It would have served better if you had mapped out their exact position, for then Arthur, they would have been secretly retrieved. It would have been far better if you had yielded to temptation, if your spirit had been a reflection of your physical strength.

But you did not follow either course, you have been King of Arms to the end, protecting that which was entrusted to your care.

After conferring with G., I now charge thee with their protection, even after your death.

We are living in a changing world Arthur, the nations are becoming restless. Even the stability that is Kilmorna House is threatened by dark forces. Why not return to England Arthur and live out your days in grace and

317

favour . . . you court danger by remaining where you are.

Finally, Arthur, forget the foolishness of which you wrote. While my admiration and friendship has deepened for you over the years, you must realise the limitation of my compassion.

My allegiance is to my King, my life is dedicated to the monarch. I would gladly lay it down for him or sadly, lay down the life of another if must be.

Come home, Arthur, where you will be safe. Where you can have halcyon days. Where you can live out under my protection.

For the last time
Goodbye old friend
K.S.G.

This letter strengthened the belief that the letters were forgeries. Although the third letter is not dated, from the references in it it appears that it was written during the reign of King George (K.G.). And it is written after 1917, as it refers to Sir Arthur's childless marriage. The letter suggests that Sir Arthur wanted to clear his name before he died by revealing his honourable motive for participating in the theft. However, his accomplice, with a veiled threat to kill him, strongly rejected Sir Arthur's proposal. Instead he suggested that Sir Arthur return to the safety of England.

It is interesting that Sir Arthur refused to give up the jewels — he was their custodian to the end. The letter gave a plausible reason for Sir

Arthur's possible involvement in the theft. As their custodian, he had the most to lose by their disappearance. His personal interests lay in status and titles, not money, and his honesty had never been questioned. This letter, however, suggested a patriotic motive, which was in keeping with the man's character. Sir Arthur could easily have got involved, if it had been for King and country, or with the expectation of being raised to the peerage by his monarch.

The *Kerryman* newspaper serialised the three letters and the publicity aroused a great stir in the local community, which quickly spread to the national arena. Days after the publication of the third letter, a treasure hunter from Cork arrived and was spotted scouring in the ruins of Kilmorna House with a metal detector. Nothing was ever found.

After a short time *The Kerryman* reporter received an anonymous phone call asking him to examine some further evidence. Following instructions, he drove outside Listowel, where he was met by an intermediary who showed the reporter items which he said were looted from Kilmorna House. These included an antique (Ansol) clock, two candlesticks, and a spectacle case with Lady Vicars' initials thereon.

Finally the caller showed the reporter a section of a map and a message which was written on oilskin. He explained that a week after Sir Arthur's shooting, three men had searched the ruins. It was claimed that one of these was Paddy McAuliffe, a highly-respected stone mason in Listowel at the time. It was rumoured by the caller that Sir Arthur had employed McAuliffe to build a secret compartment in the gable some years earlier and it was here that they found the three letters and the map. They divided the map in three parts, each taking a section. The portion he showed to the reporter had been given to him by his father. Written on the map, in the same handwriting as that of the three letters, was this short note along with a heraldic riddle indicating the location of the buried jewels:

Arthur, I have copied your lines and map. The heraldry, though I am no expert, presents few problems, but the omission of the various directions of the compass, makes it impossible. In the event of something happening to us, say, unforeseen, be so good as to make it right.
One hundred paces blazoned per pale with fifty more blazoned per fess
Only in lines with a gules tinted sun.
Two lions passant show true sanguine
Concealed from sight by a sable lie.
Approaches band sinister by banded oak
Per bend indented, the earth, now walled.
Embattled walls with embrasures therein
The Fleur de Lis with the Cross Moline lies
There on the vert showing the purpure proof.
Safely lies the marks of monarch's honesty
Bearing the tincture or Argent, azure of herald.

The caller said that he had no idea who had the other two portions of the map, but he hoped that the publicity generated by *The Kerryman* might induce them to come forward.

The use of a heraldic riddle was in keeping with Sir Arthur's profession. And a line in the riddle appears to refer to a tree that no longer exists. The 'banded oak' may have referred to one of the two trees planted in Kilmorna by Charles Stewart Parnell when he visited almost a century ago. In a terrible act of insensitivity, Parnell's tree was cut down.

Meanwhile news of the letters and map had already spread to England and a reporter from *The Telegraph*, arrived to investigate. His colleague from *The Kerryman* promised to help him meet the person with the map. On the night before *The Telegraph* reporter returned to London, we met him at the Listowel Arms hotel to discuss the affair. Around 11pm, he was paged to the reception desk where two men awaited him.

Once outside the hotel, he was blindfolded, bundled into a car, and driven to an isolated area. Fearing they were followed, his abductors stopped to switch cars. The two related the story of how the letters surfaced from the secret compartment, and showed him a selection of land deeds belonging to Lord Listowel. It was almost 2am before the reporter returned to the hotel, frightened. The two men had warned him to keep secret their identities and not to relate to us what they had told him.

Almost a year went by with no developments.

Then late one night, one of the researchers, Michael Murphy, received a phone call, instructing him to go down to the orchard wall of Kilmorna House, where he would find an object of great historical interest relating to the Irish Crown Jewels, and that he would need a wheelbarrow to remove it. The caller concluded the conversation by saying that he had found what he wanted and that this was his last contact with us.

Not knowing what to expect, Michael Murphy first called the police, informing them of the conversation and said that he was going to examine the orchard wall a short distance from his house. The police arrived as he was making his way up the driveway. In his wheelbarrow was a large cement tablet similar to a headstone, which had the following inscription:

> *Tolle Lege*
> *Audi Partem Alteram*
> *Causa Finitia Est*
> A.V. K.G.S.

On each side of the inscription was a lion's head, and a key. In a corner of the stone was the initials P.McA. Jutting out of the back of the slab were four rusted iron rods freshly cut. A rectangular stain on the back of the slab indicated that a box had been attached to these rods.

The first line of the inscription is from the Confessions of St Augustine. The second line is a well-known legal principle, however, the third line is a pun on a church edict. It translates as:

Pick up and Read
The other party has a right to be heard
The affair is 'one of deceit' (*instead of 'the
case is closed'*)

P. McA. could be identified as Paddy McAuliffe, the local stone-mason, who died in 1921. The cement tablet appeared old and weather-worn and emitted a strange odour. We reasoned it would be typical of Sir Arthur to use Latin. The word *finitia* (not *finita*, which means finished) suggested to us that the author was versed in old French. It is an etymological derivation of the French word *finesse* meaning deceit and is not readily found in a Latin dictionary but would have been well-known to Sir Arthur due to his knowledge of French heraldry.

Before there was time to analyse the age of the cement slab, the police in Listowel tipped off *The Kerryman* and it got full coverage in that week's edition. The news quickly spread to Dublin, and the National Museum was most anxious to know the facts. Many of the national papers covered the story and talk-show hosts were phoning hoping to get an interview. Before long, we were contacted by French television and an American documentary producer. Visitors descended on Kilmorna hoping to get a first-hand glimpse of the stone. One of the bars in Listowel offered to buy the stone as a curiosity. Meanwhile, a sample of the slab was taken to Enterprise Ireland, in Dublin, for analysis and a synopsis of the results are as follows:

Although concrete was readily available in the 1920s, the aggregate mix that is now commonly used in concrete was not. In that period a natural gravel aggregate was used, the stones of which would be characteristically rounded from the effects of the ice age. Also the gravel stones would be of various size and colours. However, the aggregate mix used in this tablet contained stones of the same size, were of grey colour and had jagged edges. It was therefore man-made aggregate from a quarry, and had been ground up in a machine which was not used in that period, except for large railway projects. Similarly, the paint residue on the rusted metal rods contained Titania which was not available till around the 1950s. Inside the stone were reinforcing angle irons that displayed recent welding joints. The analysis concluded that the stone was of recent origin.

This established that the whole affair, including the letters and map, had been an elaborate hoax by a group in the community.

The fact that the letters, map and stone were subsequently discovered to be a hoax was never publicised in the newspapers so the story is included here to set the record straight. Many have been led to believe that the jewels were discovered behind the tablet in the orchard wall of Kilmorna House.

The hoaxers had spent many hours researching the story, and displayed tenacity and perseverence in promoting their mischief. Maybe they got their inspiration from a previous hoax that took place when in 1983, the granddaughter of Mrs Farrell, the cleaning lady at the Office of Arms in Dublin Castle, told the police that the jewels were buried in the Dublin mountains. Taking the claim seriously, the police and army scoured the area with metal detectors, but found nothing.

Though individuals known to us should not have wasted time on the hoax, the deluge of publicity that followed it convinced us that the public is still greatly interested in the Irish Crown Jewel affair.

Other titles in the
Charnwood Library Series:

FALLING SLOWLY

Anita Brookner

Beatrice and Miriam are sisters, loving but not entirely uncritical; each secretly deplores the other's aspirations. Their lives fall short of what they would have wished for themselves: love, intimacy, exclusivity, acknowledgement in the eyes of the world, even a measure of respect. Each discovers to her cost that love can be a self-seeking business and that lovers have their own exclusive desires. In search of reciprocity, the sisters are forced back into each other's company, and rediscover their original closeness.

THE LADY ON MY LEFT

Catherine Cookson

Alison Read, orphaned when she was two years old, had for some years lived and worked with Paul Aylmer, her appointed guardian. Paul, an experienced antique dealer whose business thrived in the south-coast town of Sealock, had come to rely on Alison, who had quickly learned the trade. But when he had asked her to value the contents of Beacon Ride, a chain of events was set off that led to the exposure of a secret he had for years managed to conceal. As a result, Alison's relationship with Paul came under threat and she knew that only by confronting the situation head-on would her ambitions be realised.

FLIGHT OF EAGLES

Jack Higgins

In 1997 a wealthy novelist, his wife and their pilot are forced to ditch in the English Channel. Saved by a lifeboat crew, they are returned to land at Cold Harbour. But it is the rediscovery of a fighter pilot's lucky mascot — unseen for half a century — that excites the greatest interest at the disused airbase. The mascot's owners, twin brothers Max and Harry Kelso, were separated as boys and found themselves fighting on opposite sides when the Second World War broke out. They were to meet again under amazing circumstances — and upon their actions hung the fate of the war itself . . .

ON BEULAH HEIGHT

Reginald Hill

They needed a new reservoir so they'd moved everyone out of Dendale that long hot summer fifteen years ago. They even dug up the dead and moved them too. But four inhabitants of the dale they couldn't move, for nobody knew where they were — three little girls, and the prime suspect in their disappearance, Benny Lightfoot. This was Andy Dalziel's worst case and now fifteen years on he looks set to re-live it. It's another long hot summer. A child goes missing, and as the Dendale reservoir waters shrink and the old village re-emerges, old fears and suspicions arise too . . .